Inventor 2022 Training Guide

Know to speed up your connected engineering workflows

Linkan Sagar

www.bpbonline.com

FIRST EDITION 2021
REPRINT 2023

ISBN: 978-93-91392-00-0

Distributors:

BPB PUBLICATIONS
20, Ansari Road, Darya Ganj
New Delhi-110002
Ph: 23254990/23254991

DECCAN AGENCIES
4-3-329, Bank Street,
Hyderabad-500195
Ph: 24756967/24756400

MICRO MEDIA
Shop No. 5, Mahendra Chambers,
150 DN Rd. Next to Capital Cinema,
V.T. (C.S.T.) Station, MUMBAI-400 001
Ph: 22078296/22078297

BPB BOOK CENTRE
376 Old Lajpat Rai Market,
Delhi-110006
Ph: 23861747

Published by Manish Jain for BPB Publications, 20 Ansari Road, Darya Ganj, New Delhi-110002 and Printed by him at Manipal Technologies Limited, Manipal

www.bpbonline.com

About the Author

Linkan Sagar has done B.tech from UPTU Lucknow. His books AutoCAD, Revit, 3ds Max, SolidWorks have been much appreciated and opted in AutoCAD technology. He has extensively worked on various other software like Solidworks, SketchUP, CATIA, Staad-Pro and Revit. He has wide industry experience and worked on more than 100+ major live projects. By profession, he is Senior Design Engineer & motivation speaker.

Acknowledgement

I write books for the good future of my daughter- Jessica Sagar (Angel). I was constantly supported and guided by many wonderful people; their extended support will always be priceless for me. My mother, Archana Sagar, is a woman of substance; Like any other mother in the world, her unconditional support, caring nature, never-ending faith in me, and motivation encouraged me to finally realize that I can transfer my knowledge through writing for various other people who seek the same knowledge.

And, this is how my book writing began.

I would like to thank my sister, Shivani Sagar, who always lovingly supports, motivates, and inspires me. Many thanks to my wife, Mansi Sagar, who is a wonderful partner, she not only understands my dreams and aspirations, but is equally involved in internalizing and living it up with me. It's wonderful how she took on all the responsibilities, so that I can get space and comfort for writing this book with dedication. She stands strong with me in all the highs and lows of my life. These two women are the sources of continuous energy that keep me going.

This book is about technical skills, precision and perfection in the engineering field. And, last but not least, thanks to BPB Publications and Team for giving me the opportunity to write a book.

Preface

Book is short, lively and based on a real platform. It explains the latest release of Autodesk® Inventor® in a simple and easy manner, which is packed with user-requested updates and its enhancements to help to manage your design process, to speed up your connected engineering workflows, and to reduce the repetitive tasks. Using the real-world and imagined examples, it takes the reader through the content designing process explaining everything along the way. Projects have been explained in a step-by-step manner with the commands along with a lot of new features.

Book carries a lot for you if you are starting to learn solid work, this book is extremely simple to understand and contains projects in easy language. So far, my earlier books AutoCAD 2015, AutoCAD 2017, Autocad2018 ,3D MAX 2019, Revit 2019, Autocad2019, SolidWorks 2019 have been a success, and I hope my book Inventor 2022 will be appreciated by my beloved reader. As I receive positive feedback, and numerous people are benefiting from it, I am being more eloquent for this book with novel projects and easy language. This book carries a lot for you If you are starting Inventor for the first time. This book is extremely simple to understand and will enlighten you with the fundamentals of Inventor 2022. You can easily learn Inventor 2022 as it is a basic step-by-step book. The main objective of writing this book, after being inspired from my previous edition, is to make students enthusiastic about learning the concept of Inventor. I wish you a great future in designing.

— Linkan Sagar

Errata

We take immense pride in our work at BPB Publications and follow best practices to ensure the accuracy of our content to provide with an indulging reading experience to our subscribers. Our readers are our mirrors, and we use their inputs to reflect and improve upon human errors if any, occurred during the publishing processes involved. To let us maintain the quality and help us reach out to any readers who might be having difficulties due to any unforeseen errors, please write to us at:

errata@bpbonline.com

Your support, suggestions and feedbacks are highly appreciated by the BPB Publications' Family.

BPB is searching for authors like you

If you're interested in becoming an author for BPB, please visit **www.bpbonline.com** and apply today. We have worked with thousands of developers and tech professionals, just like you, to help them share their insight with the global tech community. You can make a general application, apply for a specific hot topic that we are recruiting an author for, or submit your own idea.

PIRACY

If you come across any illegal copies of our works in any form on the internet, we would be grateful if you would provide us with the location address or website name. Please contact us at **business@bpbonline.com** with a link to the material.

If you are interested in becoming an author

If there is a topic that you have expertise in, and you are interested in either writing or contributing to a book, please visit **www.bpbonline.com**.

REVIEWS

Please leave a review. Once you have read and used this book, why not leave a review on the site that you purchased it from? Potential readers can then see and use your unbiased opinion to make purchase decisions, we at BPB can understand what you think about our products, and our authors can see your feedback on their book. Thank you!

For more information about BPB, please visit **www.bpbonline.com**.

Table of Contents

1. Introduction of Inventor 2022 .... **1**

2. Getting started with Inventor 2022 .... **5**

Starting Screen 5

GUI (Graphical User Interface) 6

How to start sketch 7

3. Setting And Manage **11**

Unit setting 11

Application option 12

Mouse control 13

4. Sketch **15**

Create tools 15

Modify tools 18

Move *18*

Copy *20*

Rotate *20*

Trim *21*

Extend *21*

Split *22*

Scale *23*

Stretch *23*

Offset *25*

Pattern 26

Rectangular *26*

Circular *27*

Mirror *28*

Project 29

Project geometry *29*

Project cut edges *31*

Project flat pattern ... *32*
Project to 3d sketch ... *33*
Insert ... 35
Insert image ... *35*
Import points ... *36*
Insert AutoCAD file ... *39*
Format ... 40
Construction ... *41*
Centerline ... *42*
Line Type, Color and Line width ... *42*
Show format ... *43*

5. Part Design ... 45
Extrude ... 45
1. Input geometry ... *48*
2. Behavior ... *48*
3. Output ... *50*
4. Advanced properties ... *50*
Revolve ... 51
Sweep ... 52
Loft ... 57
Coil ... 59
Emboss ... 61
Rib ... 64
Decal ... 67
Import ... 68
Unwrap ... 70
Derive ... 71
Hole ... 72
Fillet ... 75
1. Constant ... *75*
2. Variable ... *77*
3. Setbacks ... *78*

Chamfer 79
1. Distance *79*
2. Distance and angle *80*
3. Two distances *81*
Shell 82
Draft 83
1. Fixed edge *83*
2. Fixed plane *85*
3. Parting line *87*
Thread 90
Combine 92
Thicken/offset 95
Split 97
Direct 100
Delete face 103
Move bodies 103
Bend Part 105
Copy Object 107

6. Work Features 109
Plane 109
Type 1 offset from plane: *110*
Axis 117
Point 120
UCS 125

7. Surface 127
Trim 127
Patch 132
Stitch 133
Ruled surface 133
Extend 135
Sculpt 135
Replace face 138

8. Sheet Metal **141**
How to open Sheet Metal option? 141
How to change sheet thickness and material? 143
Flange 146
Contour Flange 148
Lofted Flange 150
Hem 153
Bend 155
Fold 159
Contour Roll 162
Cut 163
Corner seam 164
Punch tool 167
Rip 168
Unfold 169
Refold 172

9. Assembly **173**
How to start ASSEMBLY? 173
How to use constrain? 176
Copy 181
How to use constrain Axis? 182
Move 183
Rotate 184
Grip Snap 185
How to create new part in assembly? 186

CHAPTER 1

Introduction of Inventor 2022

Inventor software is the product of Autodesk Company. Autodesk's first product is AutoCAD. The Autodesk Inventor is a computer-aided design (CAD) application. It is used for 3-Dimensional design in mechanical, product simulation, visualization, and documentation. It is developed in 1999. Author of Autodesk is Jacob Sain. Most use of inventor in the mechanical sector.

Version	Date of release	What's New
1	20-Sep-99	
2	1-Mar-00	
3	1-Aug-00	
4	1-Dec-00	
5	17-Sep-01	
5.3	30-Jan-02	
6	15-Oct-02	

Contd...

Version	Date of release	What's New
7	18-Apr-03	New DWG Support for AutoCAD 2004, Autodesk Express Viewer Compatibility, Large-Assembly Design Performance
8	15-Oct-03	
9	15-Jul-04	
10	6-Apr-05	Task Scheduler, Inventor Studio, Associative import of Mechanical Desktop data, Design Accelerators, Assembly constraints use colors to differentiate between the first and second constraint selection.
11	6-Apr-06	
2008	11-Apr-07	
2009	16-Apr-08	Frame Generator, Sheet Metal, skeletal modelling
2010	27-Feb-09	The Ribbon, New FEA
2011	26-Mar-10	Dynamic Input, Direct Manipulation, Assemble tool, Visualization, iCopy, iLogic
2012	22-Mar-11	Provides easier ways to interact with 3D mechanical design data; new opportunities for sharing, accepting and updating CAD data regardless of source and complexity; and high-impact performance and productivity improvements for both users and IT departments
2013	27-Mar-12	Equation curves
2014	27-Mar-13	Express mode, Connection, Symmetrical constraint, Slot geometry, Enhanced rectangle geometry, Thin wall FEA, Frame FEA, Assembly relationship folder Mouse over grounded constraint visibility, Model & assembly simplification, Joint constraints.
2015	28-Mar-14	Freeform, Direct Edit

Contd...

Version	Date of release	What's New
2016	16-Apr-15	Multi-CAD, AutoCAD Electrical and Inventor Interoperability, Shape Generator, 3D Printing Environment, Graphics/Visualization/Studio Enhancements
2017	28-Mar-16	Modeling enhancements, expanded Any CAD support, 3D PDF export, enhanced presentation environment, guided tutorial authoring
2018	24-Mar-17	Model Based Definition, expanded Any CAD support, large assembly performance improvements, simplification/shrink-wrap enhancements, multiple rules for sheet metal parts, mesh support in drawing views
2019	10-Apr-18	Performance improvements, large assembly performance improvements, shared view collaboration, expanded hole command, iLogic enhancements, model-based definition, improved part modeling workflows, and sheet metal for manufacturing
2020	27-Mar-19	Overall GUI improvements
2021	31-Mar-20	
2022	6-Apr-21	

CHAPTER 2

Getting started with Inventor 2022

Starting Screen

There are 4 Options in the inventor's starting screen.

1. **Part:** It is used to create a single body or part of a machine. For example, to make nut and bolt. First, we can use the part option for the nut, then the part option again to make the bolt. In this way we can make 2 different parts. Its file extension format is. **ipt.**

2. **Assembly:** This option is used to make a complete product by combining all parts together. For example, both nuts and bolts can be transformed into a complete product through this Assembly option. Its file extension format is. **iam.**

3. **Drawing:** By this drawing option we can get to know about all the required details of a part or product. Such as part length, width, height and section view of part etc. The file extension of this option is. **idw.**

4. **Presentation:** To represent the joint of a part of the assembly and its connection, the presentation is used. Such as showing different parts by image and video. Its file extension format is. **ipn.**

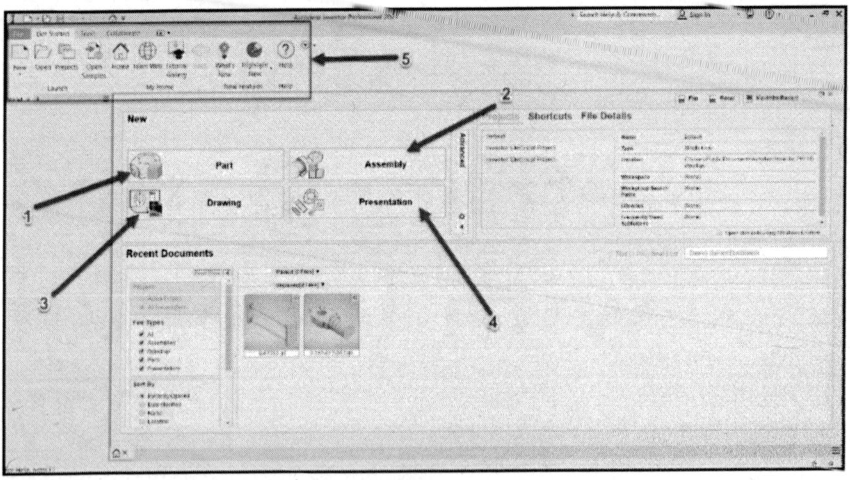

5. **Get started:** You can use the "Get Started" option if you want to work some other module or direct want to open a file, which were already made in the inventor.

GUI (Graphical User Interface)

There is a graphical user interface to enable the user to interact with the software.

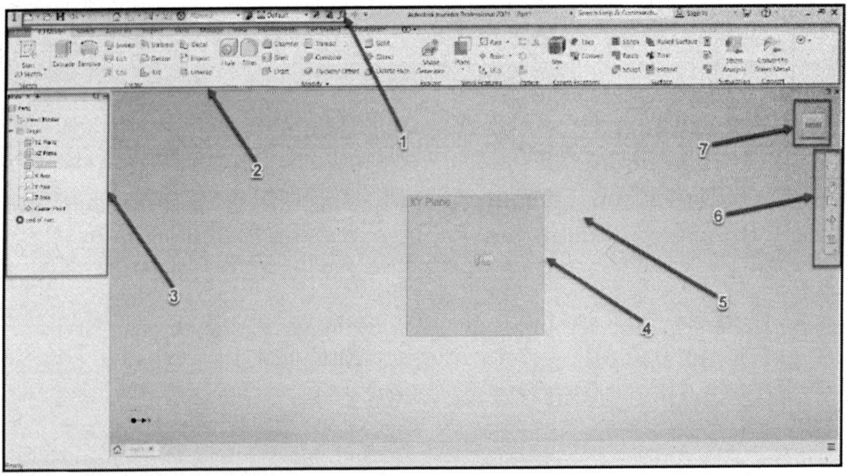

1. **Quick access:** For direct new page, file save or file open, use the Quick access toolbar.
2. **Ribbon bar:** When you open the Inventor software, you can see a ribbon bar at the top of the main window. The ribbon bar has separate tabs. In which there are different tools. For some tools, there are some sub options of the drop-down.
3. **Presentation tree:** You can see a Presentation tree at the left of the main window. It is used to simplify complex tasks. For example, if we ever want to change the sketch of the part, change the dimension, or change the height of the part, we can easily do this from the presentation tree.
4. **Plane:** There are 3 planes inside the presentation tree. It is used for sketching.
5. **Drawing area:** Drawing area is at the center of the main window. Sketches are made in the drawing area itself.
6. **Navigation bar:** You can see a Navigation bar at the right of the main window. The navigation bar has tools such as zoom, pan, and orbit. Which are used at the time of drawing or even after drawing.
7. **View control:** View control is on the top right of the navigation bar. It is used for easy viewing of any side of the drawing.

How to start sketch

First, let's start with the sketch to create any part, and to create sketch we have to select plane. The steps are given below.

Step 1: Click on "new page". Select the "Part standard template" and choose the required template. Then click on "Create". option.

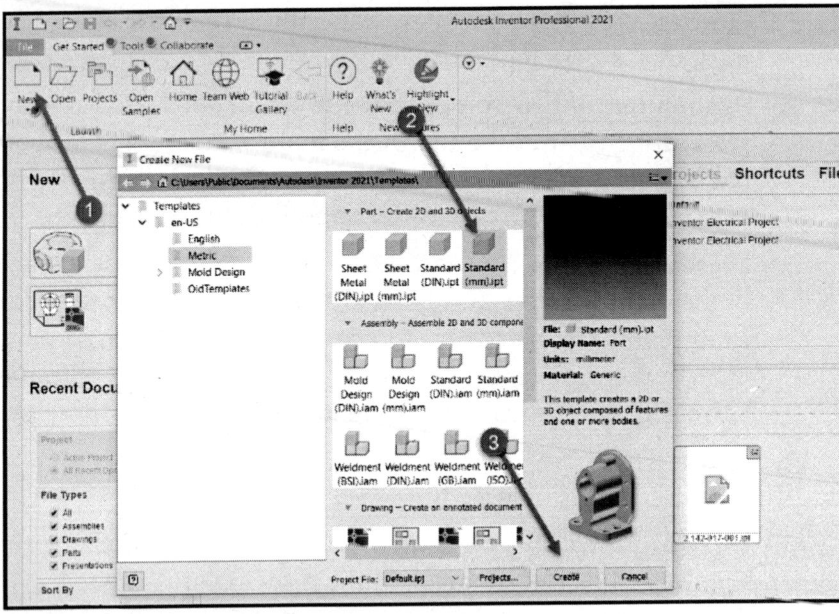

Step 2: Select the required plane. Then click on "sketch".

Step 3: Create any sketch.

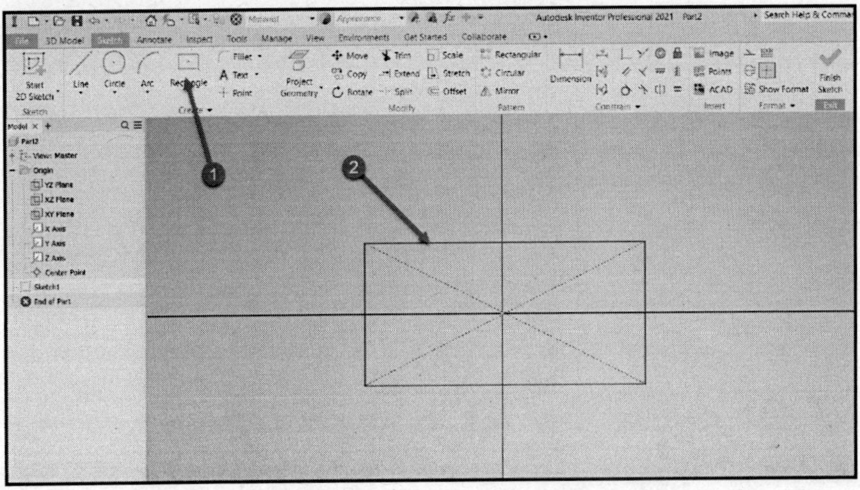

Step 4: Then give the dimension and finish the sketch.

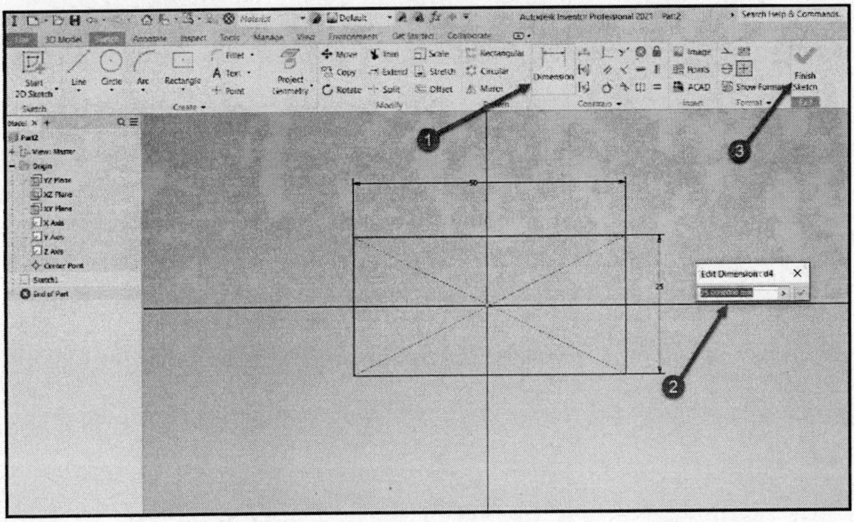

Chapter 3

Setting And Manage

Unit setting

Drawing should be done in one unit. So that its scale and dimension will correct. You can also set the required unit of drawing such as mm, meter and cm etc. Follow the steps to set up the unit.

Step 1: Ribbon bar › Tools › Document settings.

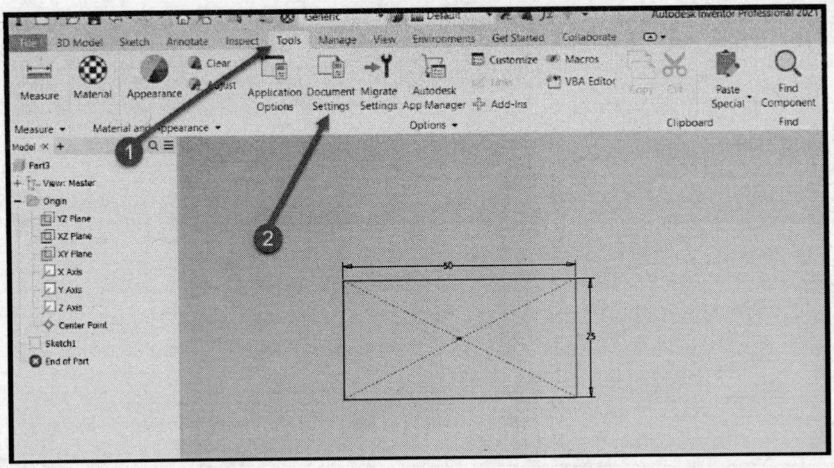

Step 2: Click on Unit tab. Set the unit length, then apply and close.

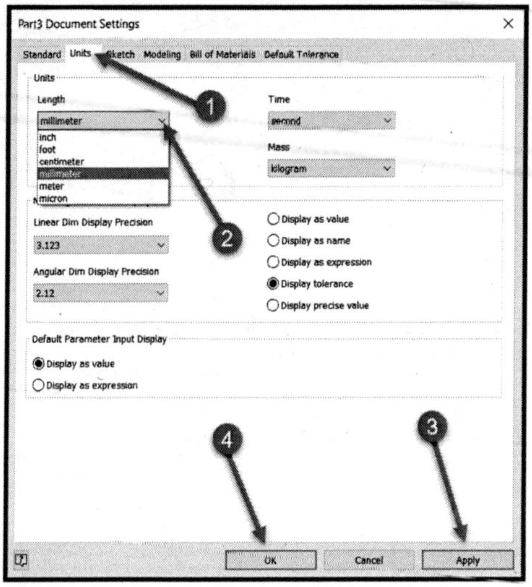

Note: If you want to change unit length as well as unit angle, precision and mass etc., then you can set it from the unit tab.

Application option

The application option is used for General setting of software. Such as file settings, save, colors and sketch settings etc. you can also change the colors of "Graphical user interface".

Step 1: Ribbon bar › Tools › Application option.

Step 2: Click on Color tab, and select the page color as you want.

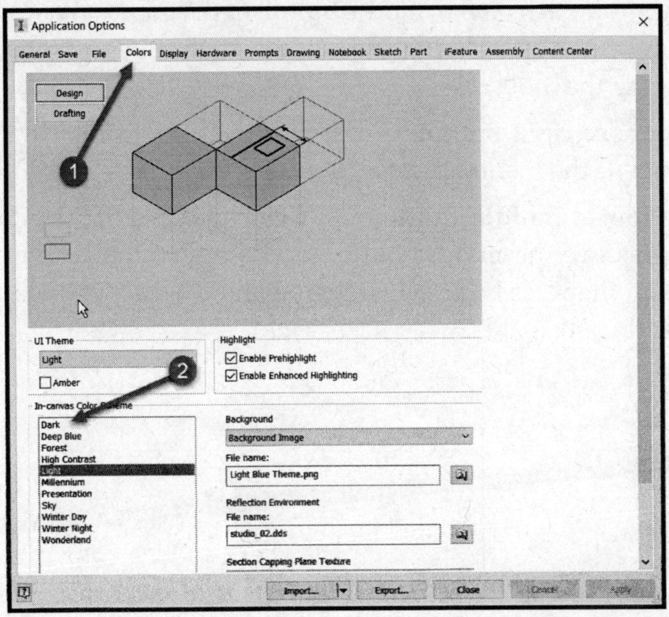

Note: With the application option, you can do different settings as per the requirement.

Mouse control

How to control the mouse. For example, zoom, selection, move and orbit etc. See the below steps.

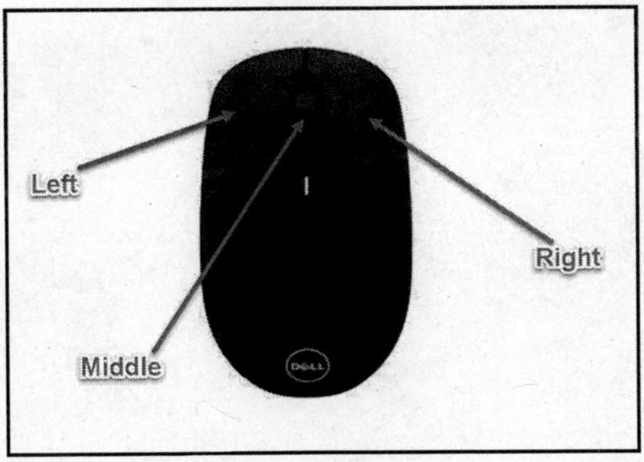

1. **Mouse left button:** Use the Mouse left button to click and select objects.

2. **Mouse middle button:** You can "zoom fit" the page, by doing double click on the middle button of the mouse. We can move the page by pressing the middle button of the mouse and drag the mouse.
3. **Mouse right button:** Clicking the right button of the mouse opens the menu option.
4. **Mouse middle button + Key board shift button:** By pressing the middle button and shift button of the mouse simultaneously or by dragging the mouse, you can rotate (orbit) the page.

CHAPTER 4
Sketch

Create tools

When you start the sketch, you can see Create tools at the sketch tab of the ribbon bar. Create tools are basic tools for the sketch such As: **line, circle, ellipse, rectangle, slot, fillet, text, and point** etc.

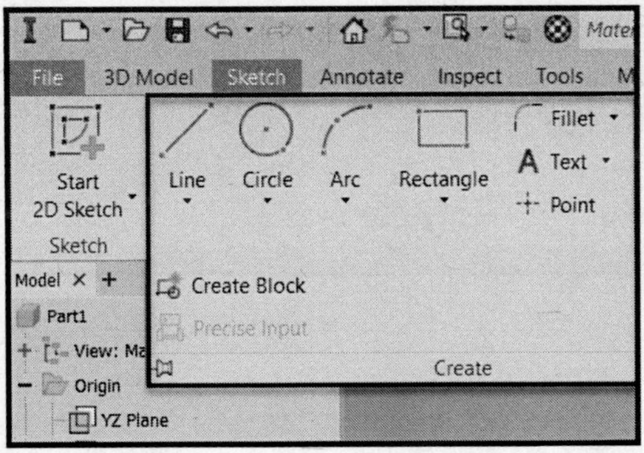

Note1: You can use the "Create Group" tool to create group of sketches.

Step 1: Click on "create block" tool.

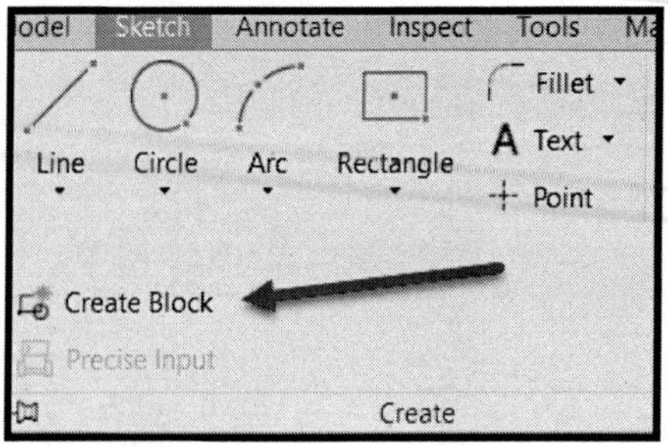

Step 2: Click on "select geometry" icon. Then select the object, which you want to block.

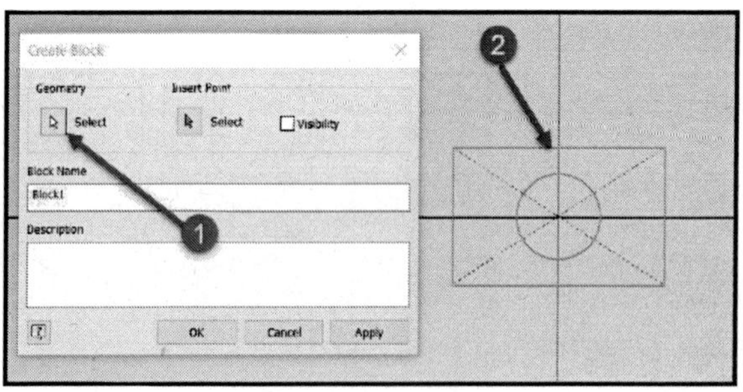

Step 3: Click on "Insert point" icon. Then specify the point for the base point of the group.

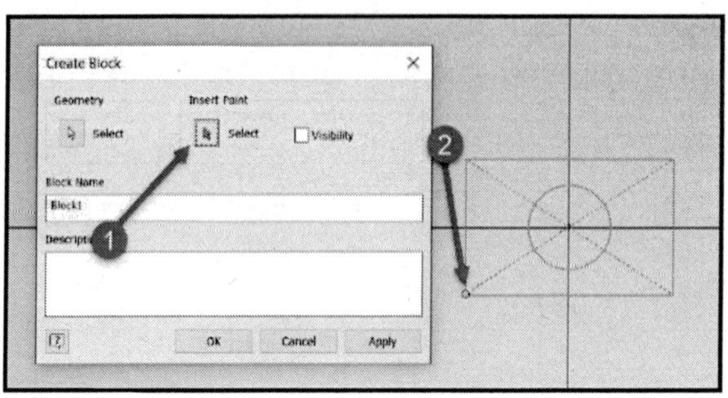

Step 4: Specify the name. Then click on apply button, and OK.

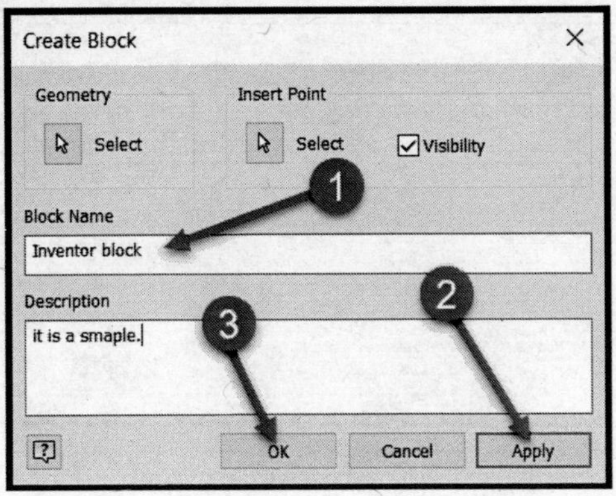

Note 2: If you want to create an object with coordinates, then you can use the precise input tool.

Step 1: Select any create a tool that you want to create. For example: circle.

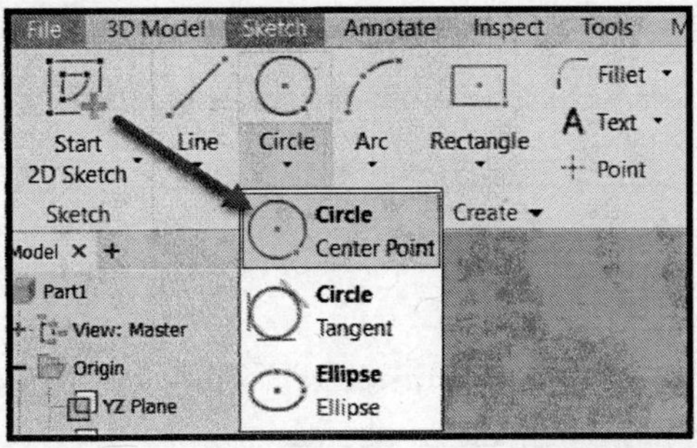

Step 2: Click on "precise input" tool

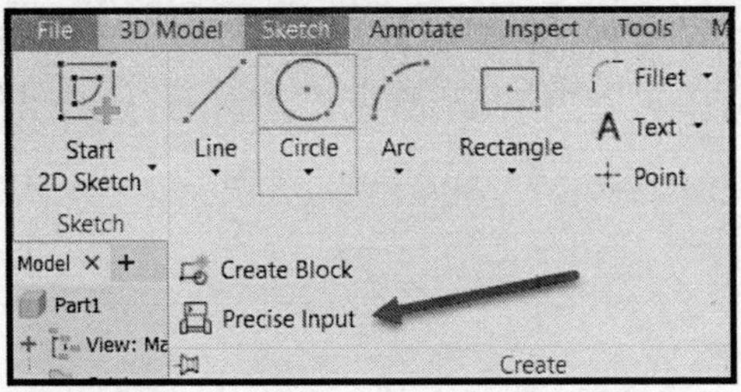

Step 3: Give values of X and Y where you want to create.

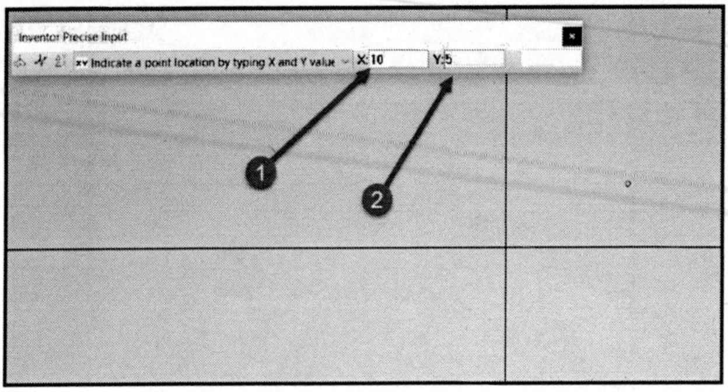

Step 4: Click on screen and specify the circle radius.

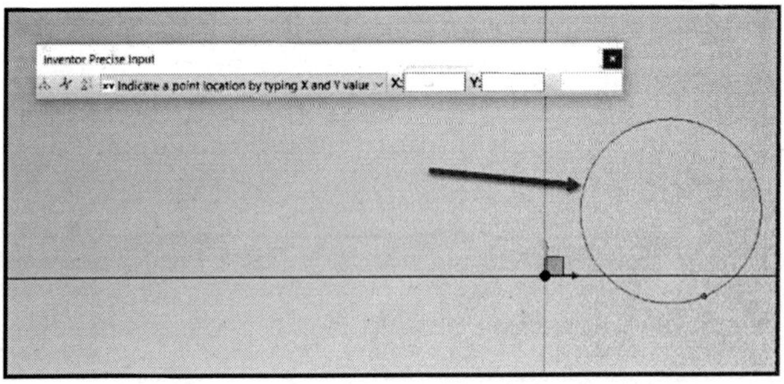

Modify tools

You can see Modify tools at the sketch tab of the ribbon bar. For any modification in Sketch, we can use Modify Tools.

Move

It is used to move a sketch object from one position to another.

Step 1: Click on move tool and select the object you want to move. Then click the base point.

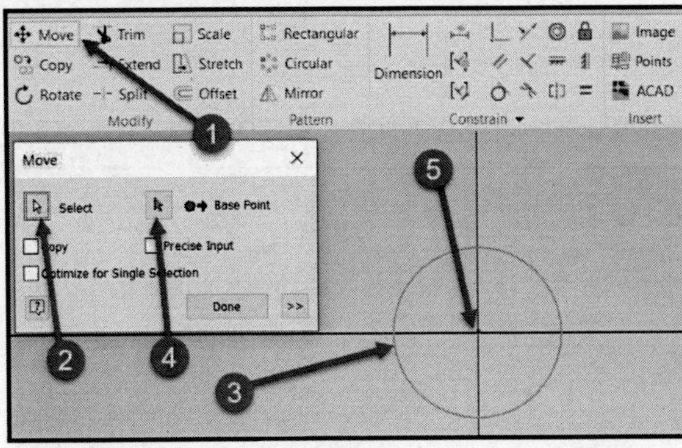

Step 2: Move the object and specify the position where you want to keep.

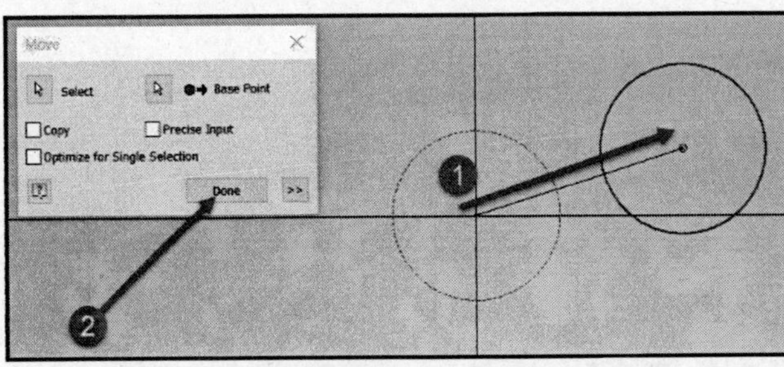

Note: You can use the press input option to move to a certain dimension.

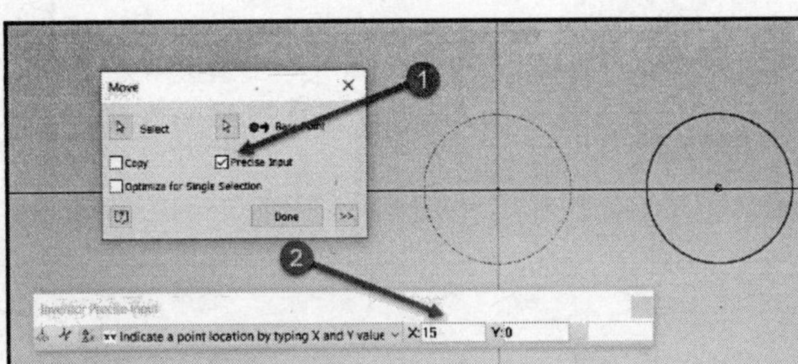

Copy

It is used to copy a sketch object. It is used exactly as a move tool.

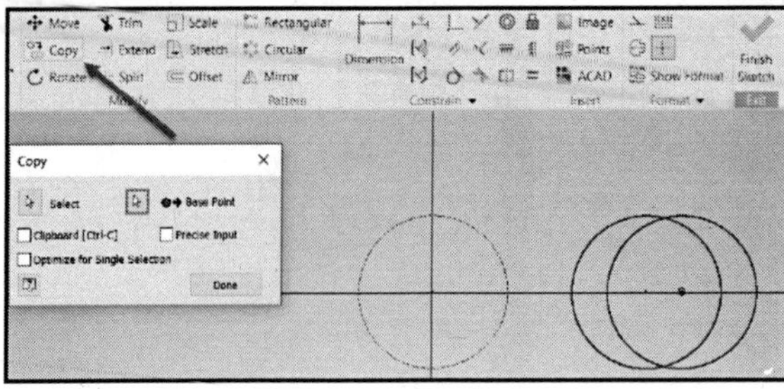

Rotate

It is used to change the angle of a sketch object. It is like a move tool but the only difference is here angle has to be given.

Step 1: Click on rotate tool and select the object.

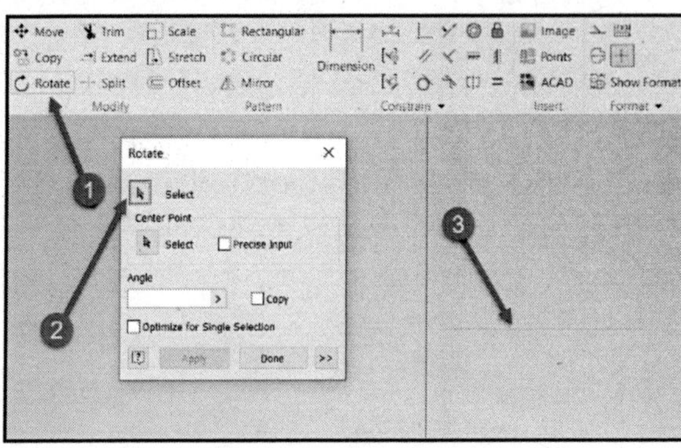

Step 2: Click on "center point" icon and click the base point of rotate. Then specify angle.

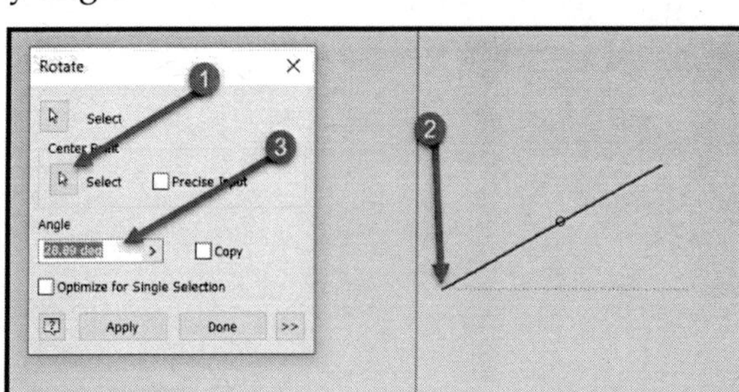

Step 3: click on apply & then on done button.

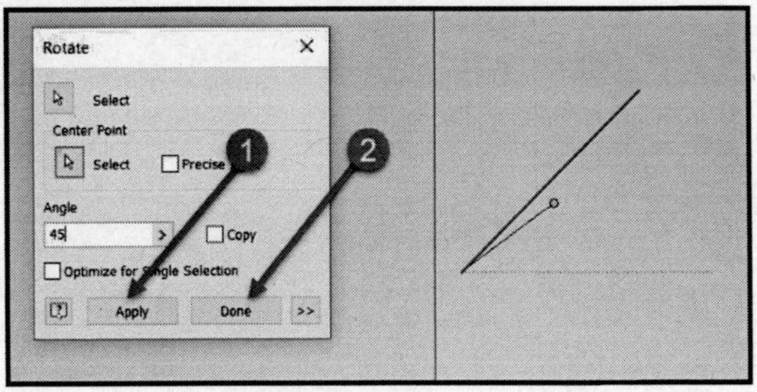

Trim

The trim tool is used in the sketch to remove the extras object. This tool is also used to delete objects.

Step 1: Click on "Trim tool".

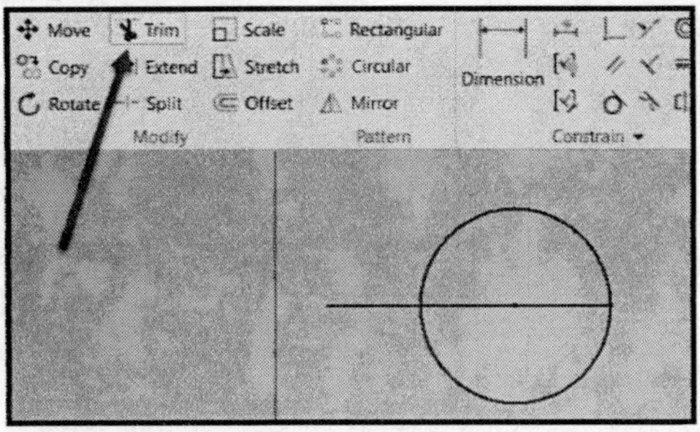

Step 2: Click on that extra object, which you want to remove.

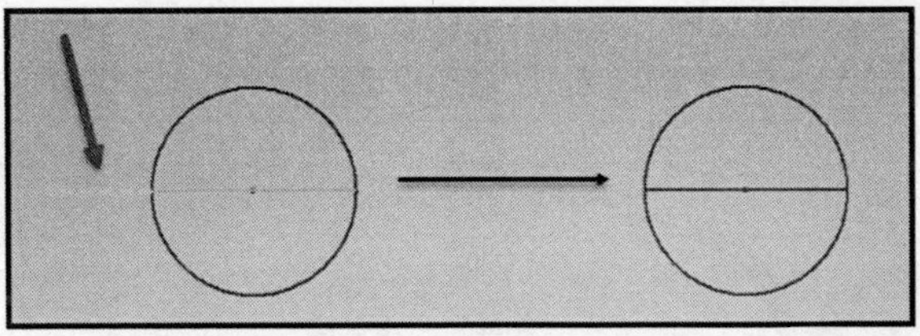

Extend

Extend tools are used to extend a sketch object.

Step 1: Click on "Extend tool".

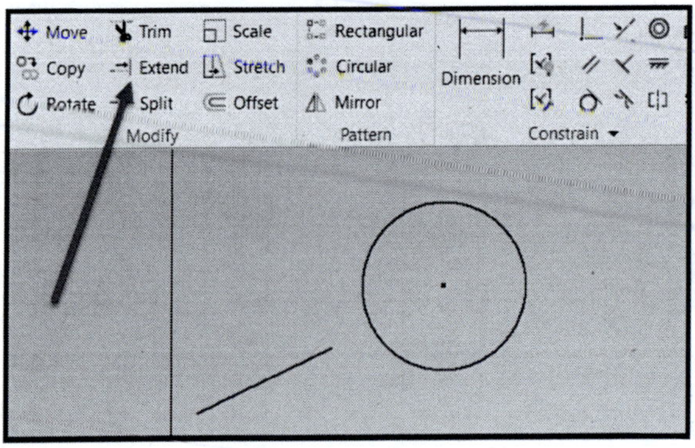

Step 2: Click on the source object, which you want to increase.

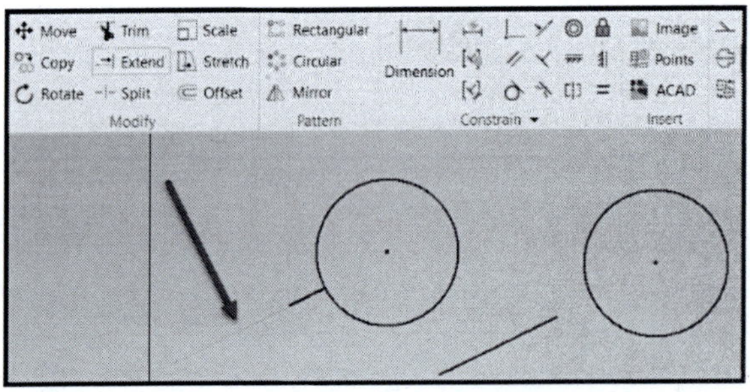

Split

It is used to break a sketch object. For example: if the circle has to be broken into 2 separate parts, it can be done with the split tool.

Step 1: Click on "Split tool".

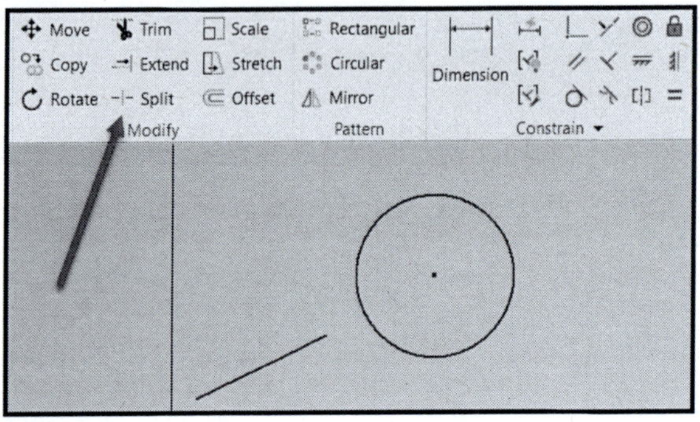

Step 2: Click on that object. Which you want to break on 2 parts. Make sure that there is also a reference line.

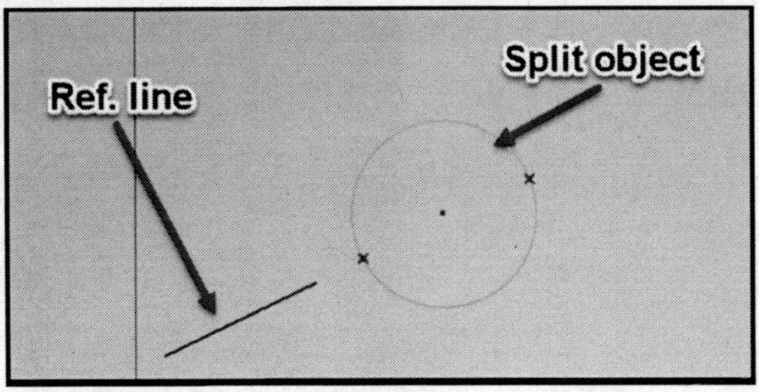

Scale

It is used to increase or decrease the scale of a sketch object. It is used exactly as a move tool.

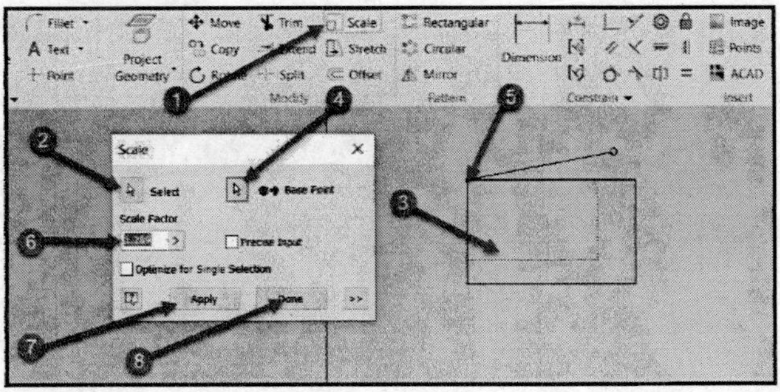

Stretch

The Stretch command is used to stretch the portion of the object partially enclosed by the polygon selection or window selection. The objects selected individually or completely enclosed by the window selection cannot be stretched. Those objects are rather moved such as ellipses, blocks, and circles.

Step 1: Click on "Stretch tool".

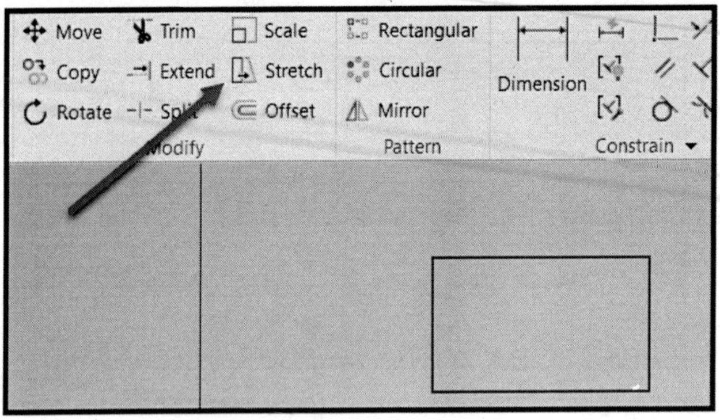

Step 2: Click on "select icon". Then select the sketch object, which you want to stretch.

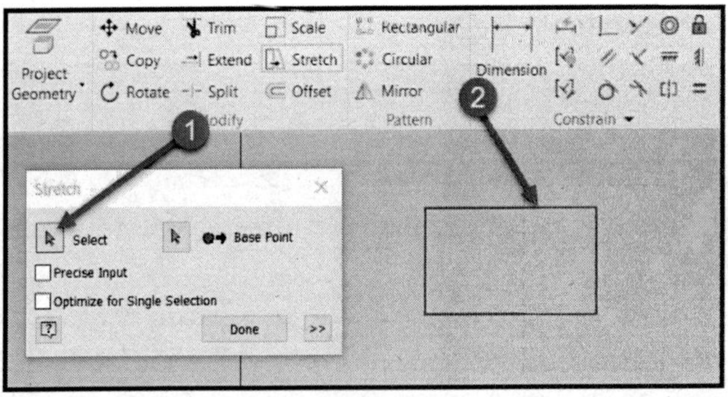

Step 3: Click on "base point icon". Then click on the sketch, where you want the base point.

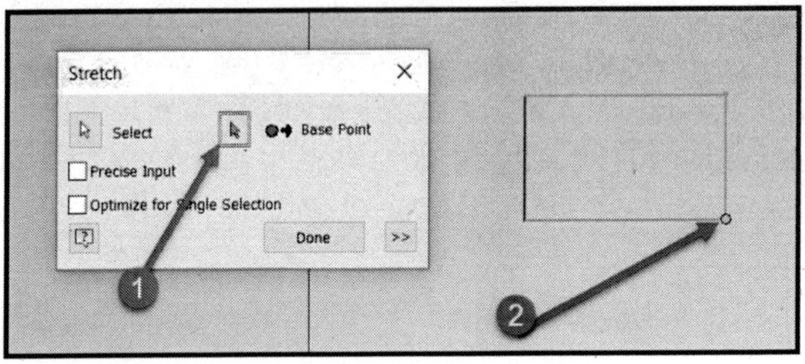

Step 4: Drag the base point and click on "done button".

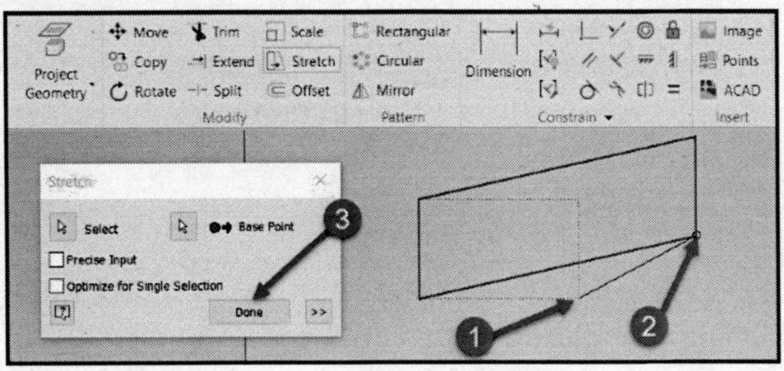

Offset

Offset one or more sketch entities, selected 2D sketch faces by a specified distance. For example, you can offset sketch entities such as splines or arcs, sets of 2D sketch. You can offset finite lines, arcs, and splines.

Step 1: Click on "offset tool".

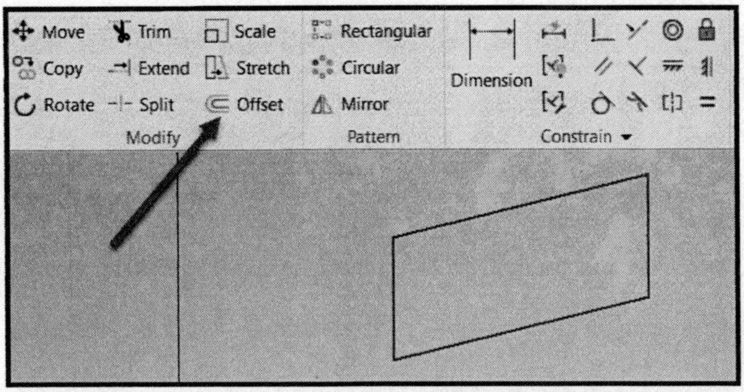

Step 2: Select the object then specify offset distance.

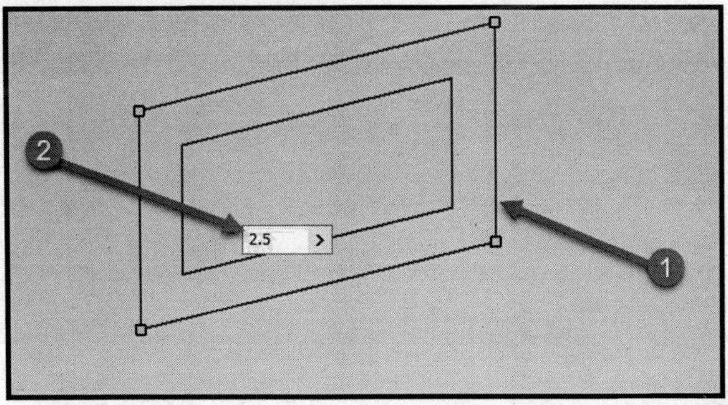

Pattern

In the sketch, when an object has to be copied more often, we use the pattern option. There are three types of patterns.

Rectangular

To copy a sketch object to a larger number in a straight direction, use the Rectangular Pattern Tools. In a rectangular pattern, you can pattern in two directions simultaneously.

Step 1: Click on "Rectangular tool".

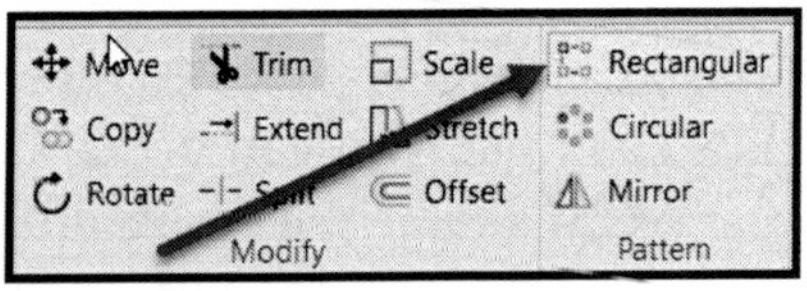

Step 2: First, click on the "Geometry icon". Then select the object, you want to pattern.

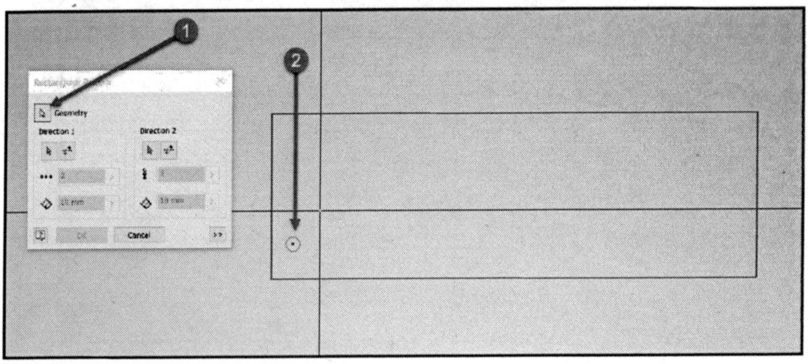

Step 3: Click on "direction1 icon" then select direction axis. Do the same for second direction.

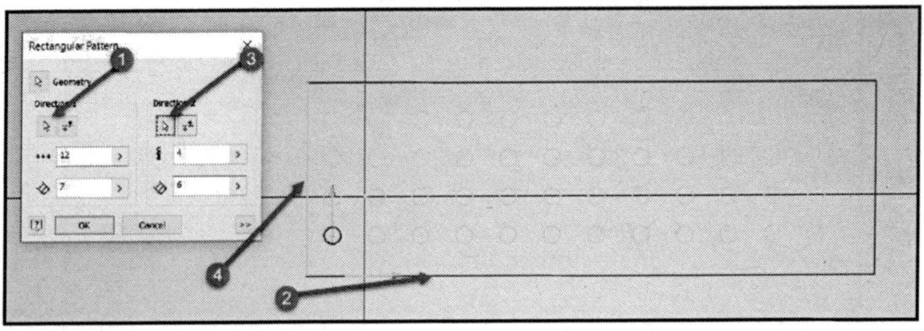

Step 4: Specify count and spacing. Then click "OK".

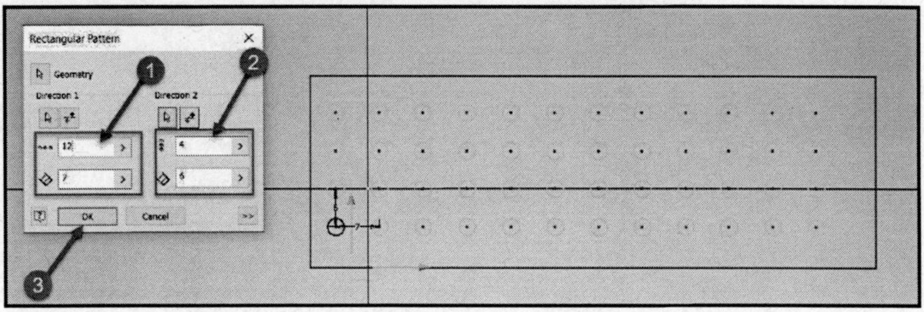

Circular

Use the circular pattern to copy the sketch object in angle. It is also necessary to have an axis point to perform circular pattern.

Step 1: Click the "circular tool".

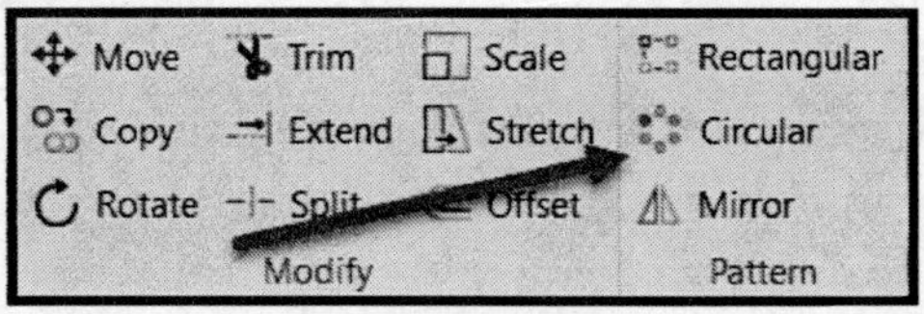

Step 2: First, click on the "Geometry icon". Then select the object. That you want to circular pattern.

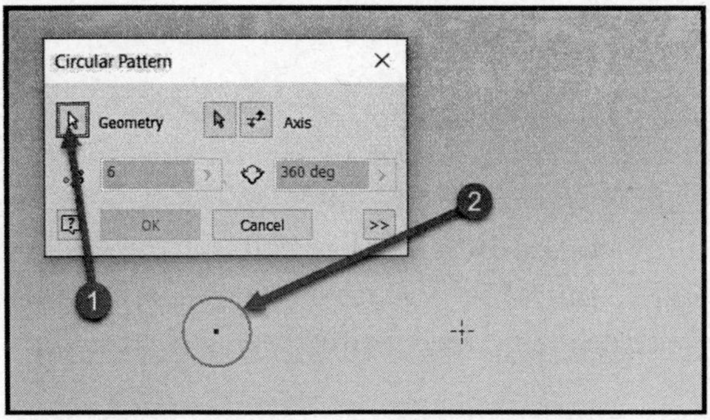

Step 3: Click the "axis icon" then select axis point.

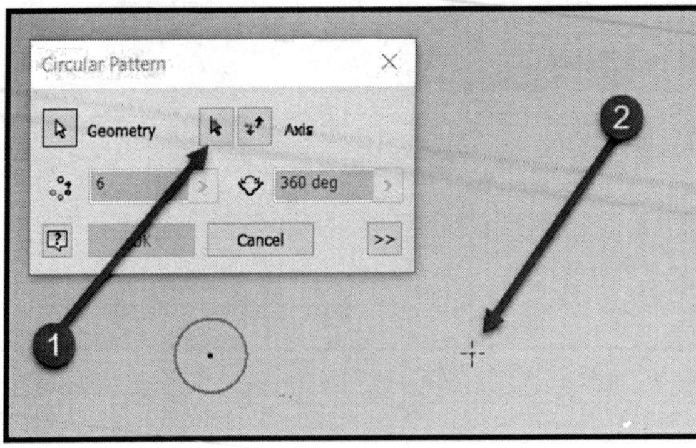

Step 4: After that, specify count and angle. Then click "OK".

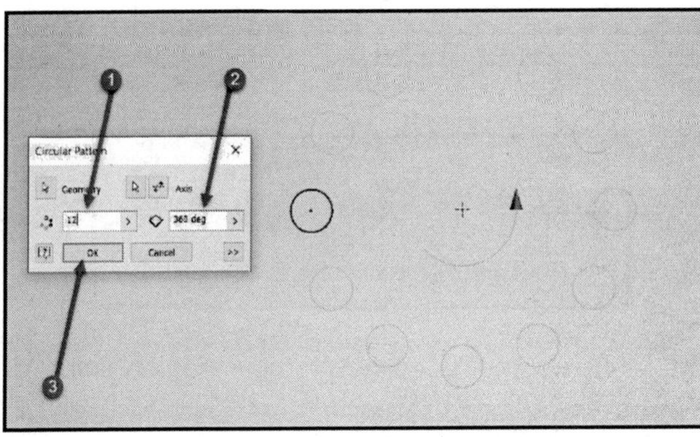

Mirror

The Mirror tool creates a mirror image of objects. You can create symmetrical drawings using this tool. Activate this tool and select the objects to mirror, and then define the 'mirror line' about which the objects will be mirrored. You can define the mirror line by either creating a line or selecting an existing line.

Step 1: Click the "mirror tool".

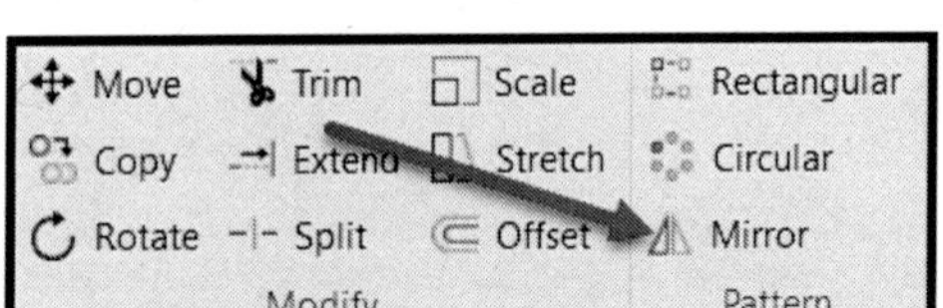

Step 2: Click on the "select icon". Then select the object. That you want to mirror.

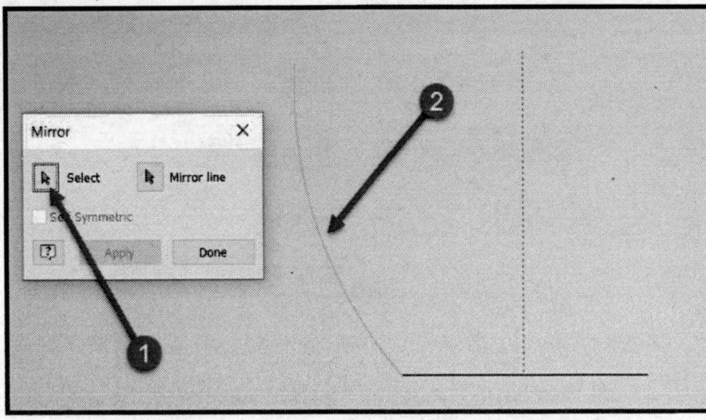

Step 3: Click on the "mirror line icon". Then select the axis line. After that, click the "apply button and done button".

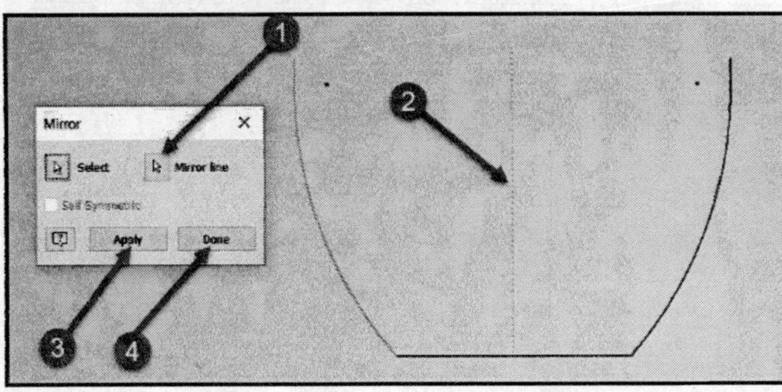

Project

Use the Project option to project the 2D and 3D edges in the sketch. The project option works only in an open sketch. Five types of project options have been given.

Project geometry

Step 1: First of all, select object face and click on sketch.

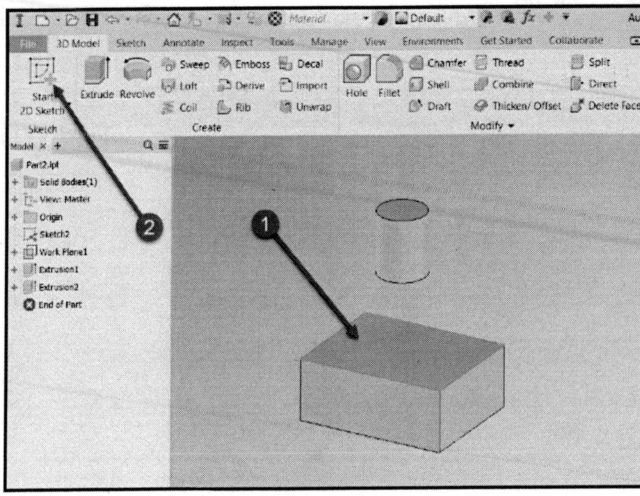

Step 2: Click on "project geometry tool".

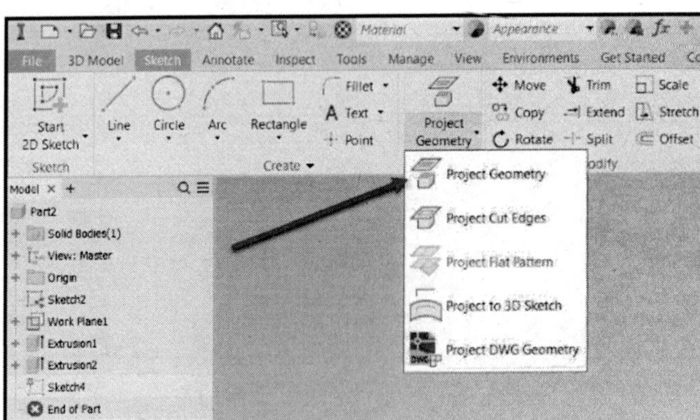

Step 3: Click the edge which you want to project.

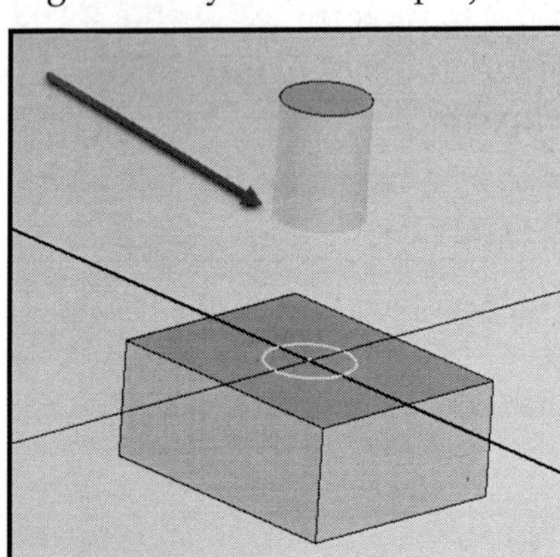

Project cut edges

Step 1: Select the plane and click on sketch option.

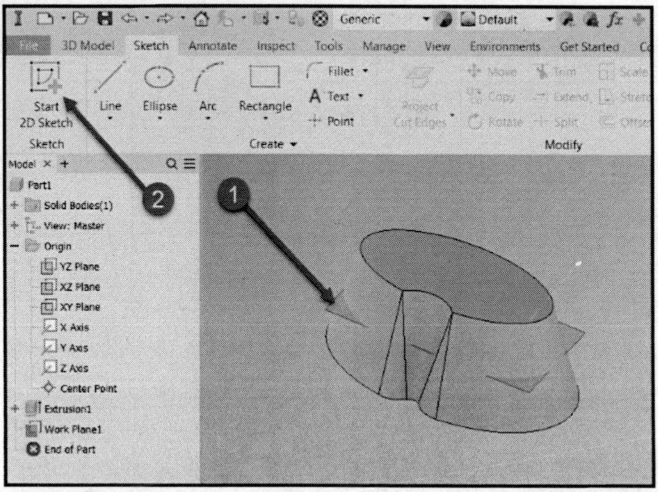

Step 2: Click on "Project cut edges tool".

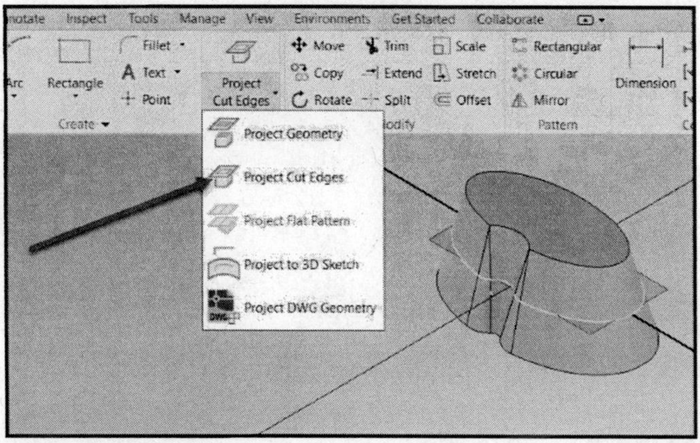

Project flat pattern

Step 1: First of all, make a sheet metal sheet with flange.

Step 2: Select the face and click on sketch option.

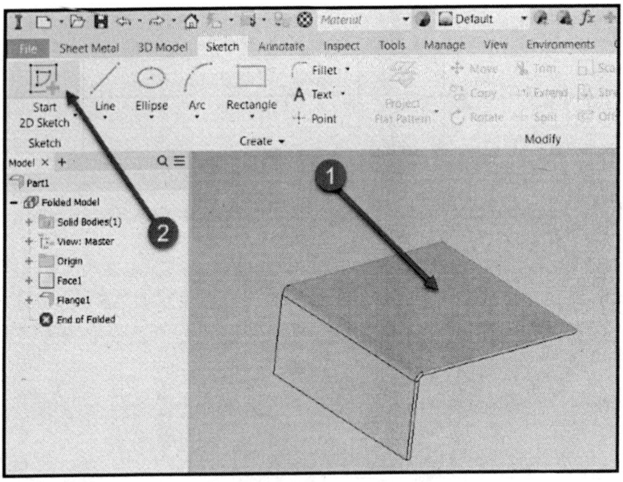

Step 3: Click on "project flat pattern tool".

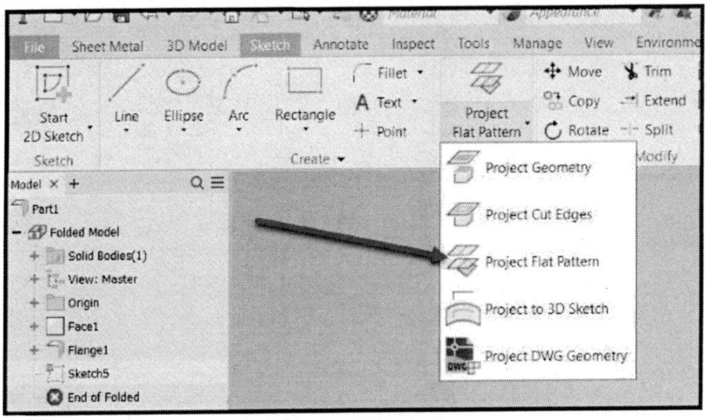

Step 4: Select the face which you want to project flat.

Project to 3d sketch

Step 1: Create a cylinder.

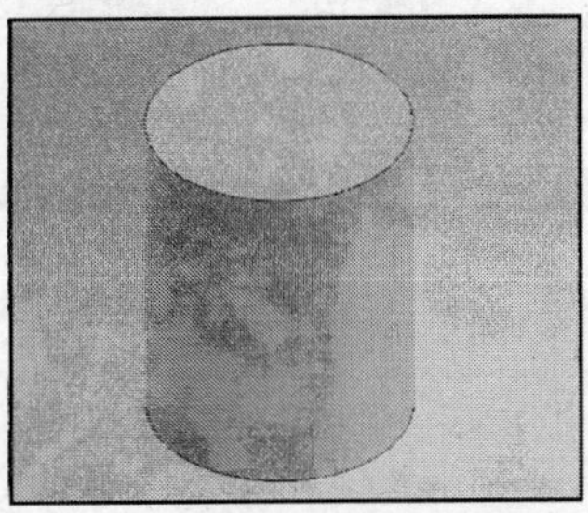

Step 2: Make another plane parallel to XY plane.

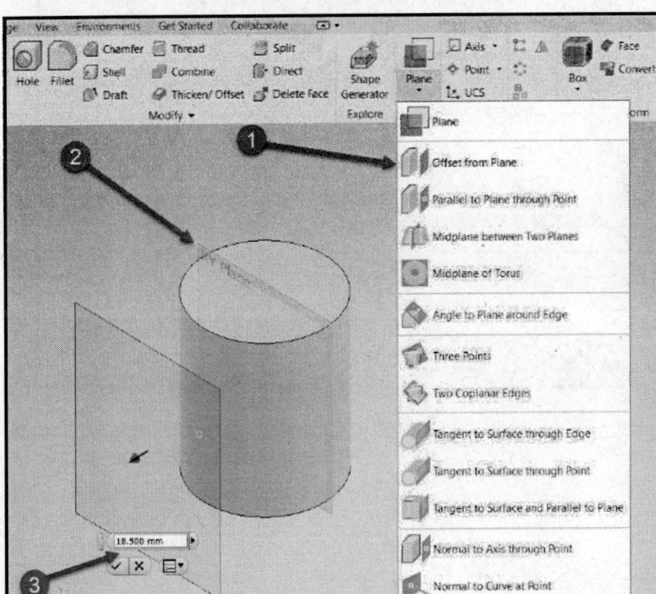

Step 3: Select the plane and click on sketch option.

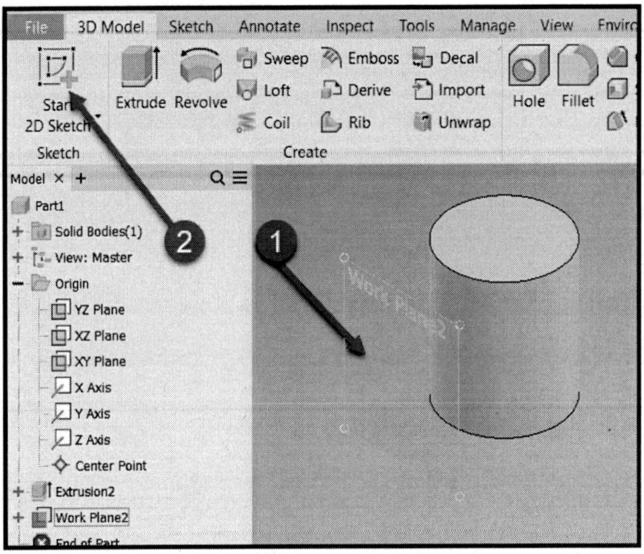

Step 4: Create a circle. Then click on "project to 3d sketch tool".

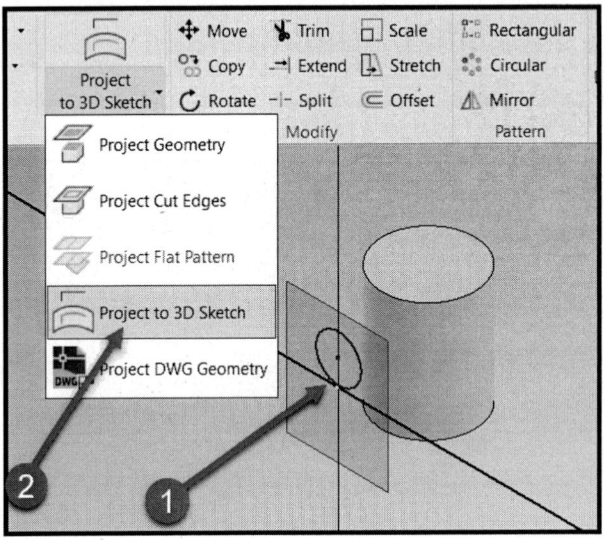

Step 5: Select the face and click on the "OK" button.

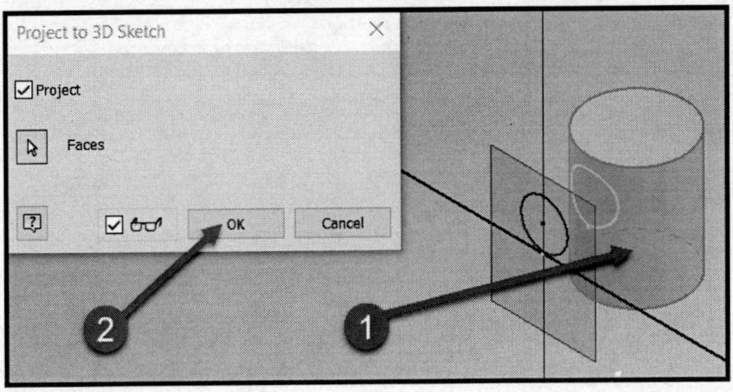

Insert

Insert image

It is used to place an image on any plane. Work can be made easier by inserting the image.

Step 1: In the sketch, Select the "face or plane" and click the "sketch" option.

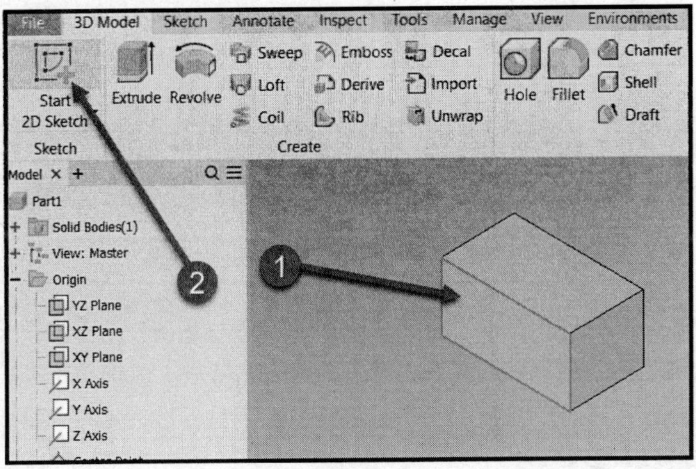

Step 2: Click the "insert image" tool and browse the image.

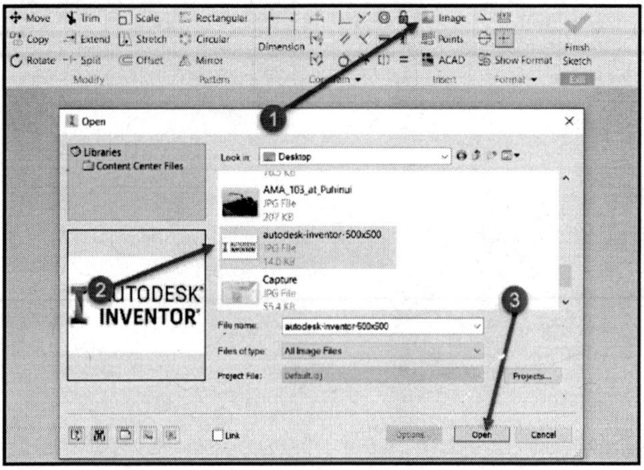

Step 3: Specify the base point of the image.

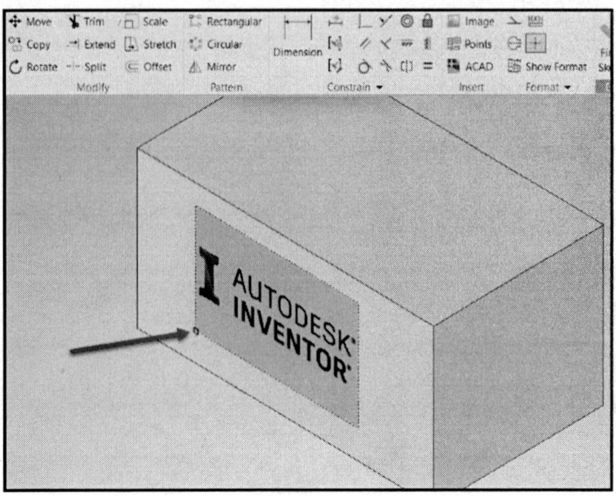

Note: Use the Modify tools to adjust the image. Such as, move, rotate and scale.

Import points

Coordinate points can be inserted through Excel in this tool. For which the value of X, Y and unit should be.

Step 1: Create an Excel sheet. In which you will give the values of the digits x, y and z. That too with the unit.

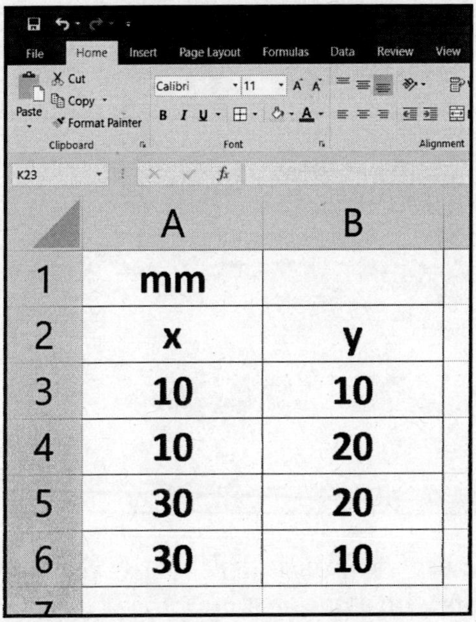

Step 2: Select XY plane then click the "sketch" option in the ribbon bar.

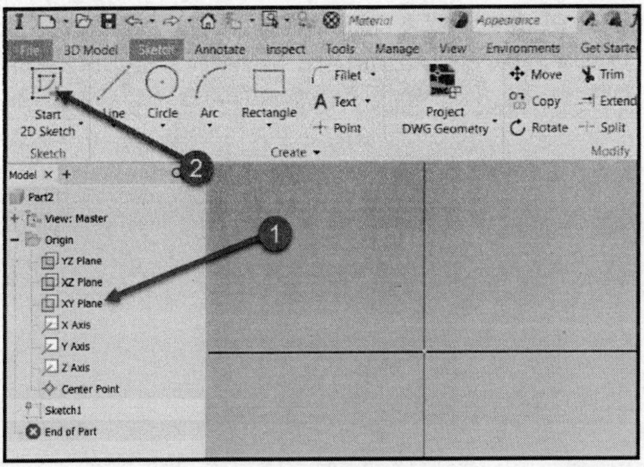

Step 3: Click the "points" tool in the sketch tab. And browse the excel file.

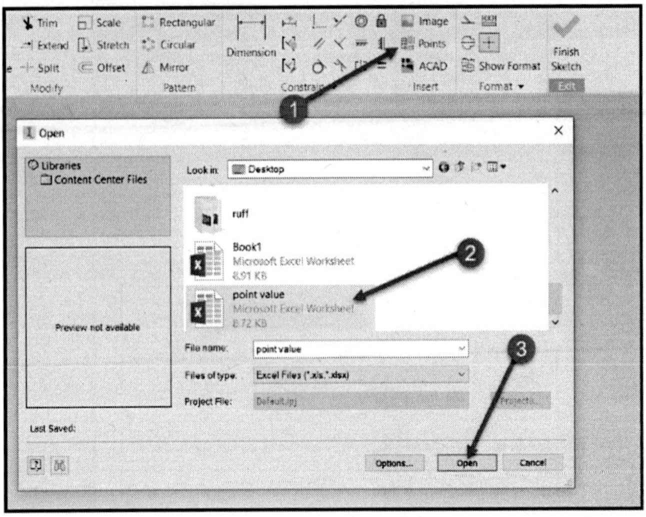

Step 4: You can use any sketch tool. Sketches can be completed by combining points with a line or spline.

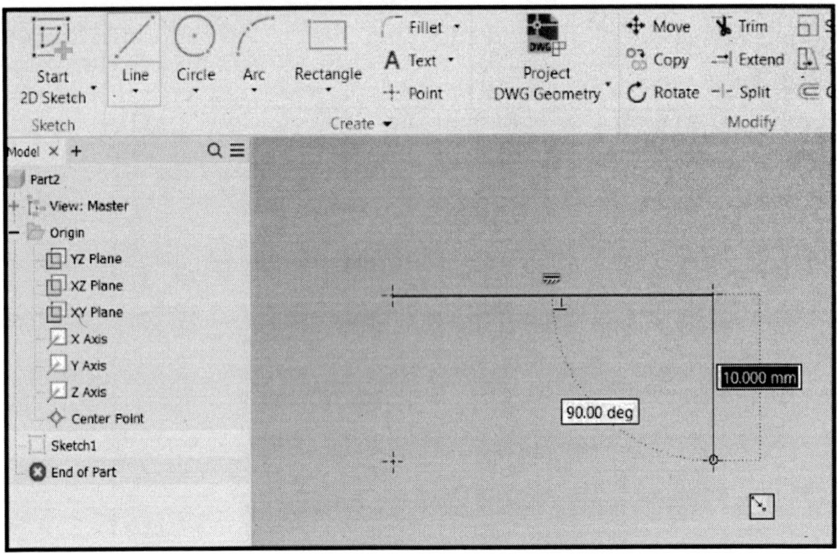

Insert AutoCAD file

It is used to Insert the Cad file. Work can be made easier by inserting the CAD file.

Step 1: Select XY plane then click the "sketch" option in the ribbon bar.

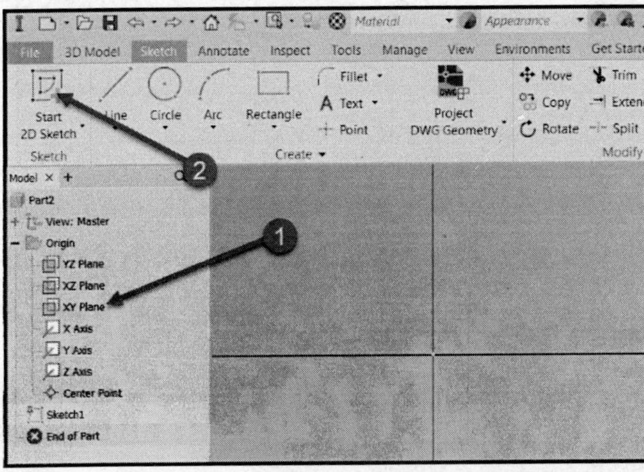

Step 2: Click the "ACAD" tool in the sketch tab. And browse dwg file.

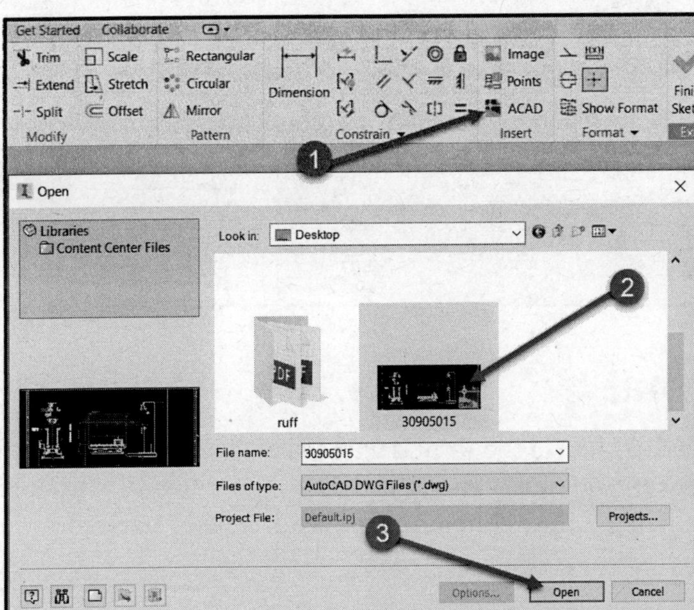

Step 3: Choose layer then click the "next" button.

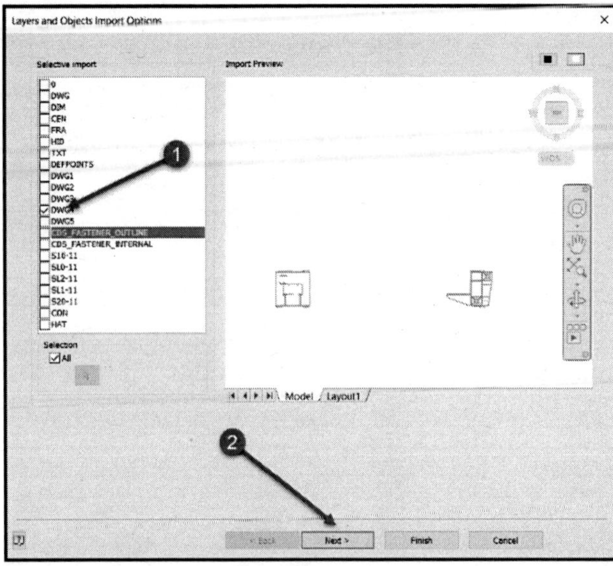

Step 4: Choose unit type then click the "finish" button.

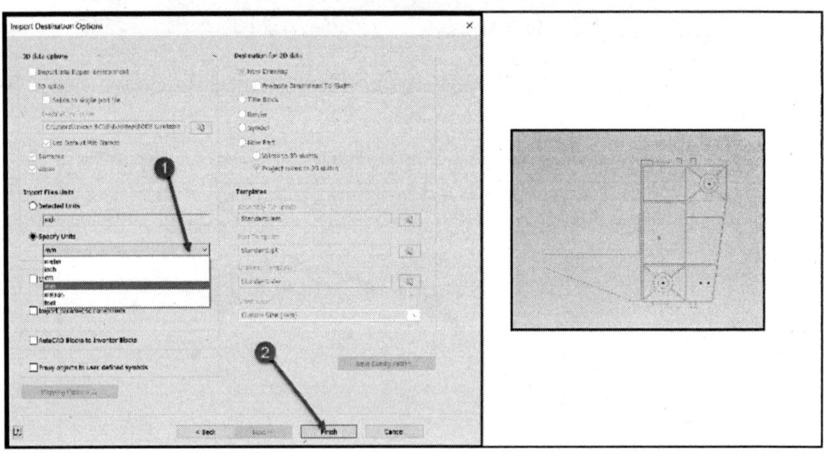

Format

It is used to change the format of the sketch object. For example, the color, layer, and line type of the sketch. From the format, the sketch can be divided into a different part. Which makes sense to be a sketch and interactive and clear.

Construction

The construction tool is used to make a sketch a reference sketch. For this, you just have to turn on the Constructions option. After this, create sketches as you do. Similarly, you can make construction sketches.

Step 1: In the sketch, Click the "construction" tool.

Step 2: Start drawing. And now you will see the difference in both sketches.

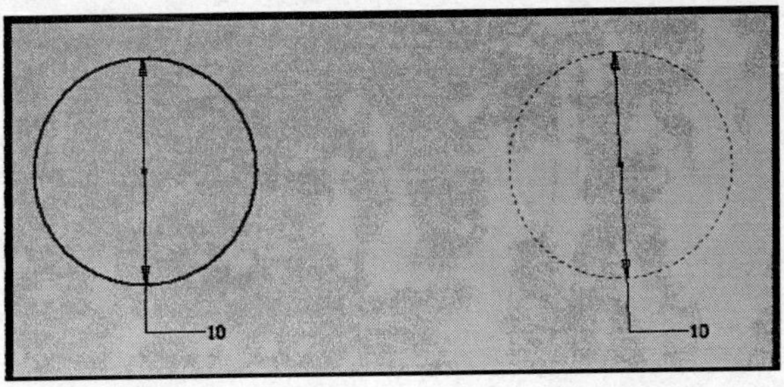

Note: 1. You can also convert a normal sketch to a construction sketch. For that, you select the sketch. Click on the construction tool.

2. The construction sketch only works for reference sketches. You cannot use it in 3D. In 3D it is used only for reference Purpose.

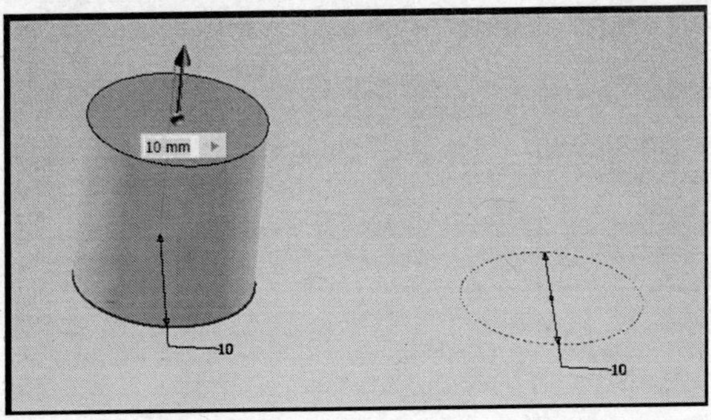

Centerline

The centerline is used to automatically draw the line between 2 lines. It also serves as a reference line. It is also used as a construction tool. You can create a centerline by turning on the Centerline tool.

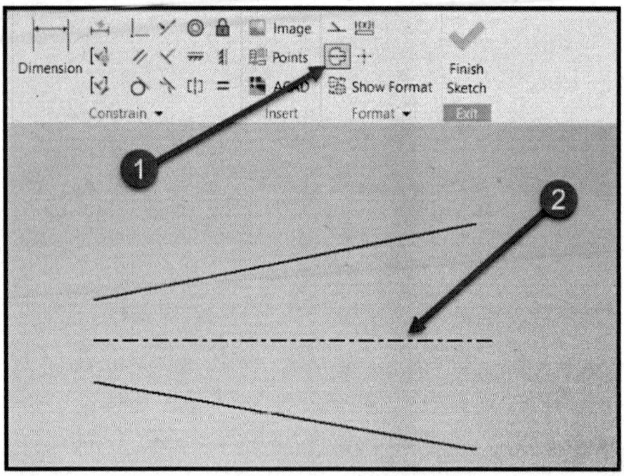

Line Type, Color and Line width

To change the format of the sketch, we use line type, line width, and color format. These are 3 different options. To use these tools, you can select the format by selecting Sketch Object.

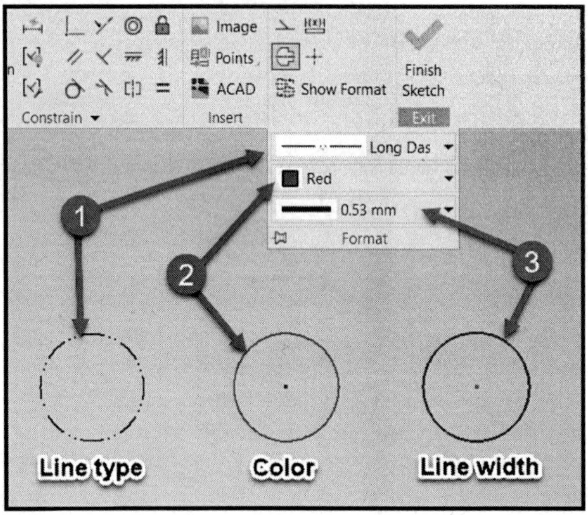

Show format

Show format works to show or hide the format on the sketch. With its help, you can show the format of all objects in the normal default format.

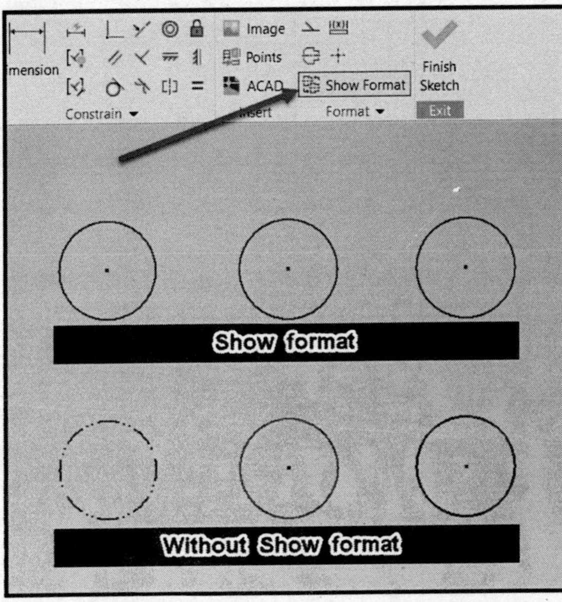

Chapter 5
Part Design

Extrude

Extrude is used to increase the height of any sketch so that you can convert it into the 3d object. Extrude converts the sketch into the body.

Step 1: First of all, select the "front" plane and click the Sketch.

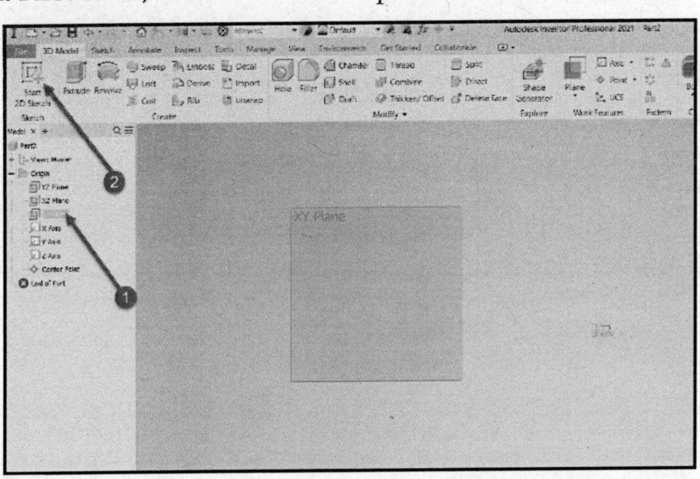

Step 2: After that, create a sketch. Then click the "finish sketch" for a close sketch.

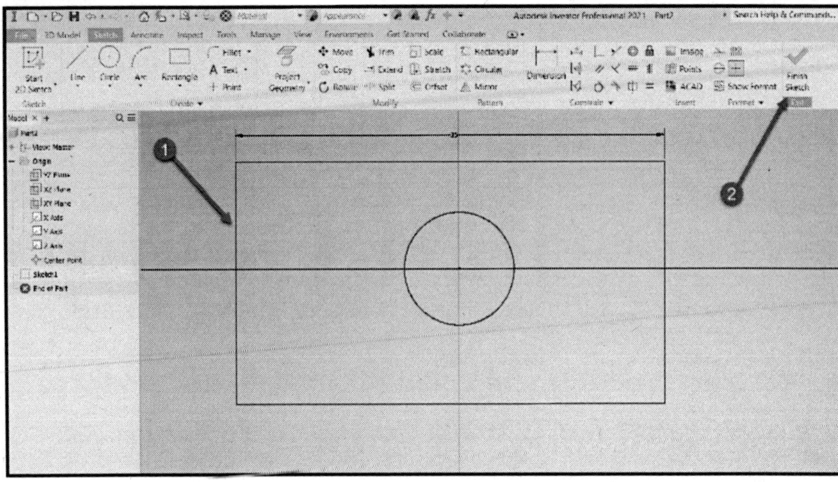

Step 3: Select the sketch profile. And click the "Extrude" tool.

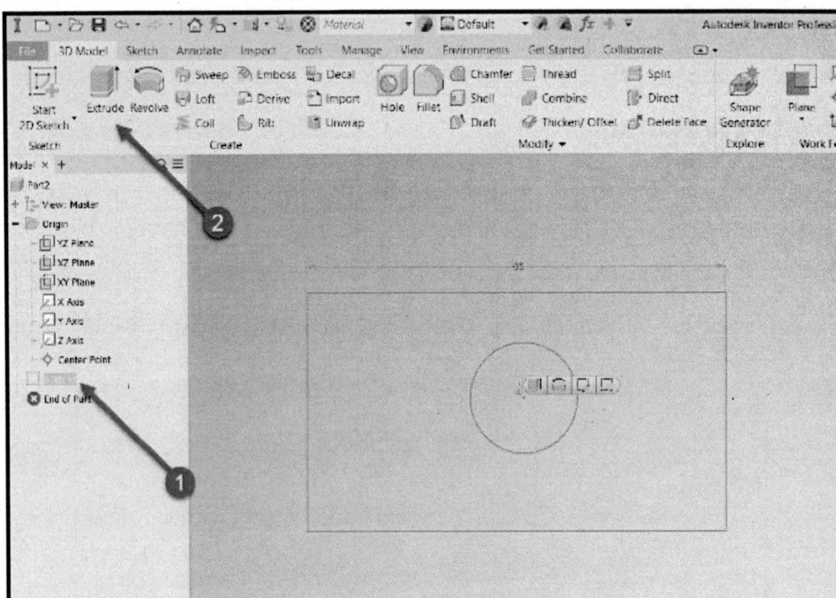

Step 4: Which you want to extrude. Select that profile.

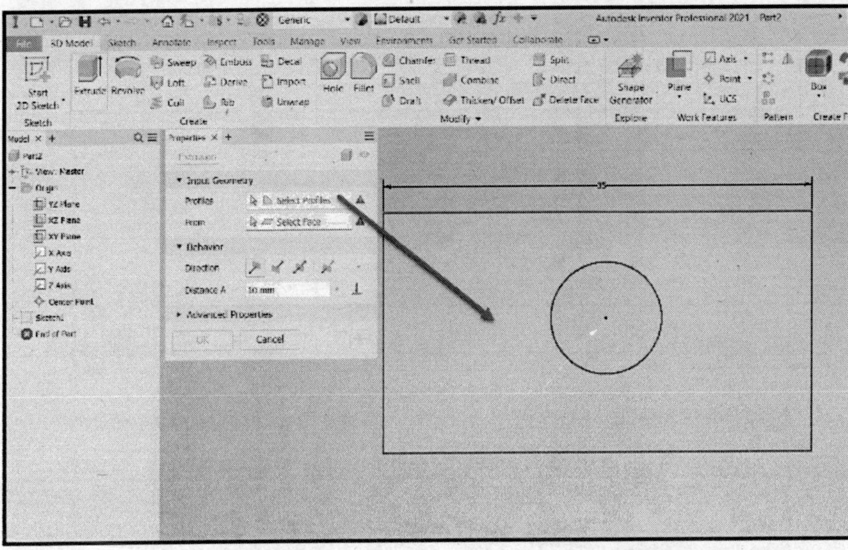

Step 5: Give the dimension then click "OK".

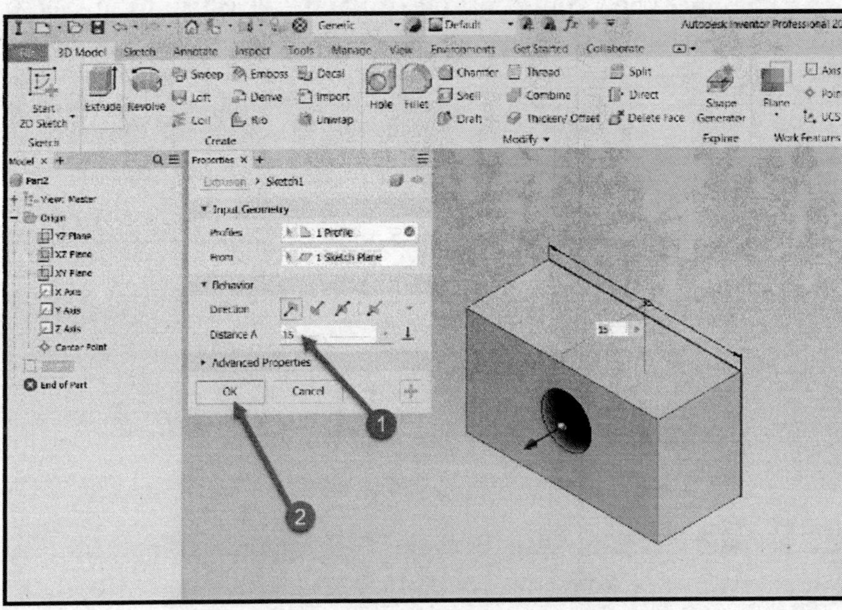

Note 1: Extrude has different options in the extrude tool. Such as, Input geometry, Behavior, Output and advanced properties.

1. Input geometry

- **Profiles:** To select particular profiles in extrude, use "the profiles" option.

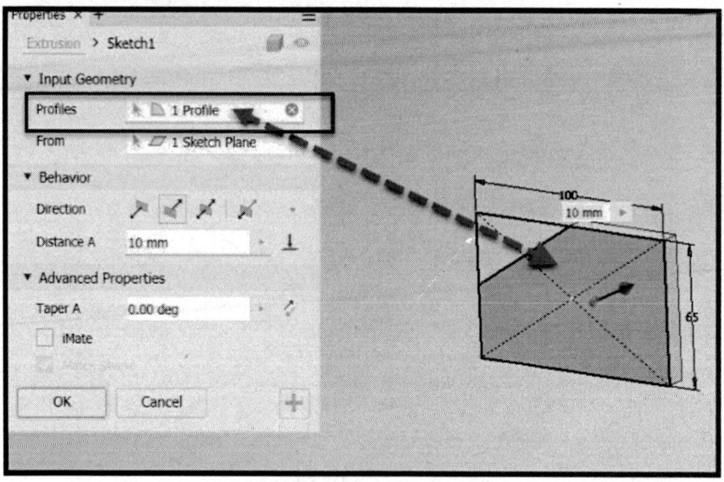

- **From:** When you want to extrude the object so from where you want to extrude it you can use it from.

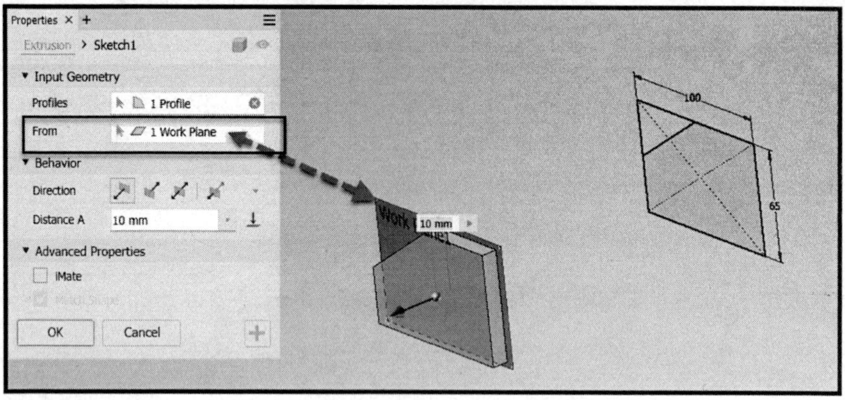

2. Behavior

- **Direction:** With this option, you can select the direction of extruding. It has 4 options.

Default

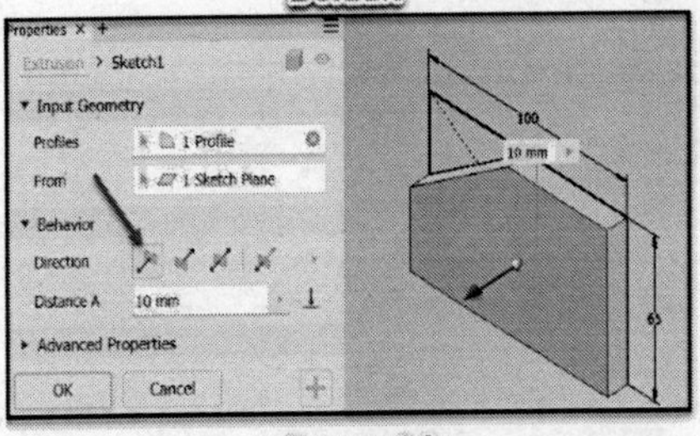

Flipped

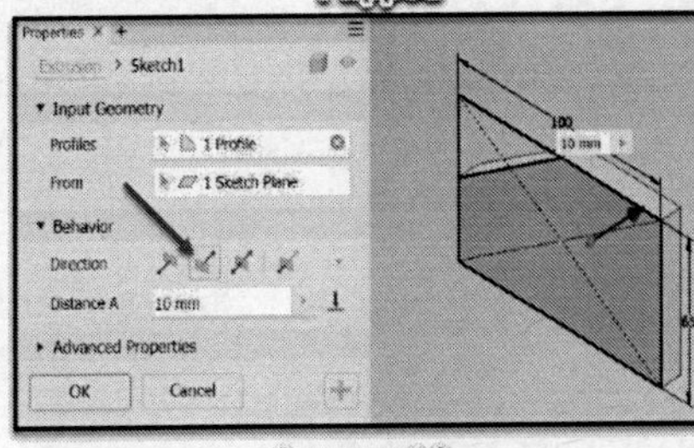

Symmetric

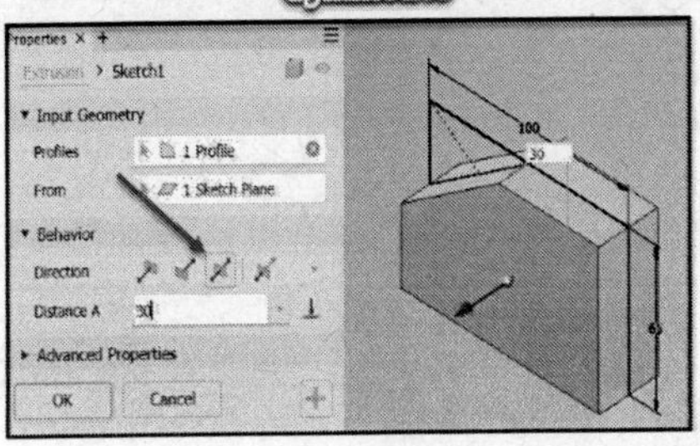

Asymmetric

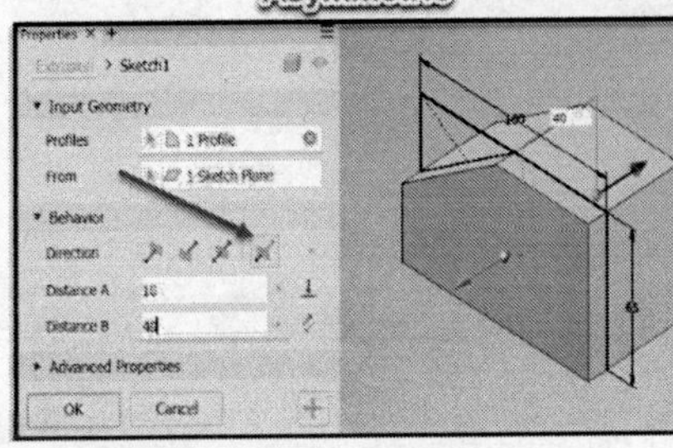

- **Distance:** For extrude, we use "distance", "to", "through all", and "to next".

Distance

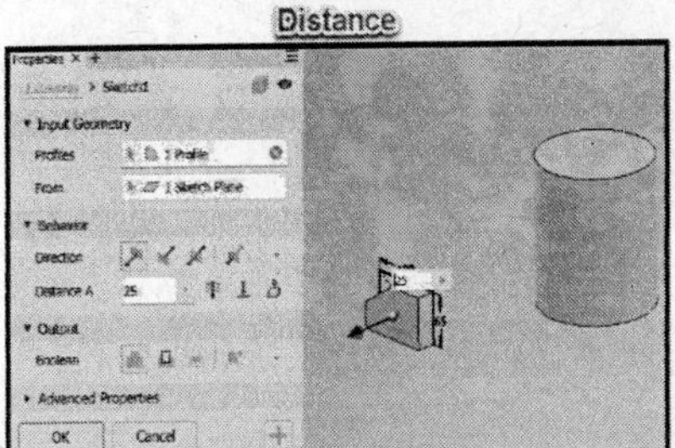

Through all

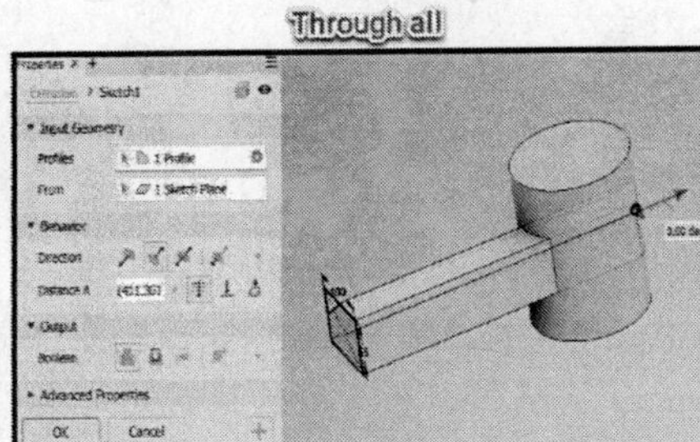

To

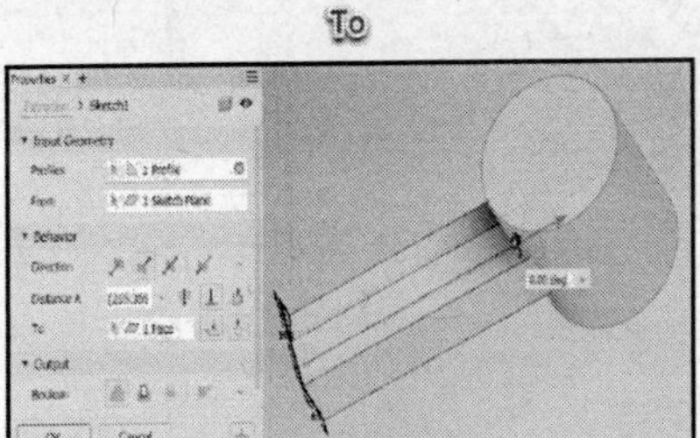

To next

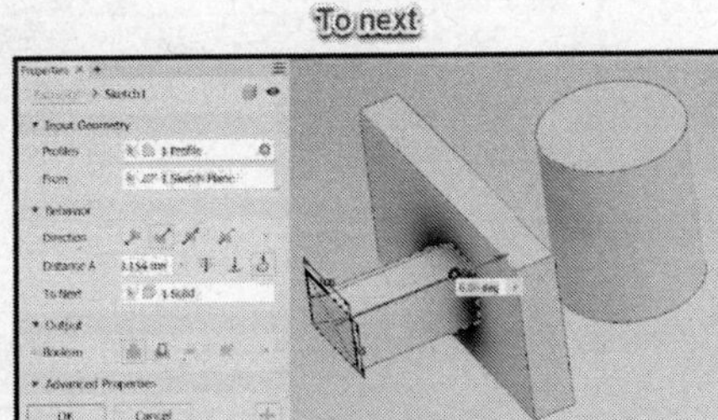

3. Output

- **Boolean:** Use the Boolean for extruding objects from another solid body to join, cut, intersect, or new body.

Join

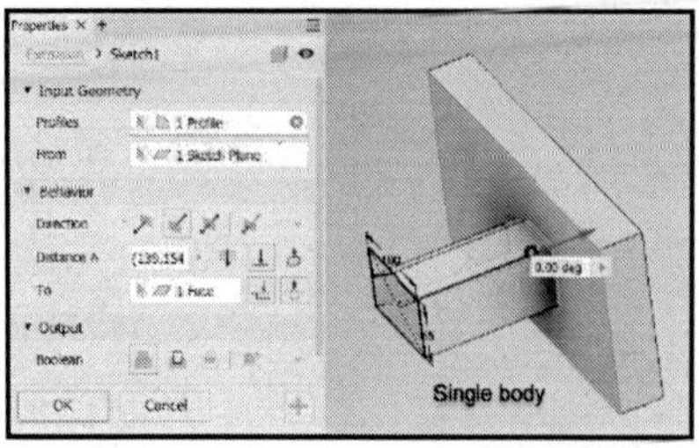

Cut

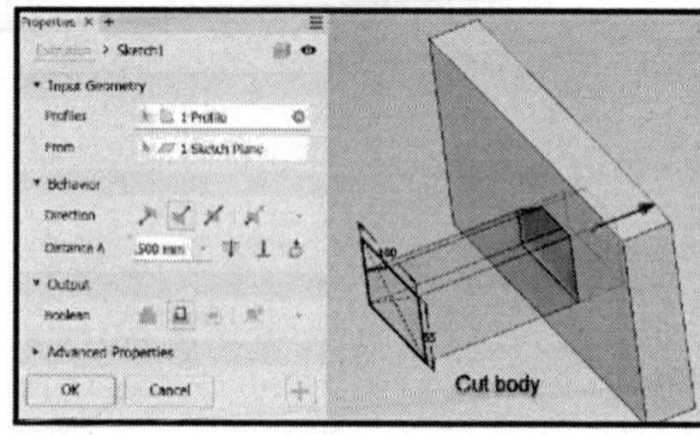

Intersect

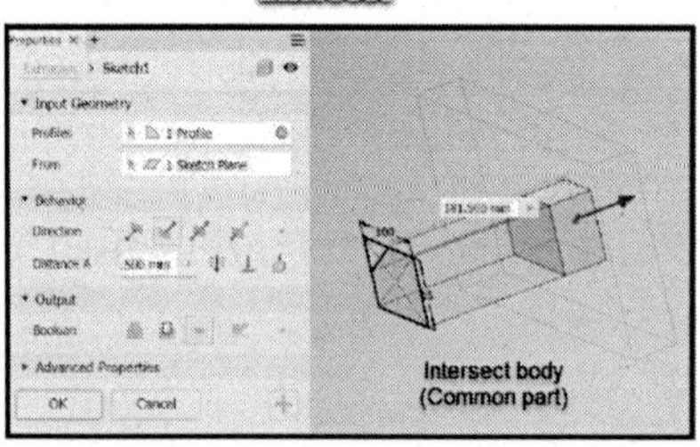

New body

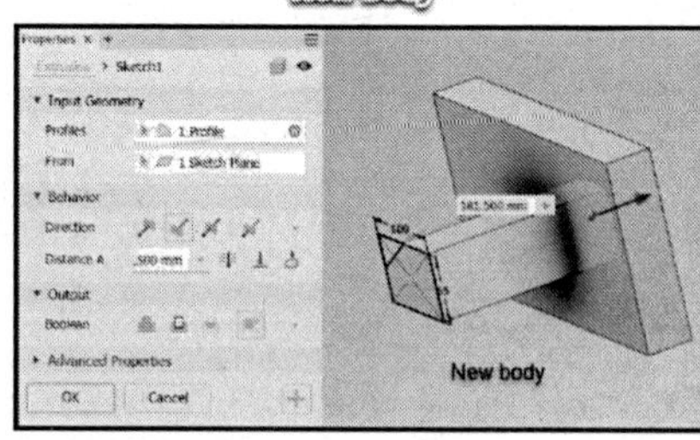

4. Advanced properties

- **Taper:** It is used to extrude the object with the angle.

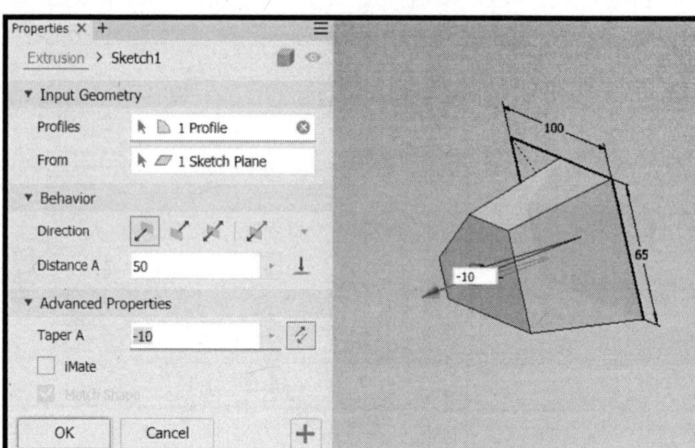

Note 2: If you want to Surface extrude. So you can also surface extrude with this tool.

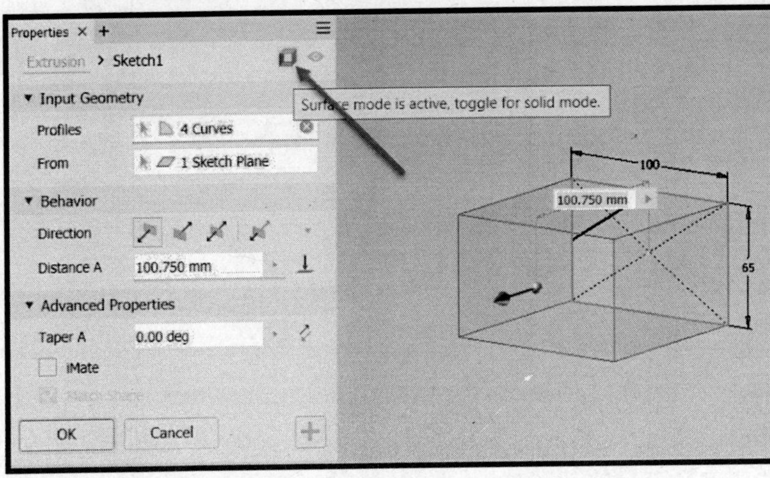

Revolve

Revolve is used to create an object circular about any axis. To use revolve sketch should be closed and there should be at least one axis.

Step 1: First of all, select the "front" plane and click the "Sketch".

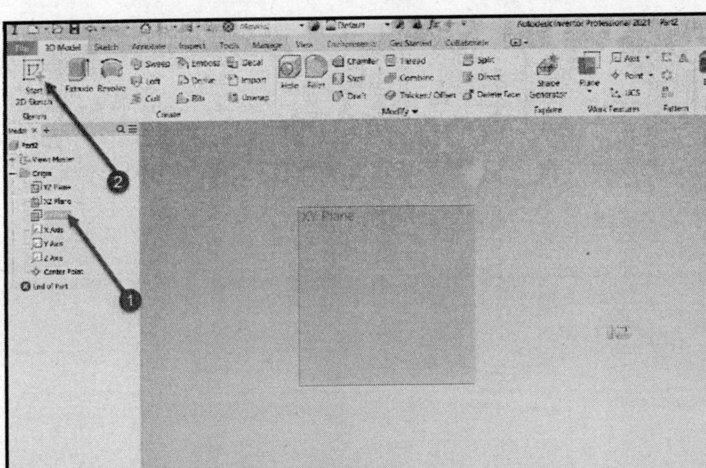

Step 2: After that create a sketch. Then click on finish sketch for close sketch. Make sure an axis is also to be made.

Note 1: Use construction option for Axis line.

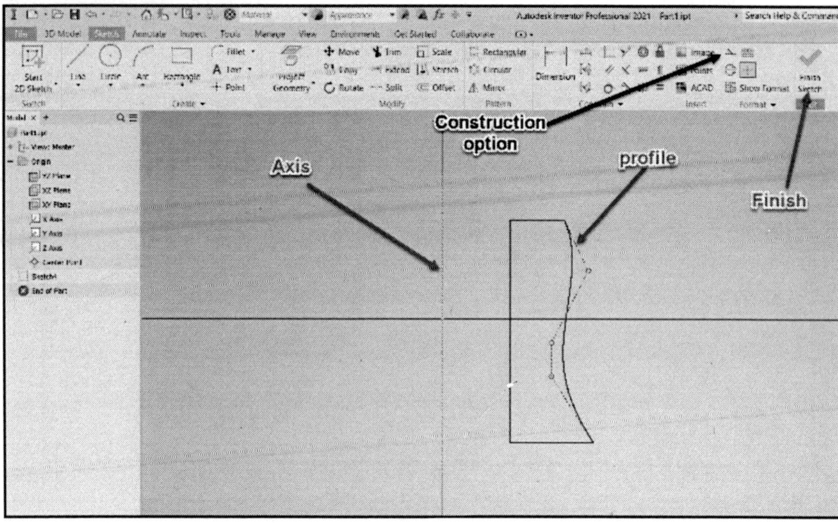

Step 3: Select axis and specify an angle for revolving. Then click OK.

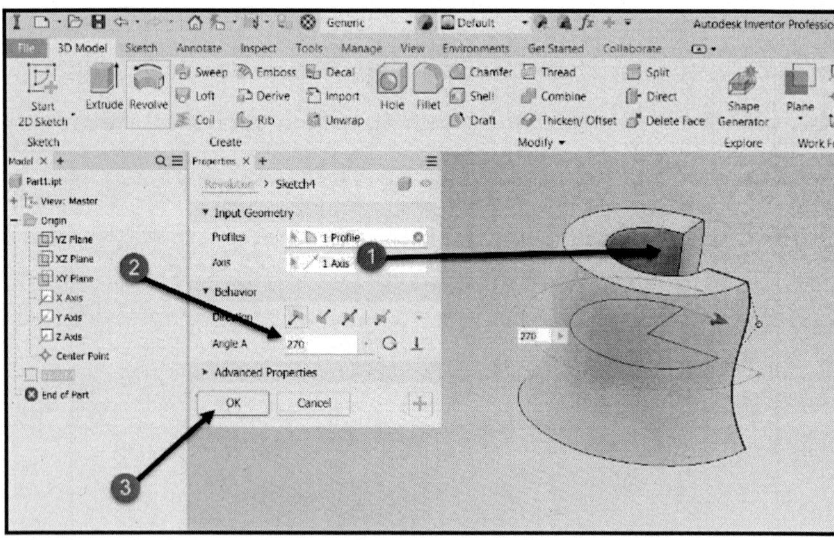

Note 2: This tool has more options. Which we use for revolving. Such as Direction, Angle, and Advance Properties, etc.

Sweep

In sweep command you can convert a path into any profile shape with the help of any profile. By following the profile path shape can be converted.

Step 1: First of all, select the "front" plane and click the "Sketch".

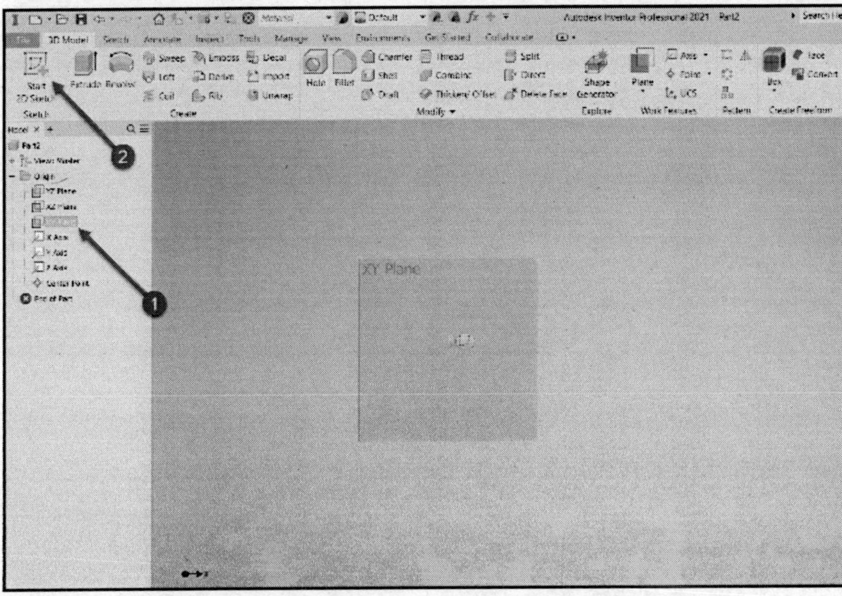

Step 2: Make a path from the spline. Then click the "finish sketch" for close sketch.

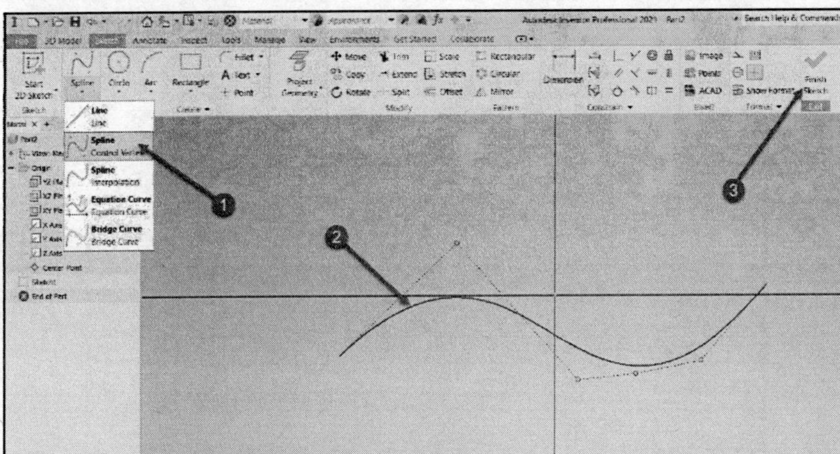

Step 3: Select sketch then click on "Normal to curve at point".

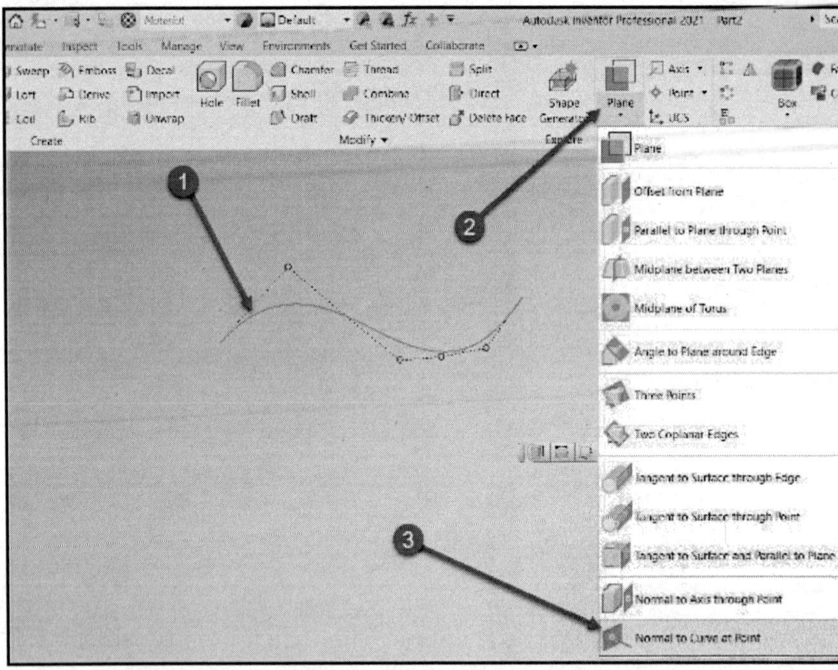

Step 4: Click the endpoint of the spline.

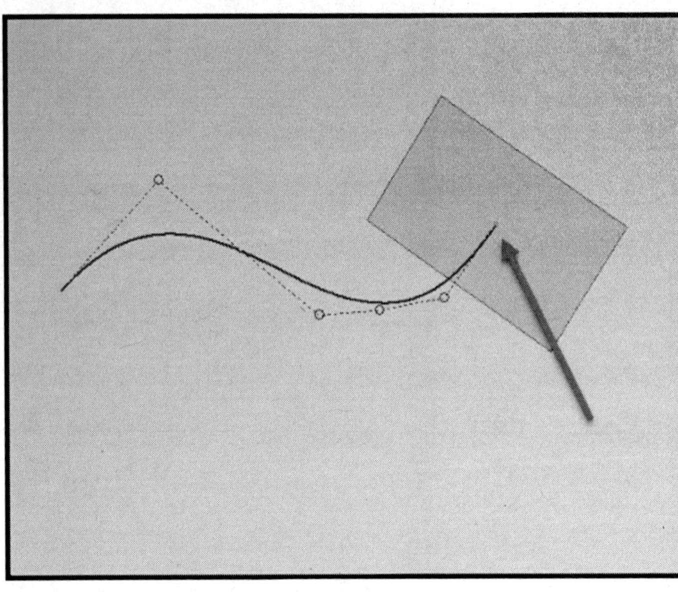

Step 5: Select new plane and click the "sketch".

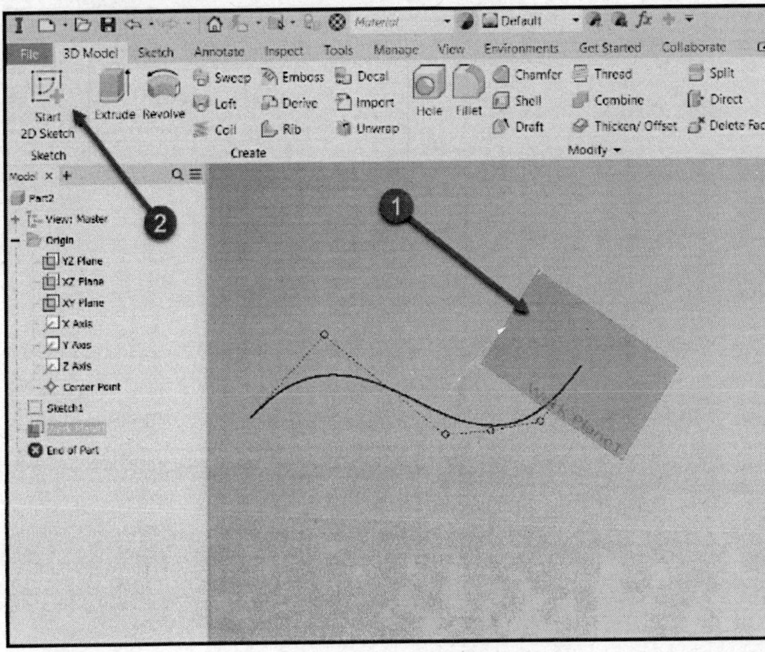

Step 6: Make a profile from the circle. Then click the "finish sketch" for close sketch.

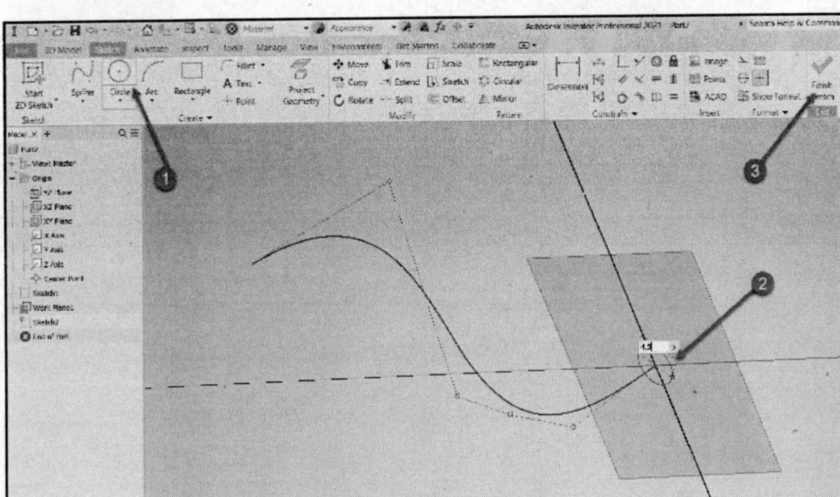

Step 7: After that, click the "sweep" tool then select profile and path.

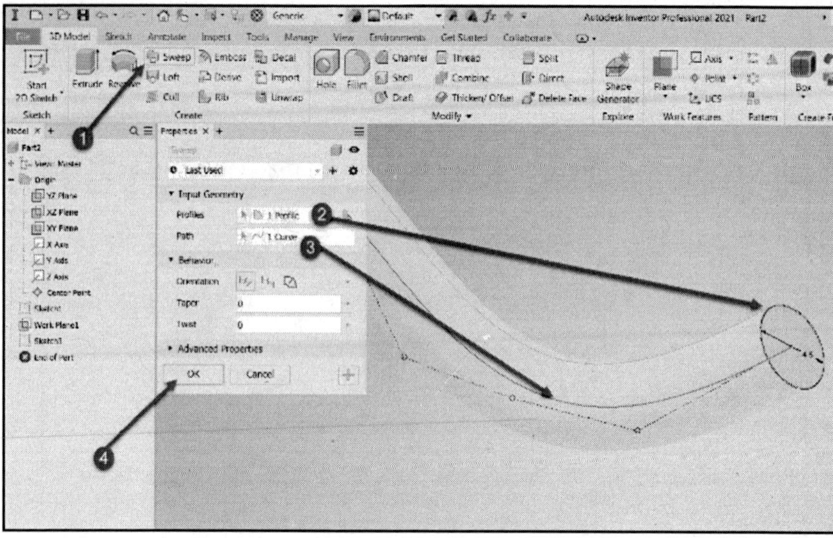

Note 1: This tool has more options. Which we use for a sweep. Such as, follow the path, fixed, guide, taper, and twist.

Follow path

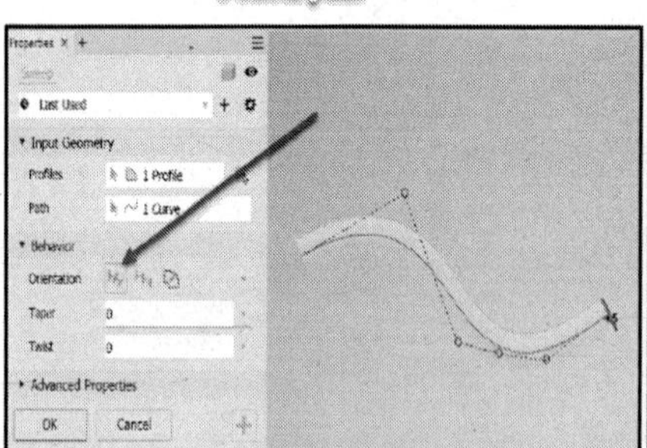

Fixed

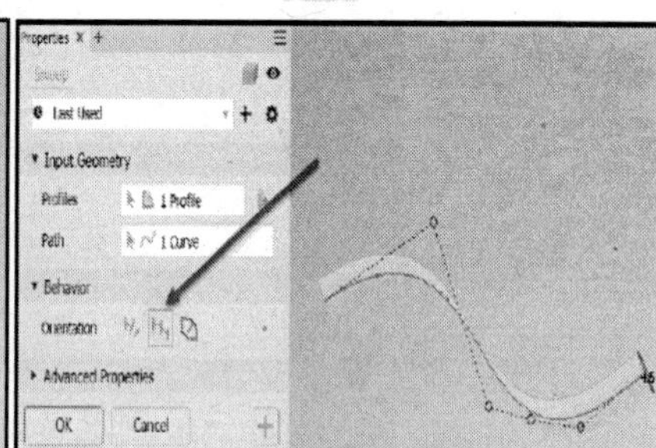

Guide

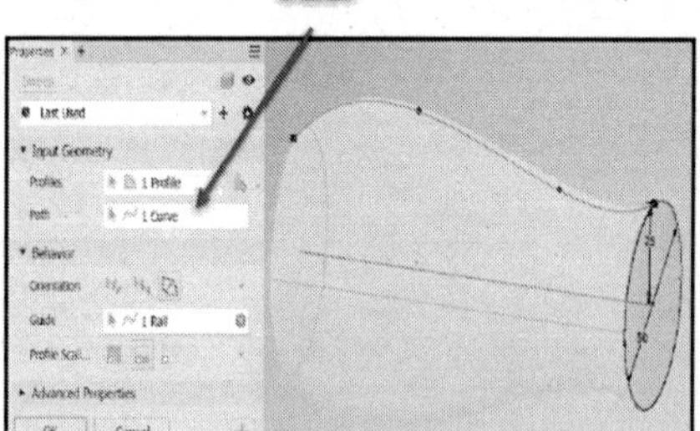

Taper

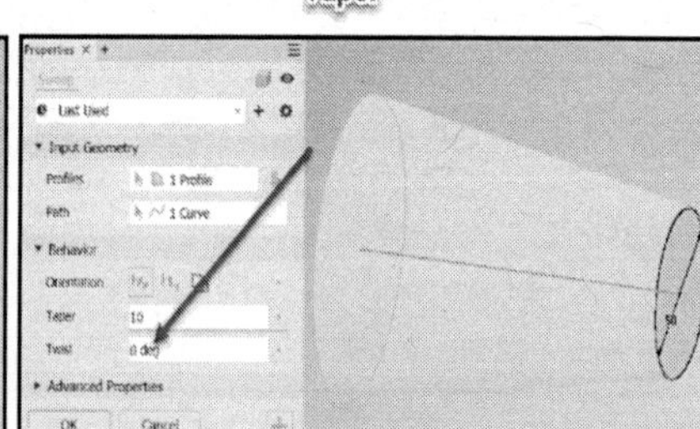

Twist

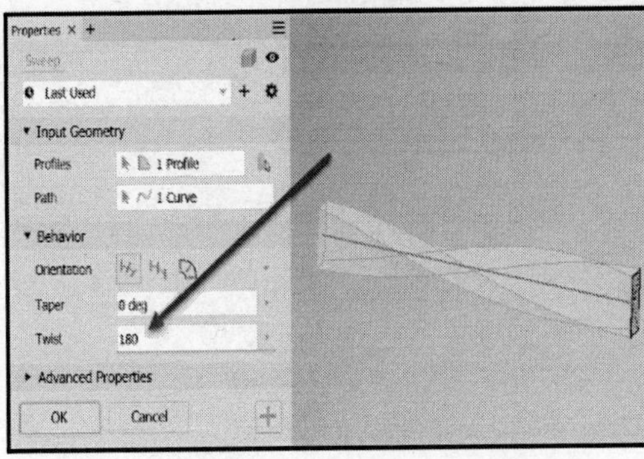

Loft

It is used to convert two or more objects into the solid body but in same shape. You can also give the direction with the help of guide curve.

Step 1: First of all, create the first sketch on the front plane and create the second sketch on another pallor plane of the front plane.

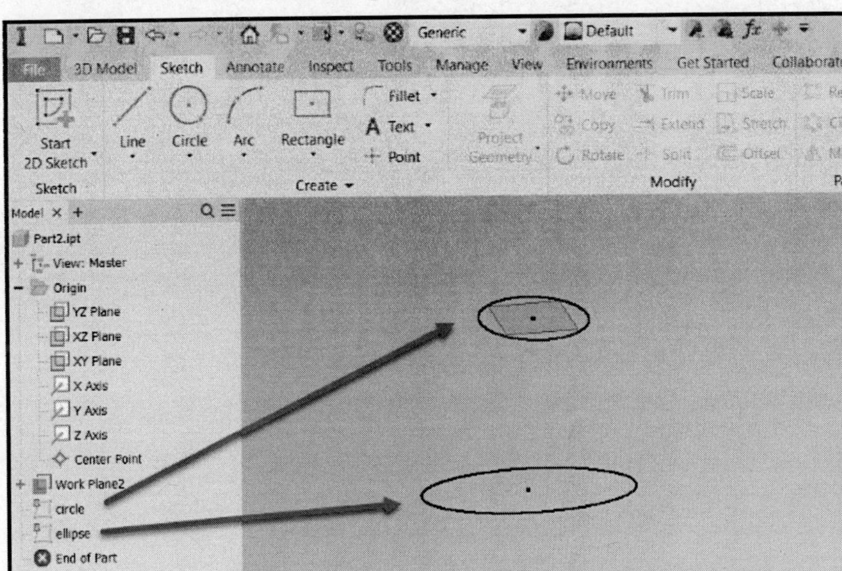

Step 2: Make two guide curves after this. But make sure to have two separate sketches. Not a single sketch.

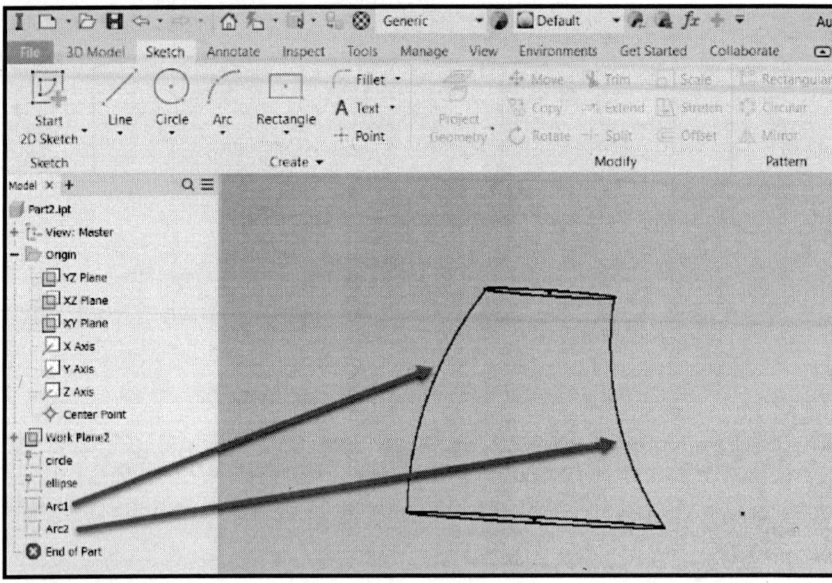

Step 3: Click the "loft" tool. Then select the first circle sketch and select the second ellipse sketch.

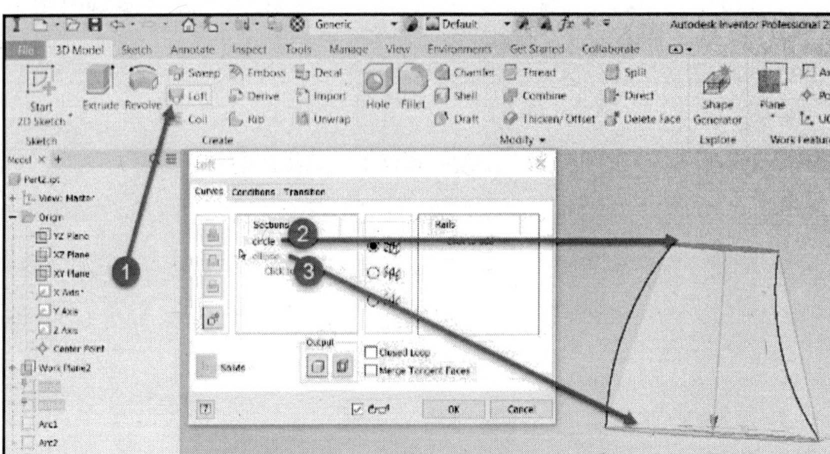

Step 5: After that, Click the "rails" option then select the first guide curve and second guide curve. Then click OK.

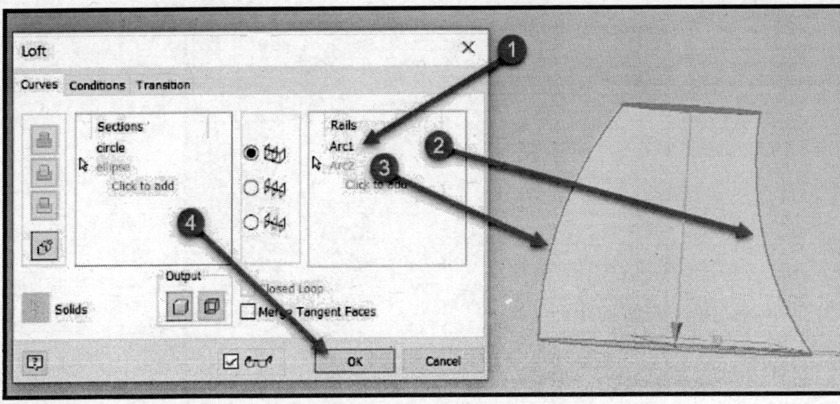

Coil

Use the coil tool to create a spring or ring shape. You can create a helix or spiral solid curve in a part.

Step 1: First of all, select the "front" plane and click the "Sketch".

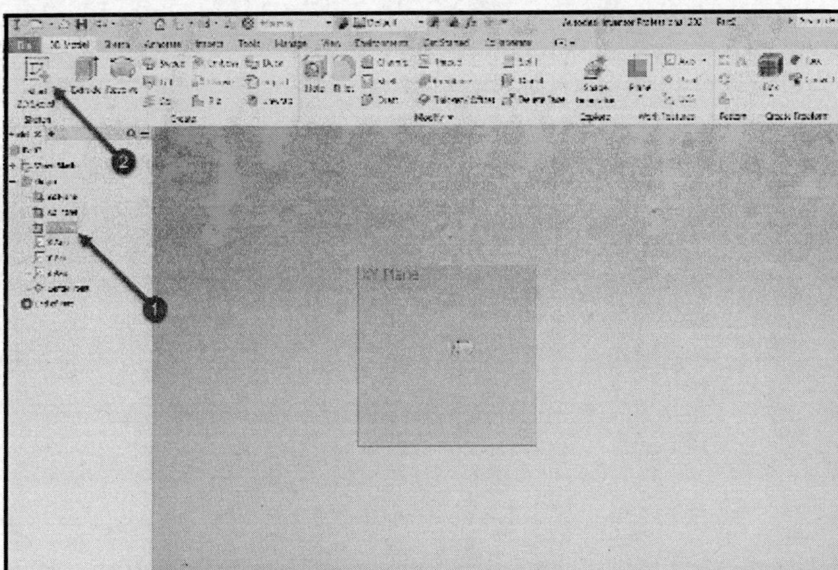

Step 2: Make a circle and an axis. Then click the "finish sketch" for close sketch.

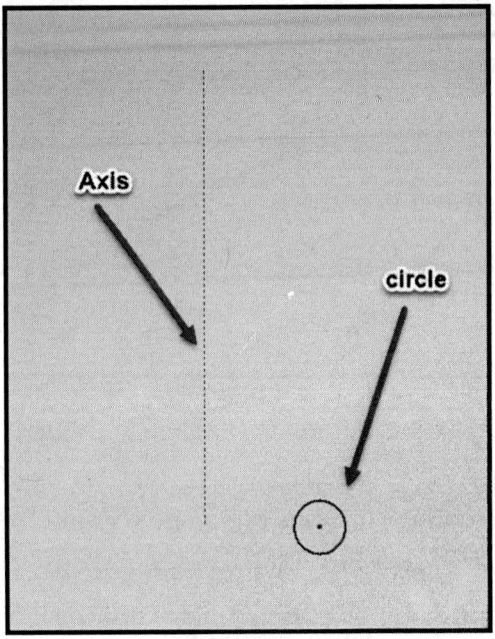

Step 3: Click the "coil" tool then select profile and axis.

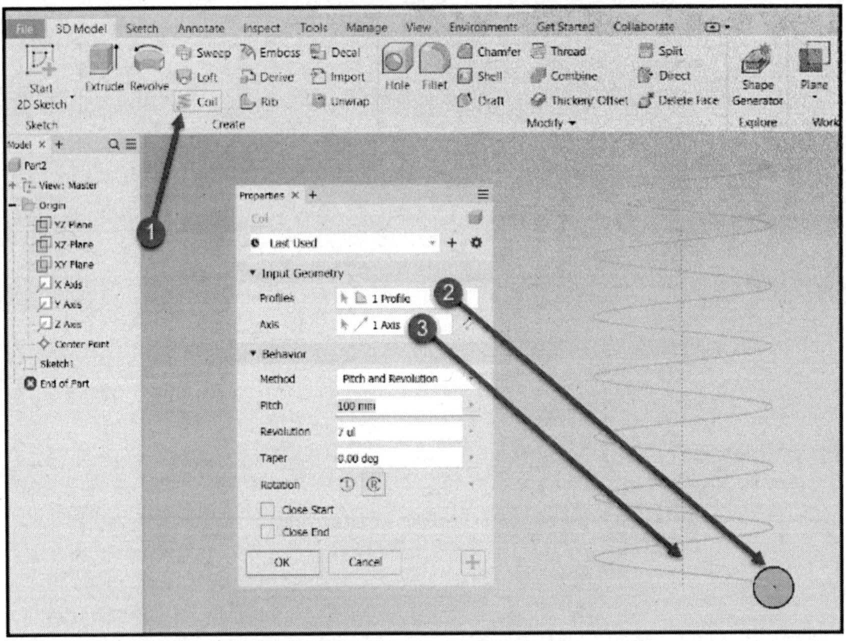

Step 4: Set up behavior. Such as pitch, revolution, and taper.

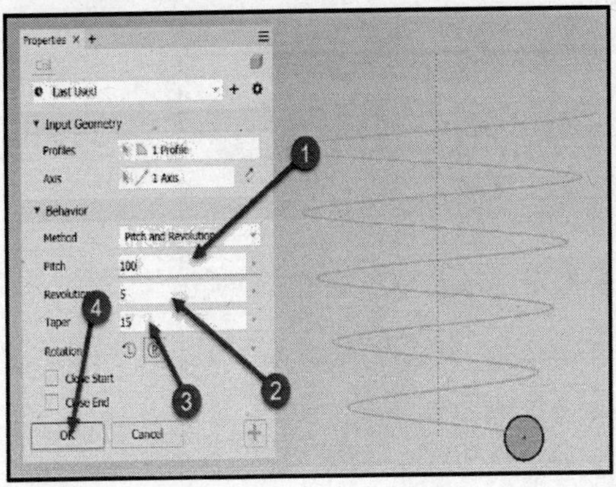

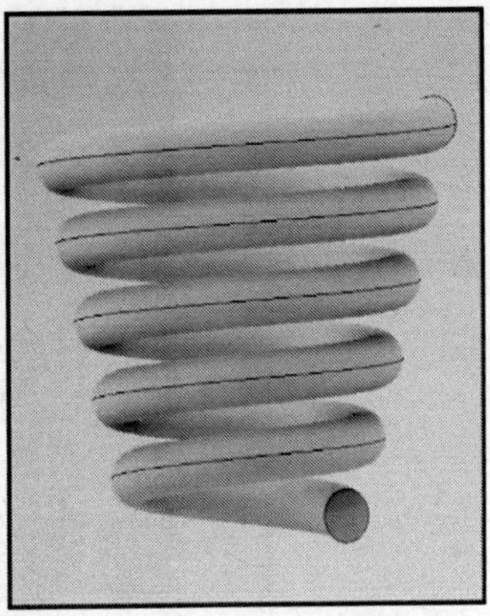

Emboss

The Emboss feature is good in Inventor. If you are trying to project a sketch around a surface and cut or add material to that part without any distortion. They are used to print an object in a solid body.

Step 1: With the help of the Circle and Extrude tool, make a cylinder.

Step 2: After making the cylinder, make a plane parallel to the vertical plane of the cylinder.

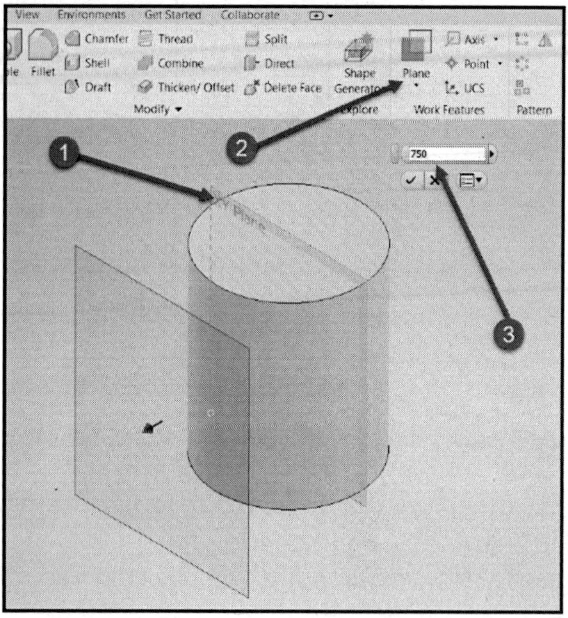

Step 3: Next, select the plane and click the sketch option. Type the text with the help of the text tool. After that, click the "Finish" button to close the sketch.

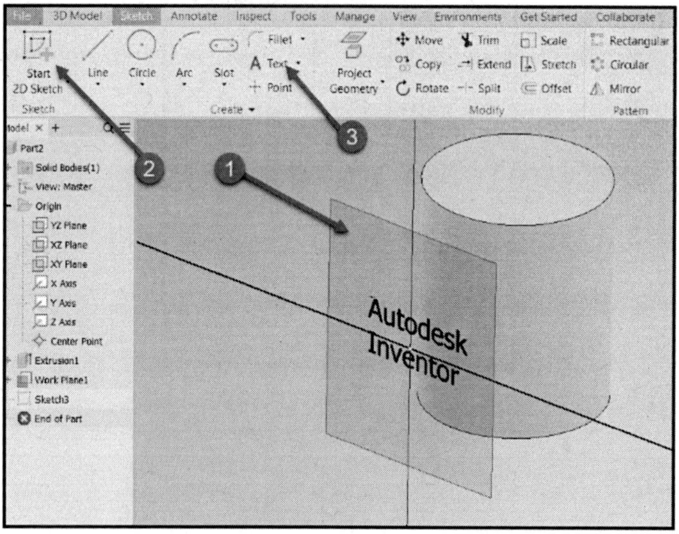

Step 4: Click the "Emboss" tool. Choose Profile (Text) and choose Emboss Type.

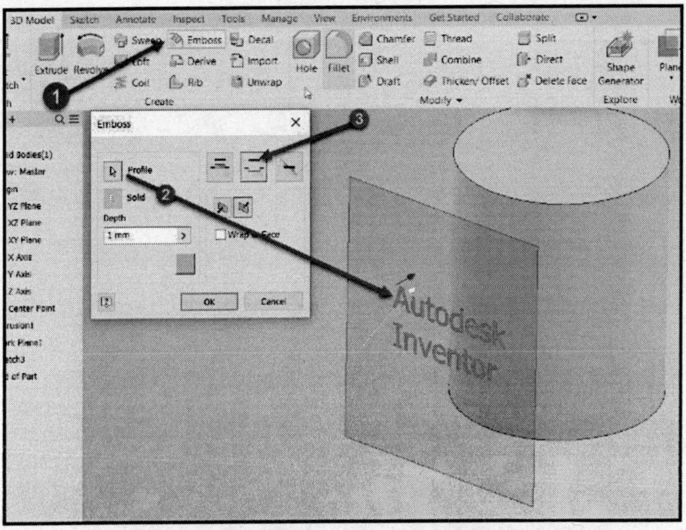

Step 5: Specify depth. Click the "ok" button.

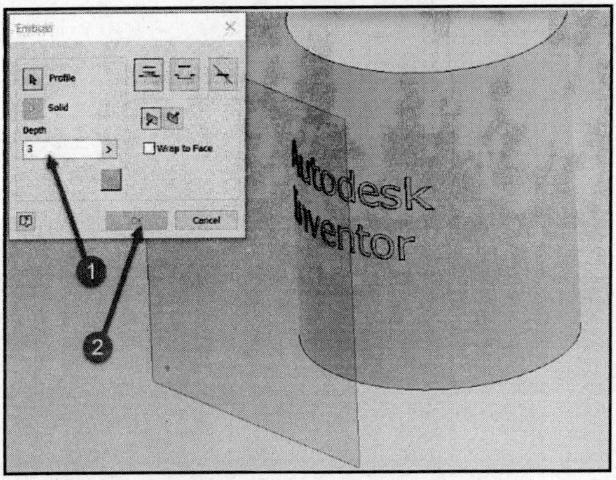

Note: The Emboss tool has 3 types of options.

1. Emboss from face
2. Engrave for face
3. Emboss /Engrave for face

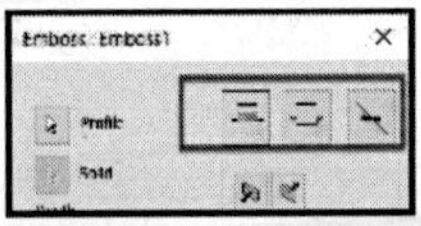

Rib

Creates a thin wall to support two faces. For which Rib uses the tool.

Step 1: Make an L-shape body. Like this.

Step 2: Select the middle plane. If is not, draw a mid-plane. And click the "sketch" option.

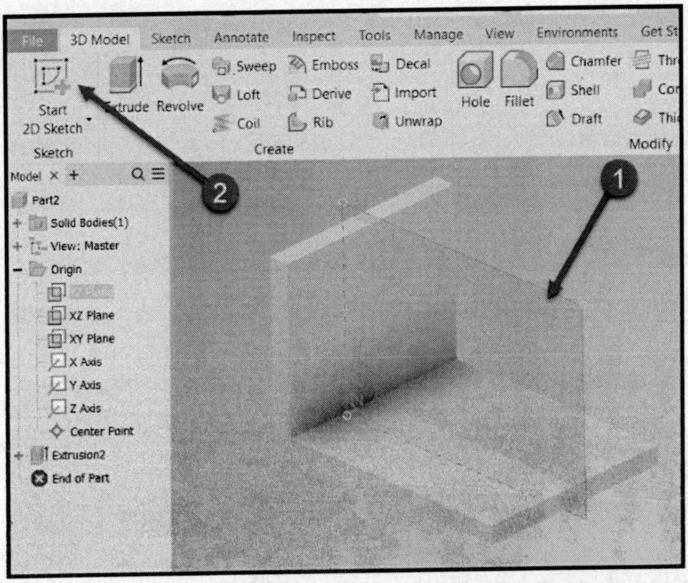

Step 3: Draw a tilted line. Click the "finish sketch".

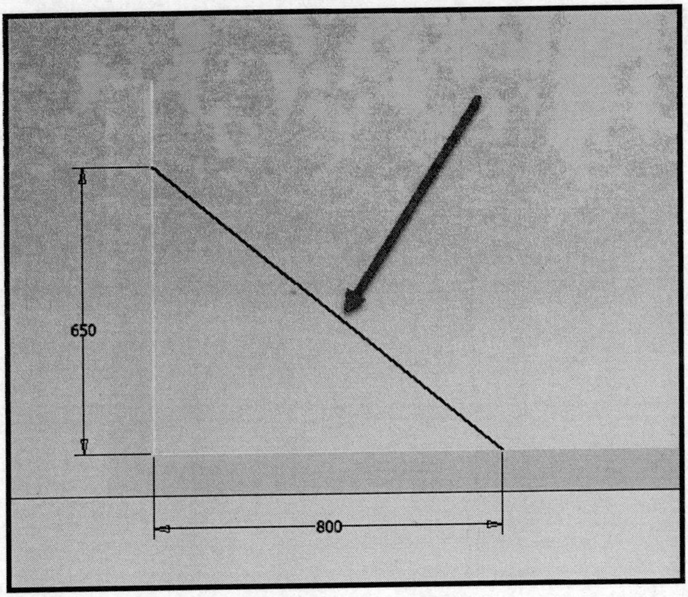

Step 4: Click the "Rib" tool. Choose the "Parallel to sketch plane" option.

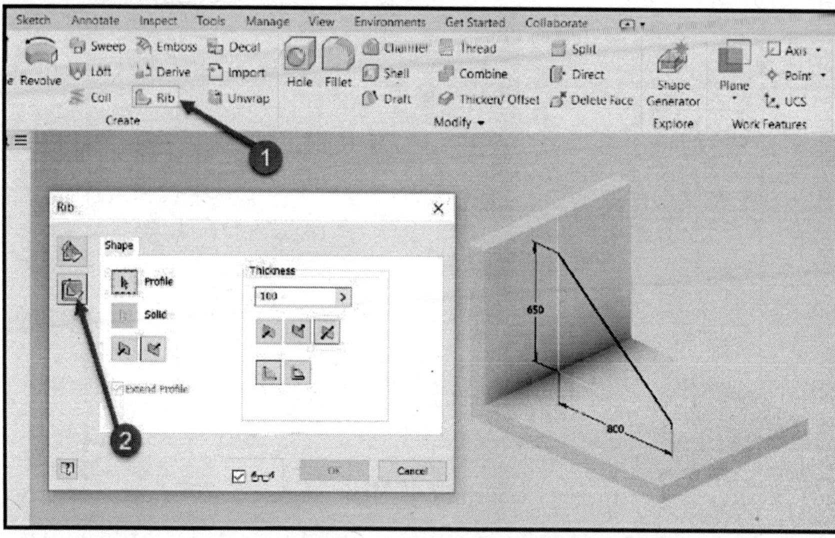

Step 5: Select the inclined line. Then specify the thickness and choose an option. After that, click on the "OK" button.

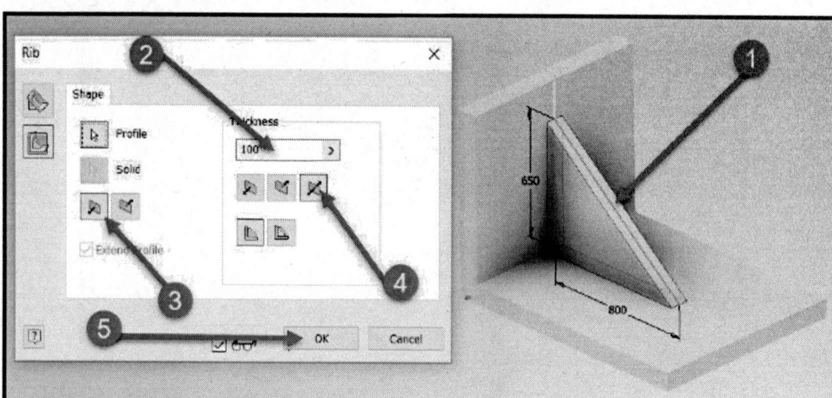

Decal

It is used to insert the image on the face of the object. We use another tool for image inserts. But after image insert, if you want to apply that image on the face of an object, then use this tool.

Step 1: Firstly, make a cylinder and a plane.

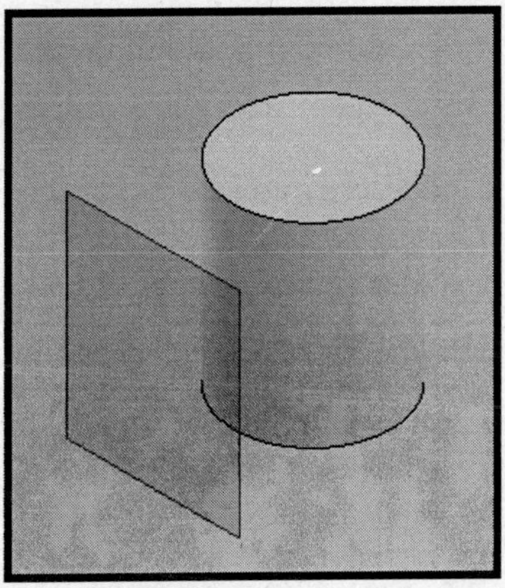

Step 2: Select "Plane" and click the "Sketch" option. After that, click the "Image" tool.

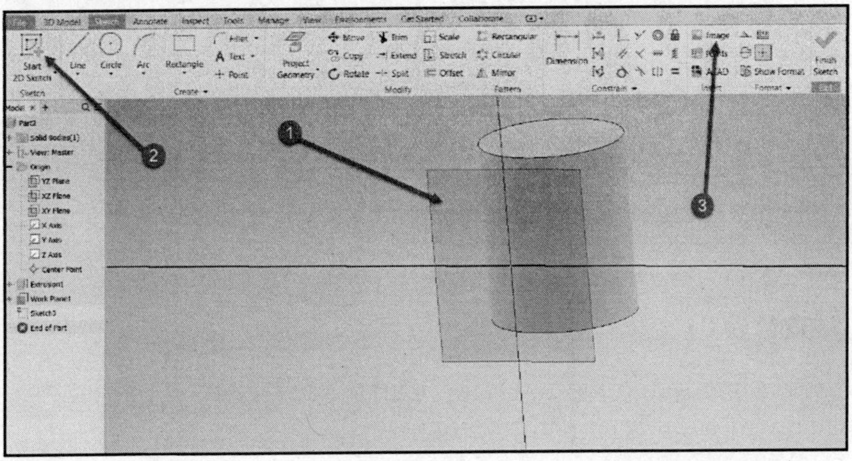

Step 3: Browse image and place. Then click the "finish sketch" option.

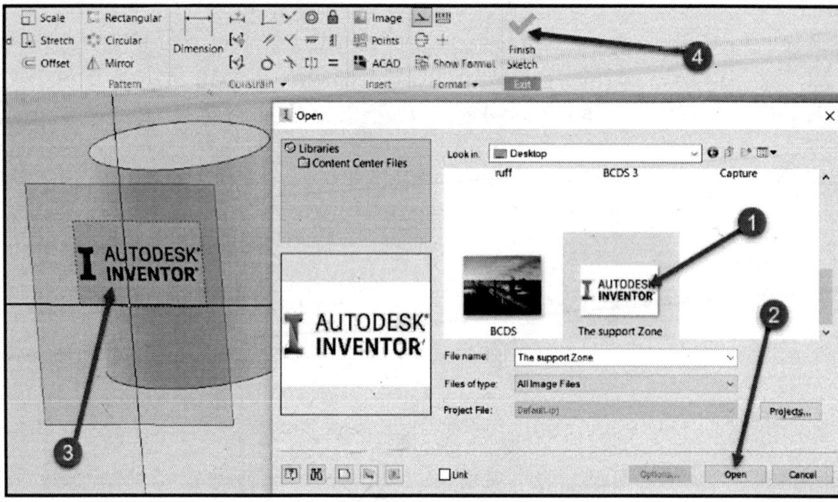

Step 4: Click the Decal tool. Then select "Face" and click the "OK" button.

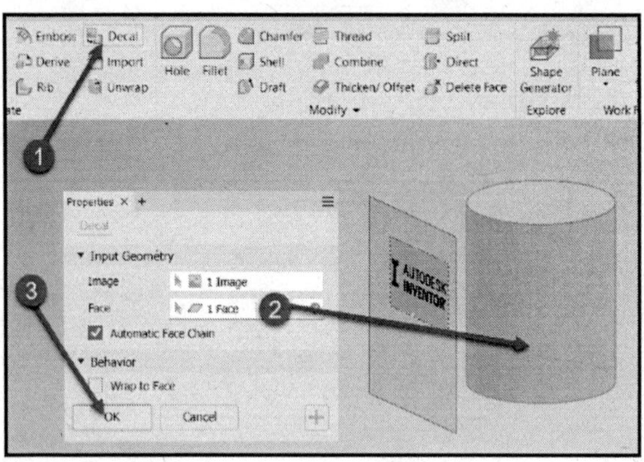

Import

Use the import tool to import the Solid or the 3D part. With this tool, we can import files of different formats.

Step 1: Click the "import" tool. And browse file.

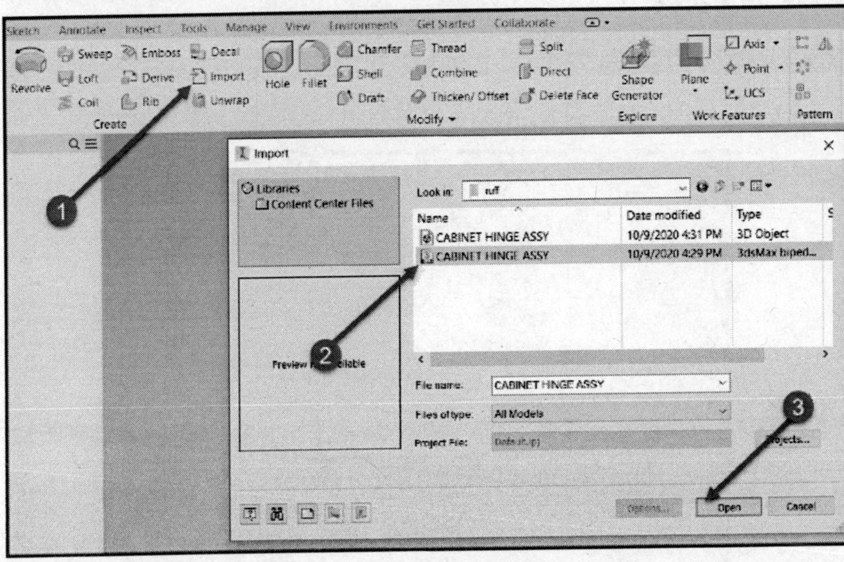

Step 2: Choose the option as you want. Then click the "ok" button.

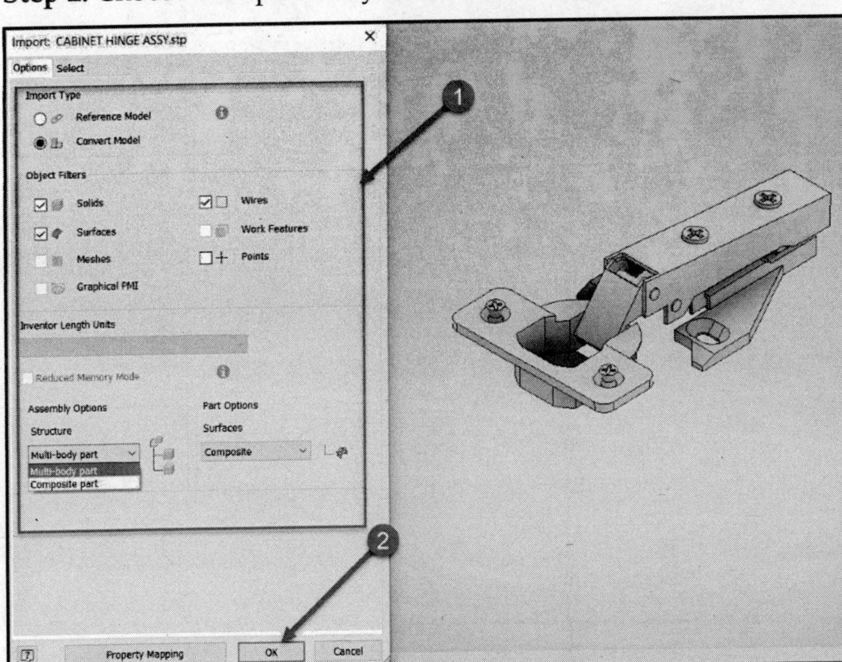

Unwrap

You can straighten any solid plate or surface with the unwarp tool.

Step 1: In the sketch, first, make an arc.

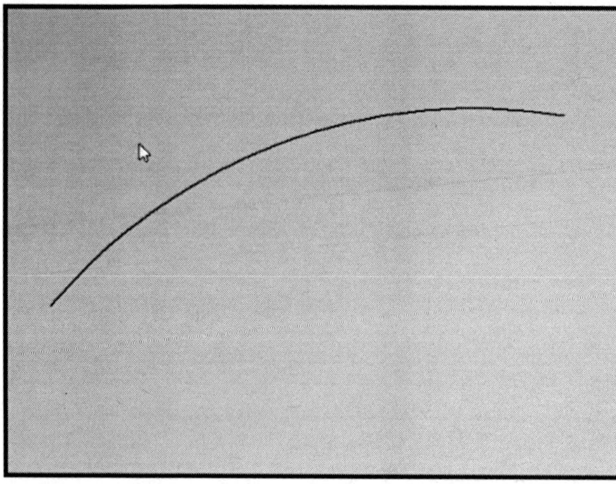

Step 2: Convert Arc from "extrude" tool to surface.

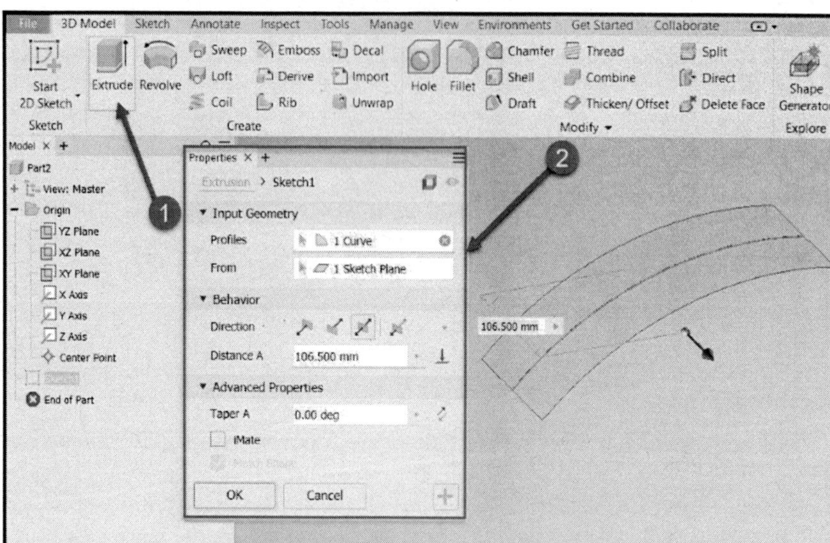

Step 3: Click the "unwrap" tool. Then select face and click the "ok" button.

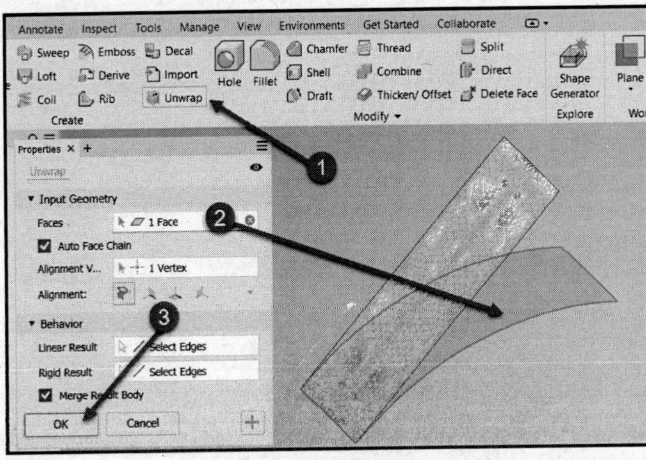

Derive

A derived part is a new part that references an existing part to copy bodies and other information such as sketches, work features, and parameters associatively. A derived assembly is a new part that references an existing assembly.

Step 1: Click the "derive" tool. And browse the file.

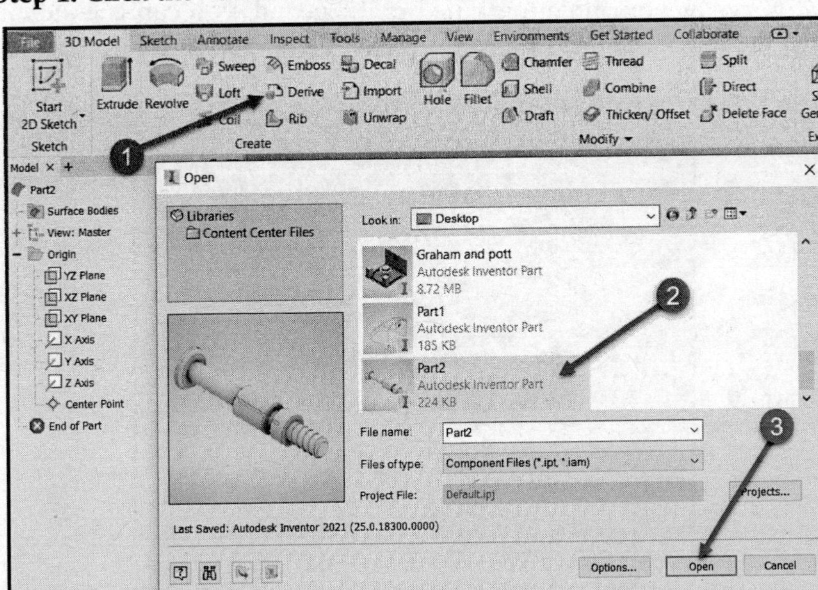

Step 2: Choose derive style, Scale factor, and design view. Then click the "ok" button.

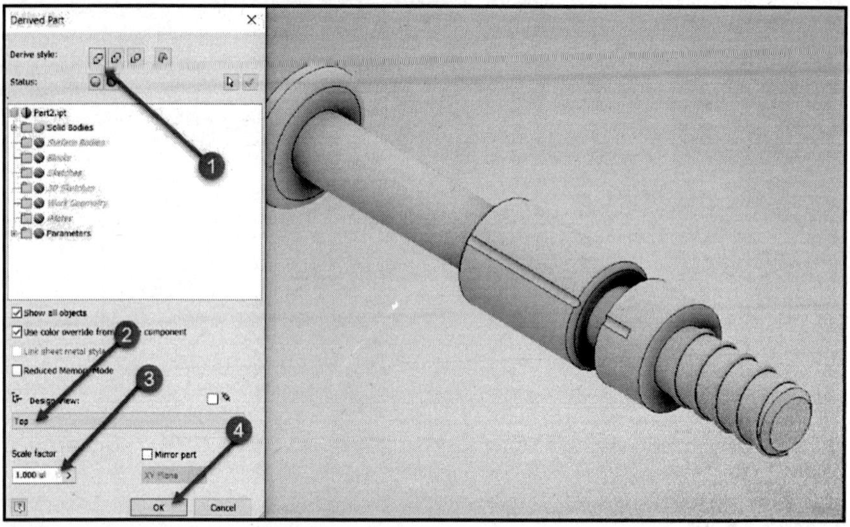

Hole

Hole tools can be used to make a simple hole or screw hole in a plate or solid body. Hole tool can be used in two ways. First, where you have to make a hole. Open the sketch there and make a point that will serve as your hole marking point. Second, you can click using the direct hole tool. To understand it better, see the step given below.

Step 1: First, make a solid body or plate.

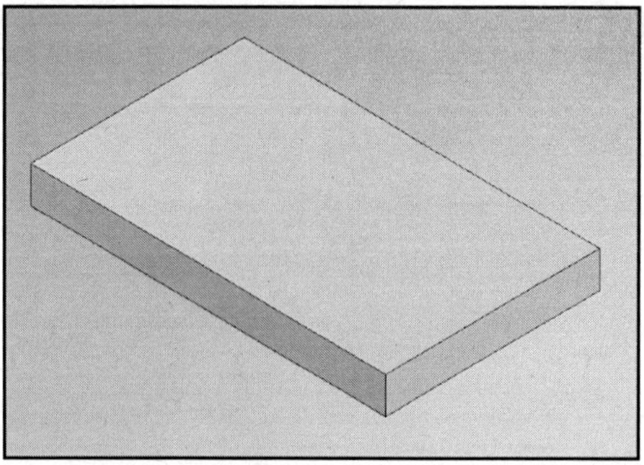

Step 2: Select the face and click the "sketch" option.

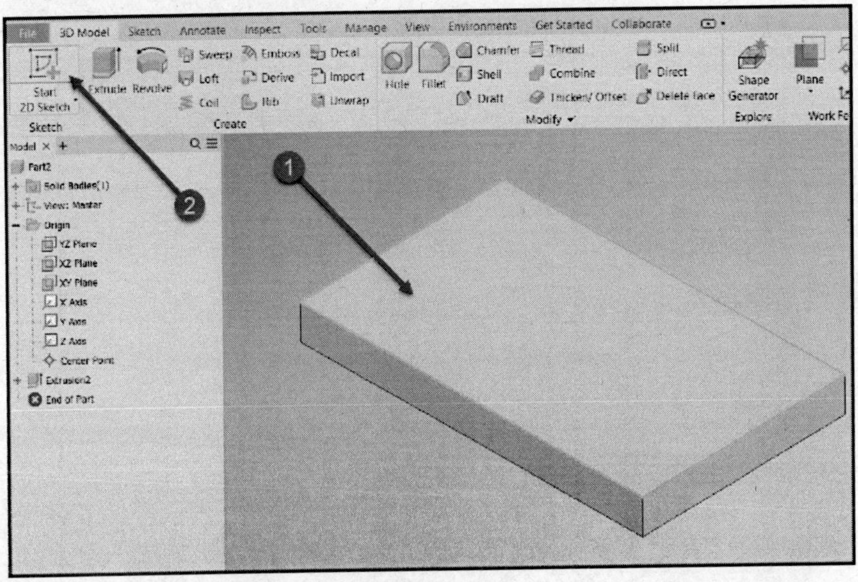

Step 3: Make a point and fix the position of the point with the help of dimension. After that, click the "ok" button.

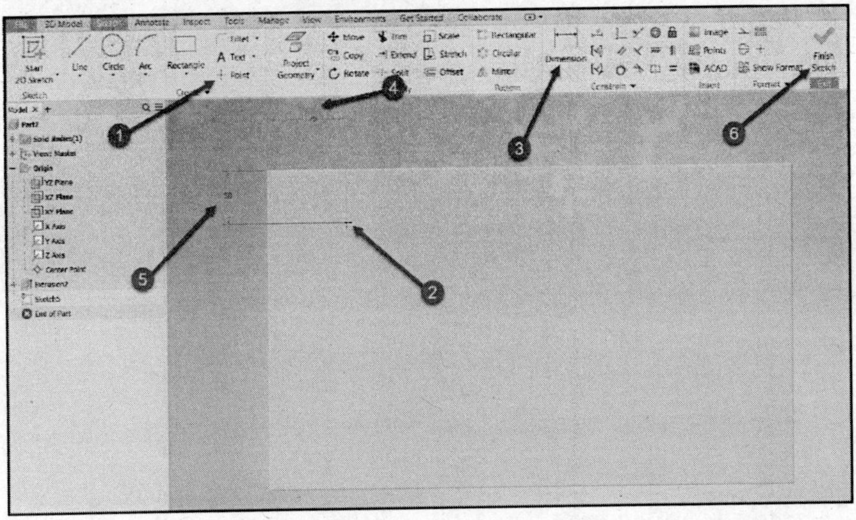

Step 4: Click the "hole" tool. And then select the hole type, fastener, and behavior. "Click the "OK" button.

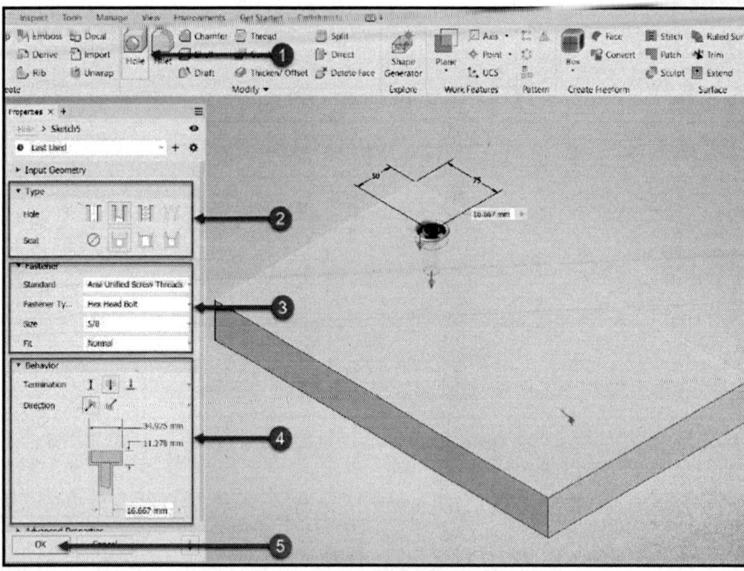

Note: You can also use the direct hole tool without any sketch point.

Step 5: Click the "hole" tool. After that, where you want to make a hole. Click that "face". And select hole Type.

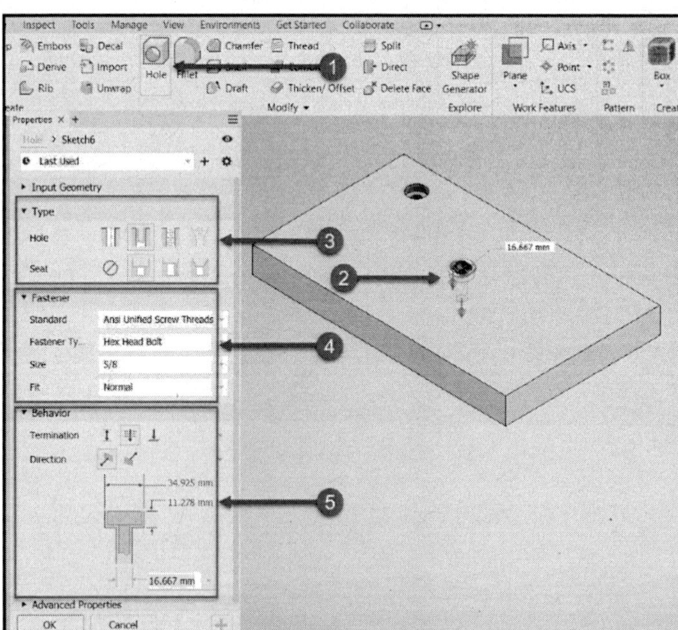

Step 6: Click the "Sketch" Options. Next, fix the hole position with the dimension tool. And click the "finish sketch".

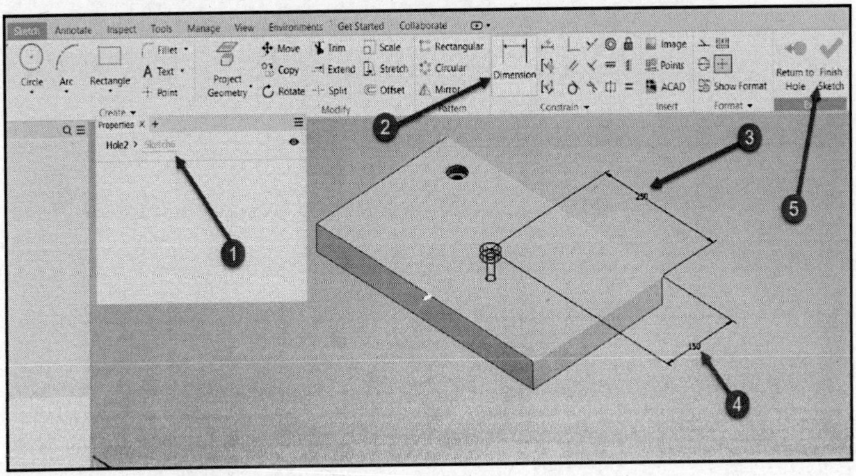

Fillet

The fillet is used to convert the corner shape into a curve. This curve can be set by radius. The fillet gives a part better flow and less resistance. The use of a fillet also eliminates any sharp edges that can be easily damaged or can cause injury when the part is handled. Fillet has 3 types.

1. Constant

Step 1: First, make a solid part.

Step 2: Click the "Fillet" tool. Set the radius in the fillet tab. Then select the edge. after that, click on Apply and OK to close the tab.

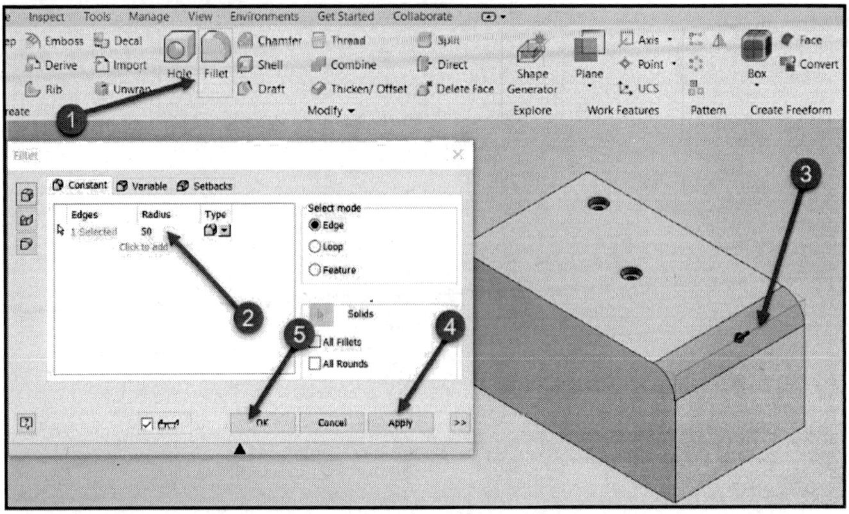

Step 3: To take a different radius, click on the "Click to Add" button in the fillet tab. And then, By filling the radius. Select the edge of the solid part.

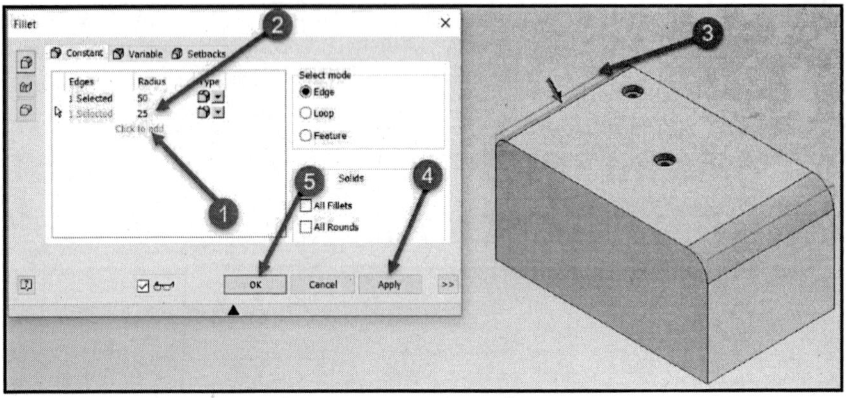

2. Variable

Step 1: Click the "Fillet" tool and click on "various" tab. After this, select the edge by filling the start and end radius.

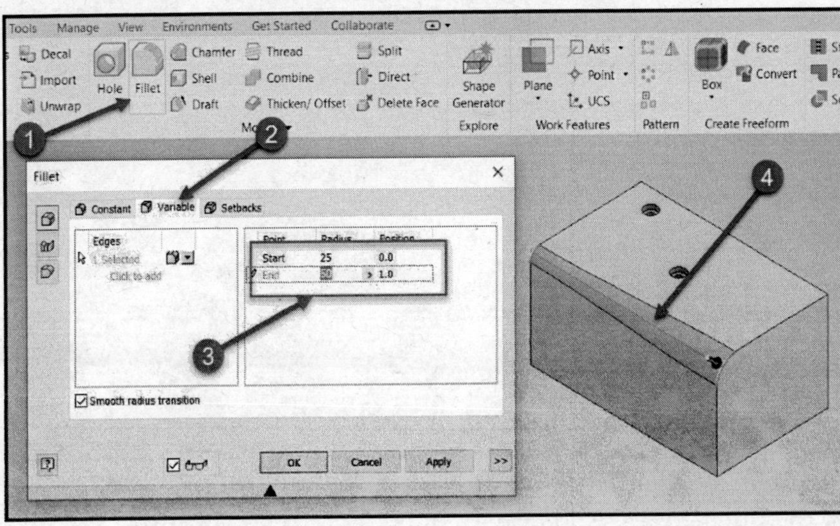

Step 2: Next, Clicking anywhere on the edge. You can also create an extra point and set its radius.

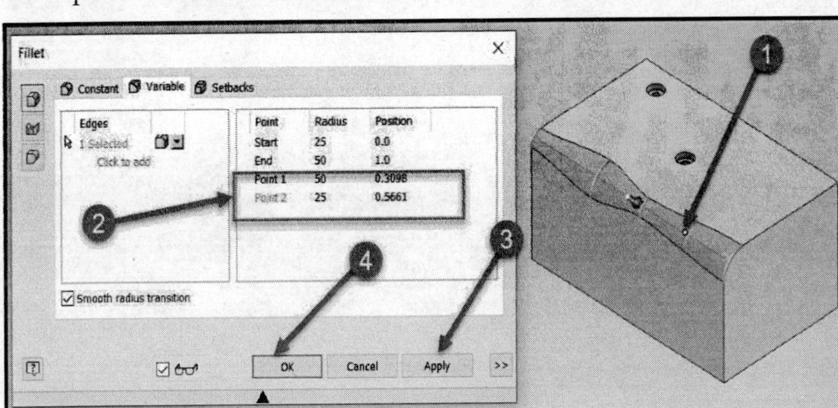

3. Setbacks

Step 1: In the fillet, click the "Constant" tab and select the edges you want to fillet. Make sure, do not click the "apply" and "ok" button.

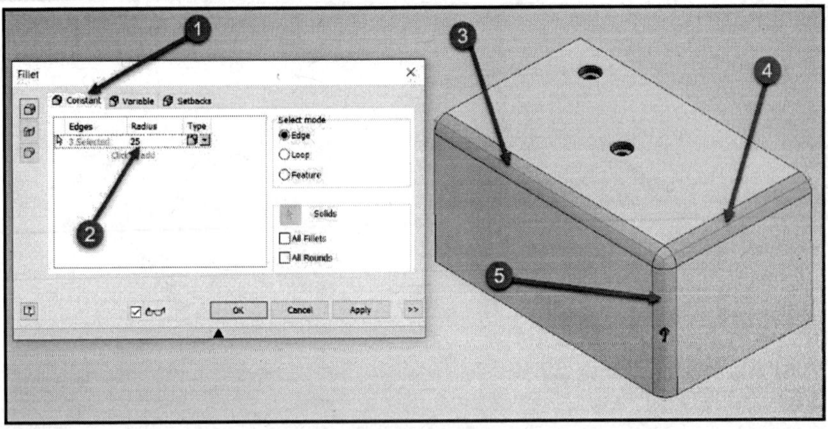

Step 2: In the fillet, click the "Setback" tab and select the corner points of the three edges. And specify the radius. Then click the "ok" and "apply" button.

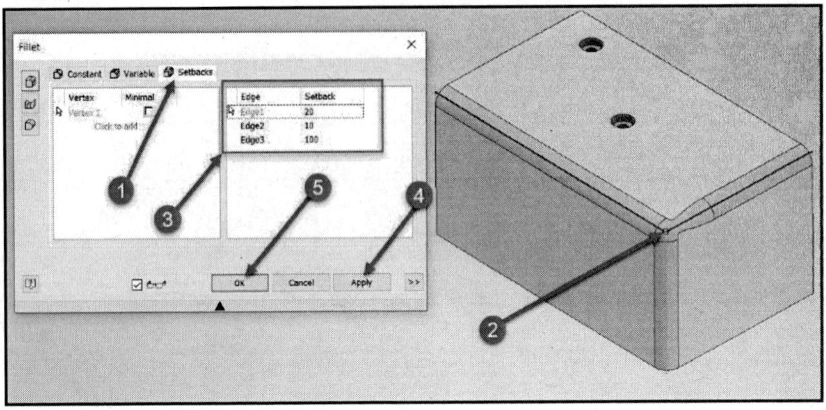

Note: We can fillet in three ways. There are three types of options. Are given below.

1. Edge fillet
2. Face fillet
3. Full round fillet

Edge fillet | Face fillet | Full round fillet

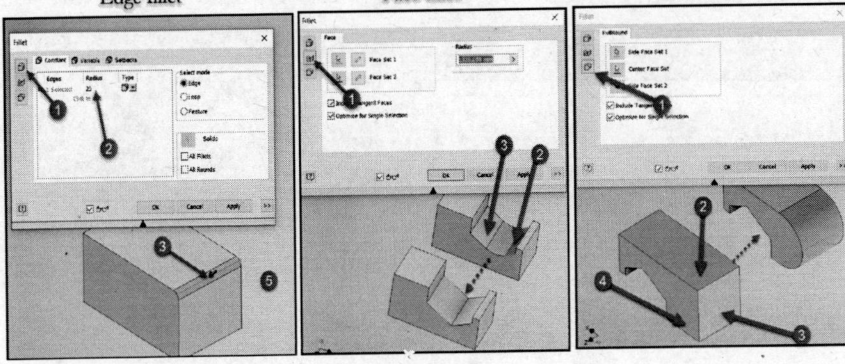

Chamfer

In a solid body, use the chamfer tool to cut the bends in the edges. Machinists use the Chamfer for "seamless" otherwise sharp edges for safety and to prevent damage to the edges. Chamfer can be used in three ways. Are given below.

1. Distance

Step 1: Click the "Chamfer" tool. Select the "distance" type in Chamfer window. And then select the edge.

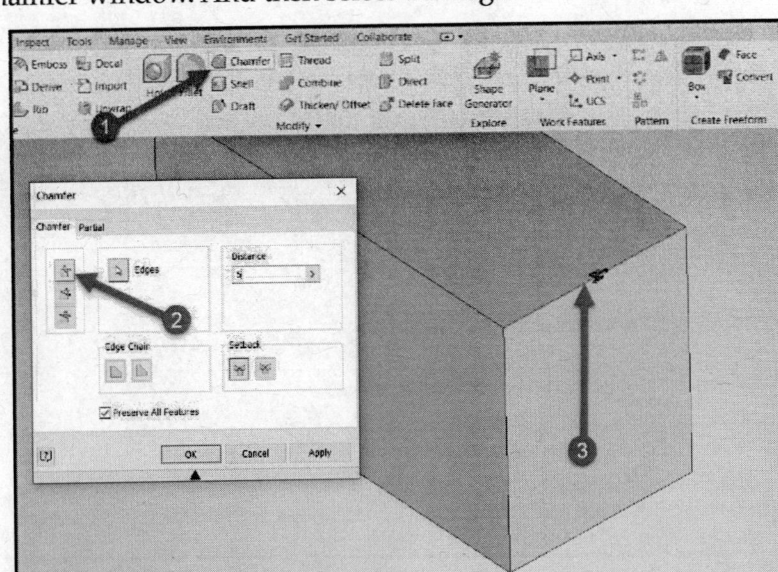

Step 2: Specify distance. Next, click the "apply" and "ok" button.

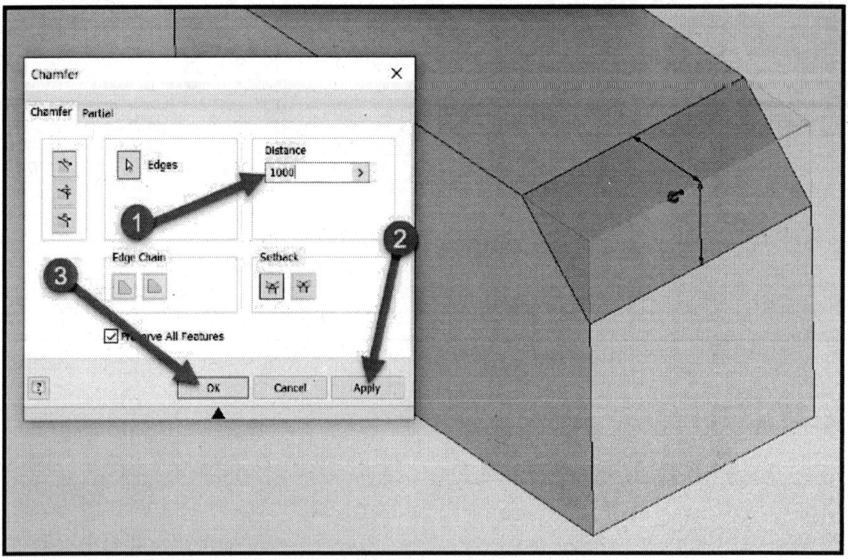

2. Distance and angle

Step 1: Click the "Chamfer" tool. Select the "distance and angle" type in Chamfer window. And then select the face and edge.

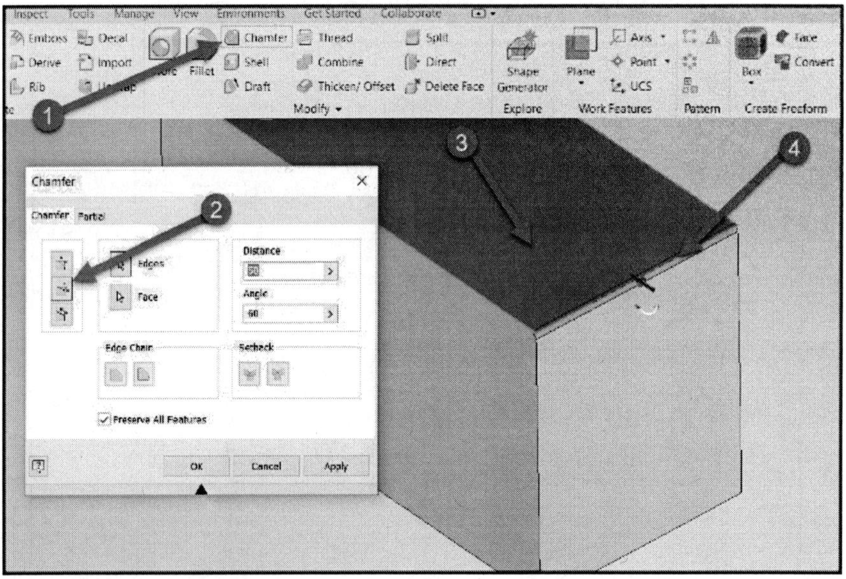

Step 2: Specify distance and angle. Next, click the "apply" and "ok" button.

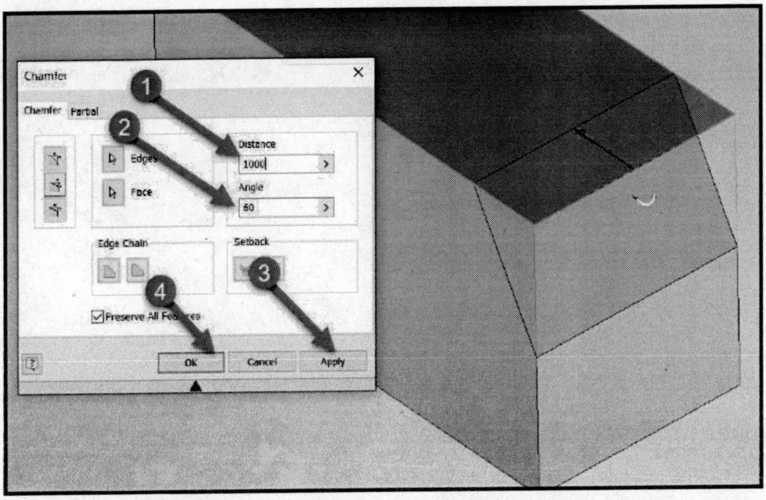

3. Two distances

Step 1: Click the "Chamfer" tool. Select the "two distance" type in Chamfer window. And then select the edge.

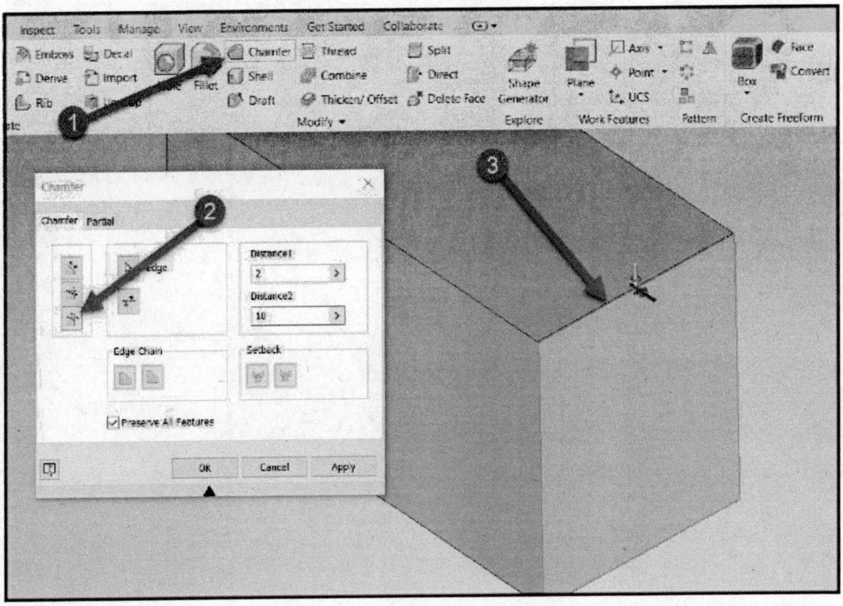

Step 2: Specify distance 1 and distance 2. Next, click the "apply" and "ok" button.

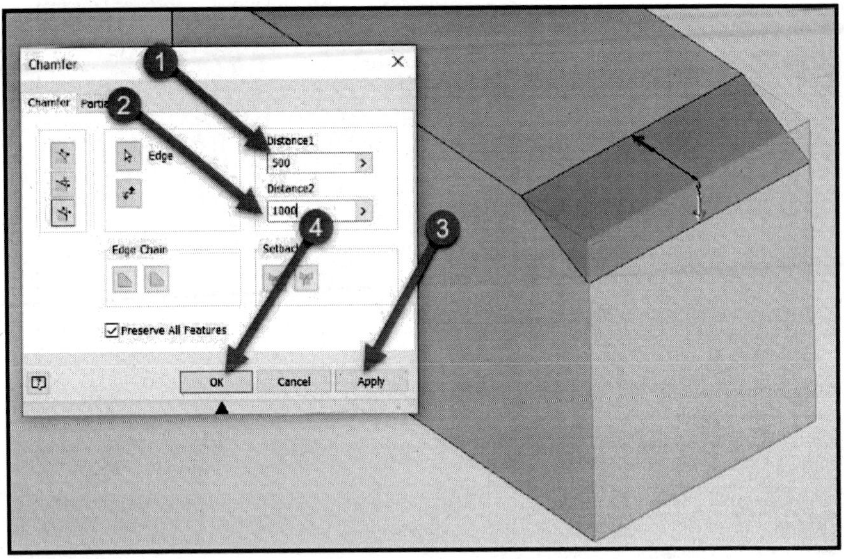

Shell

Shell tool is used to convert solid body to thin outer wall. With this, the face is removed.

Step 1: First, make a solid part.

Step 2: Click the "Shell" tool. Next, select the face and specify thickness in the shell window. Then click the "ok" button.

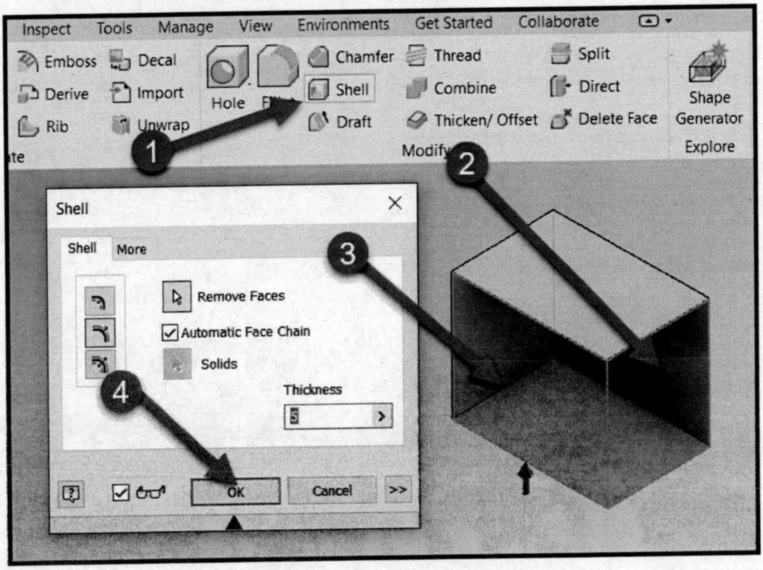

Draft

You can rotate the face of a solid body with the draft tool. Whichever angle you want to rotate can be done. The draft angle has three options. Which are given below.

1. Fixed edge

Step 1: First, make a solid body.

Step 2: Click the "Draft" tool and click the "Fixed Edge" option in the Draft window.

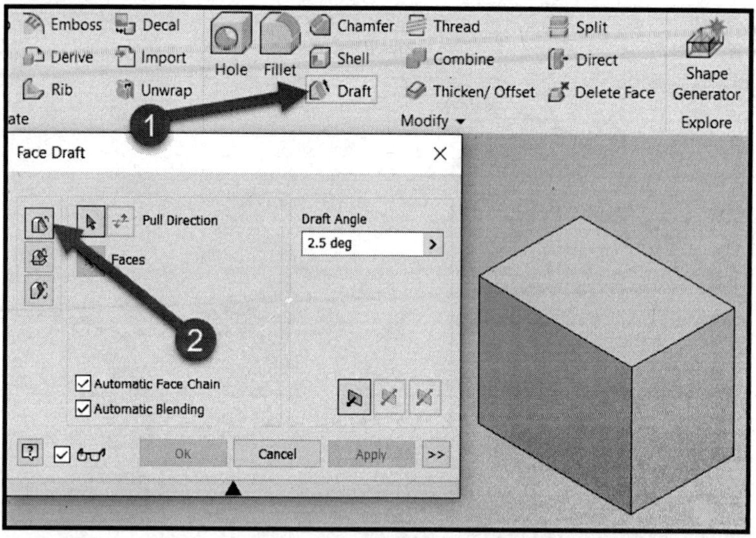

Step 3: First, select the "pull direction" face. Second, select the "face to draft" face.

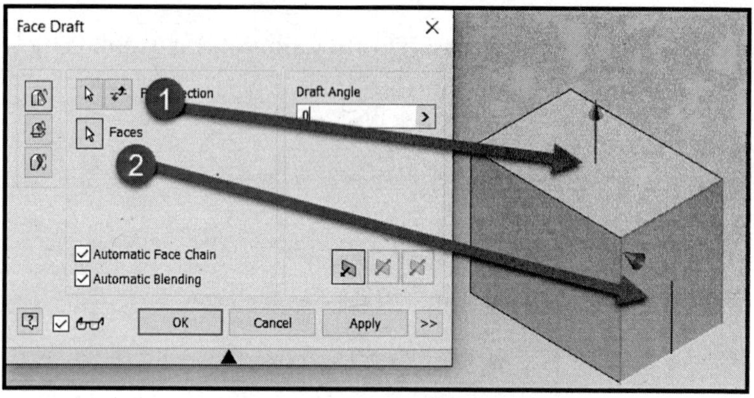

Step 4: Specify the angle. Then click the "apply" and "ok" button.

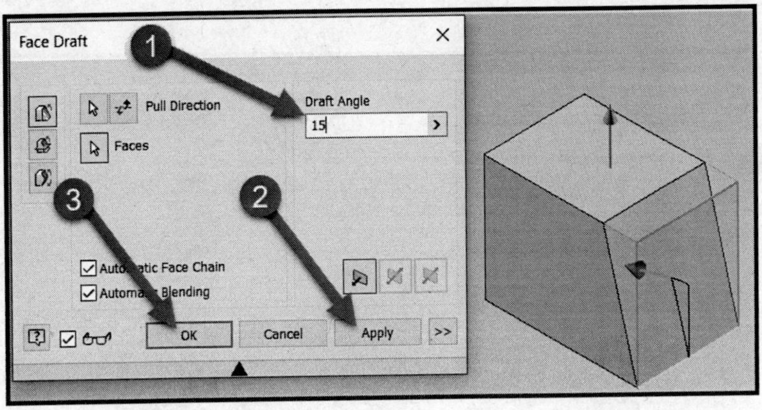

2. Fixed plane

Step 1: First, make a solid box. Second, create a plane with the "offset from plane" tool. Which is made in the middle of the solid box.

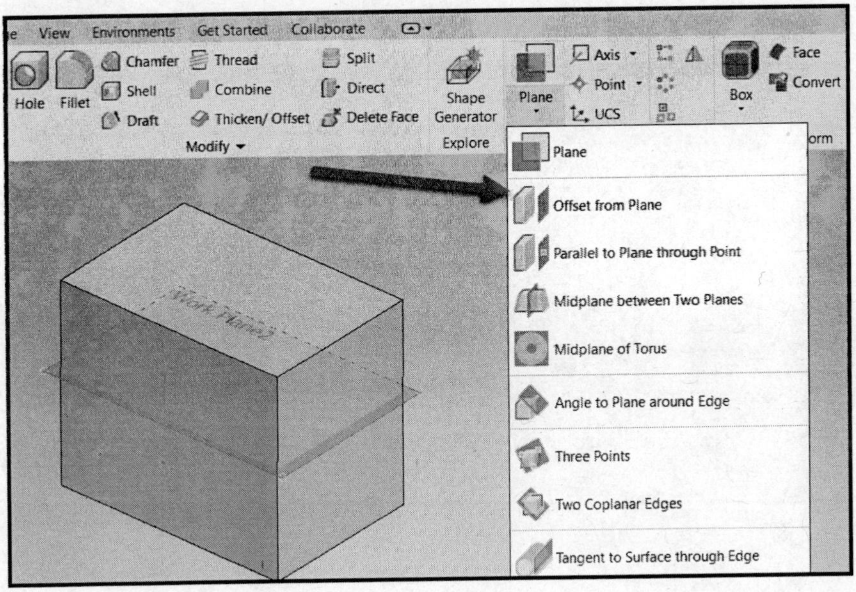

Step 2: Click the "Draft" tool and click the "Fixed Plane" option in the Draft window.

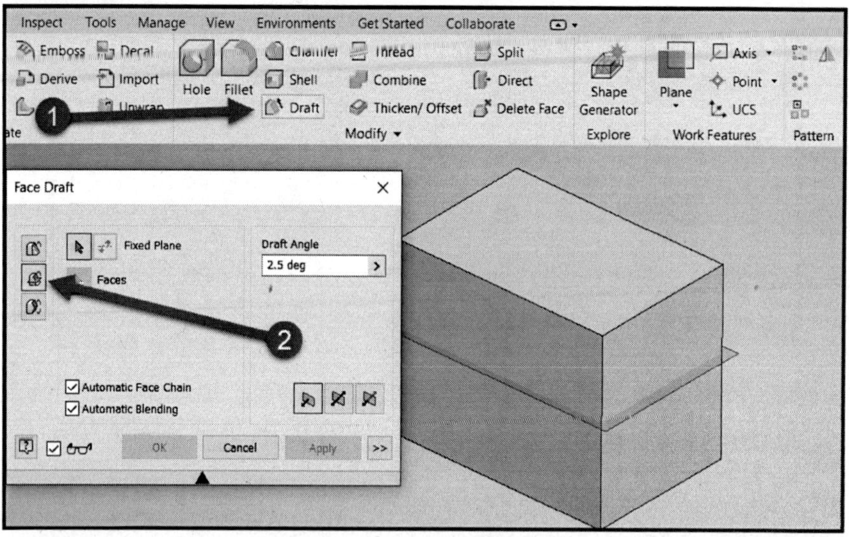

Step 3: Select the "plane" and "face to draft" face.

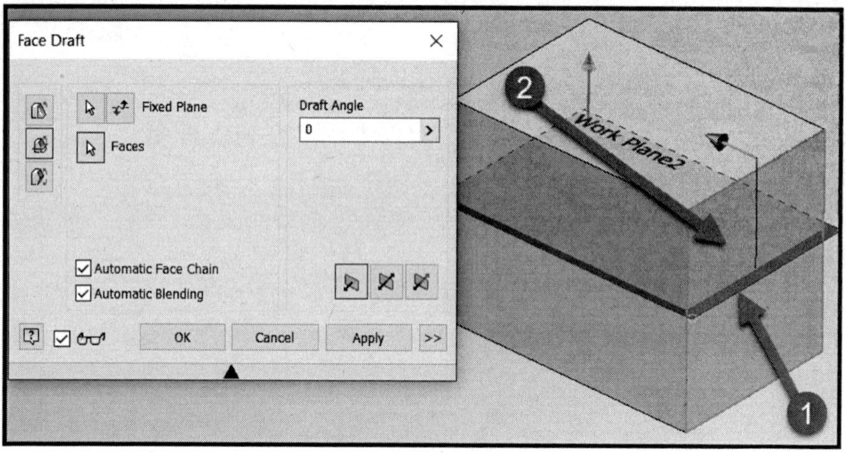

Step 4: Select the "asymmetric" option. Then specify the draft angle and draft angle 2.

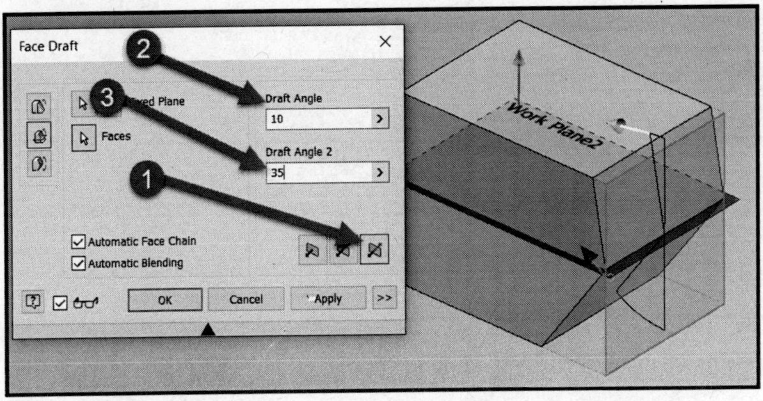

3. Parting line

Step 1: First, Make a solid box and parallel to the box a plane.

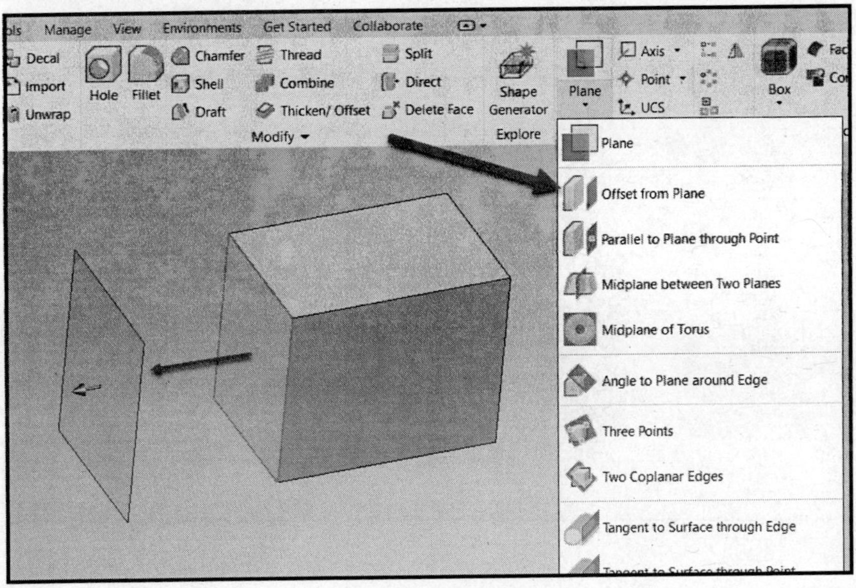

Step 2: Select the plane and click the "start sketch". And then make a tilted line. In the last, click the "Finish sketch".

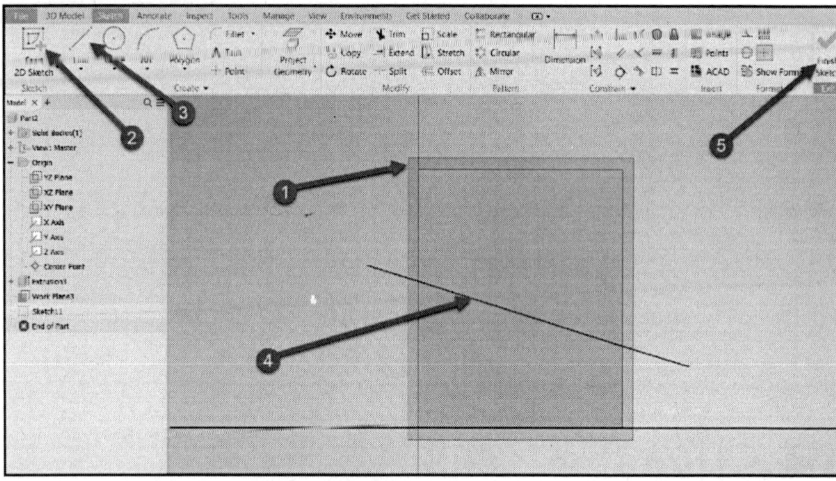

Step 3: Select the face of the box and click on "Sketch" again.

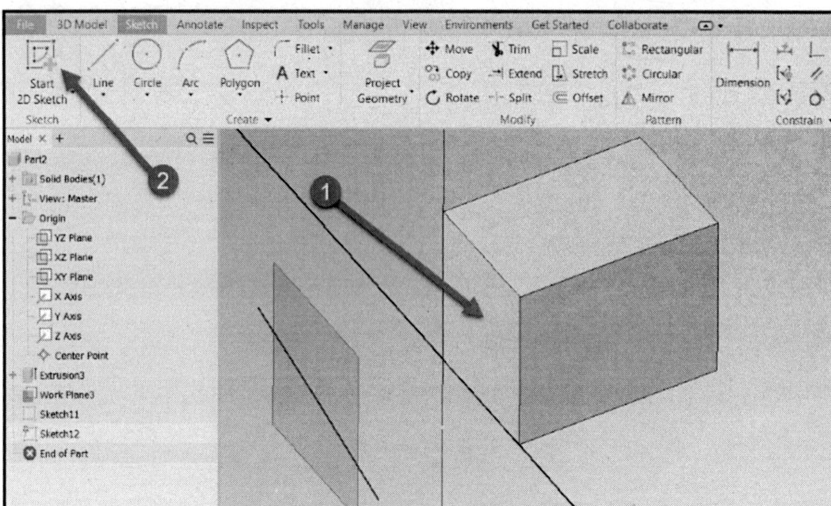

Step 4: Click the "Project Geometric" tool. And select the inclined line. Next, to close the sketch, click "Finished Sketch".

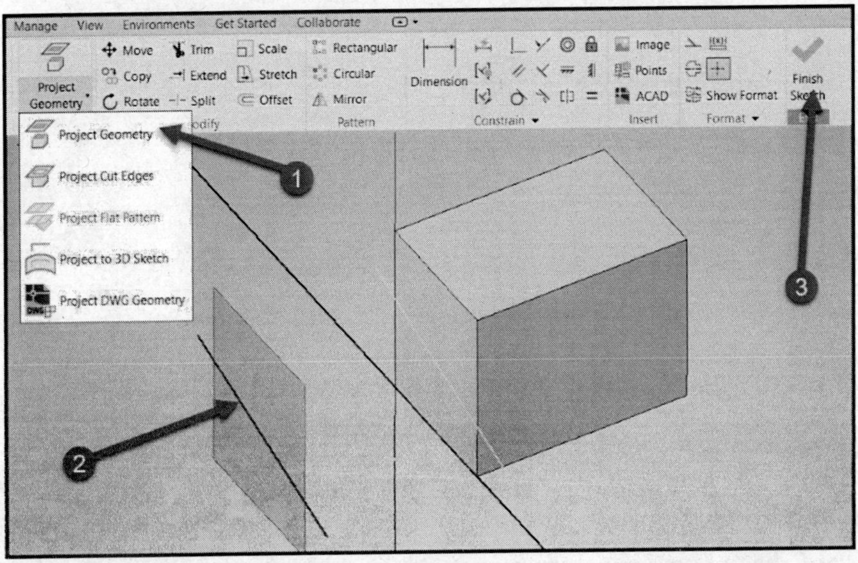

Step 5: Click the "Draft" tool. Then select the "Parting line" and "Asymmetric" option in the draft window.

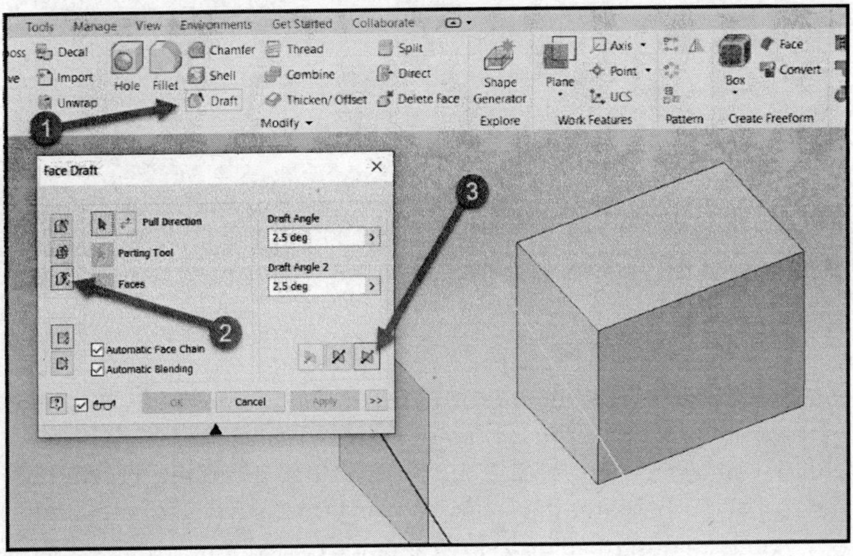

Step 6: Now, select "pull direction", "parting tool", and "face" in a sequence.

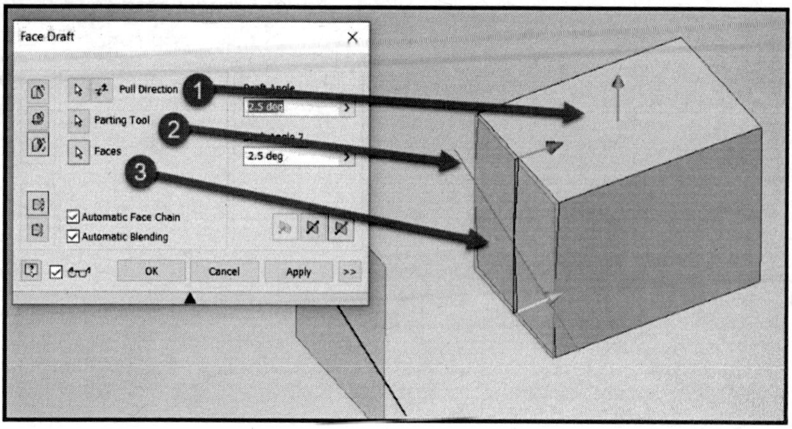

Step 7: After that, specify "draft angle" and draft angle. Then click "Apply" and "OK" button.

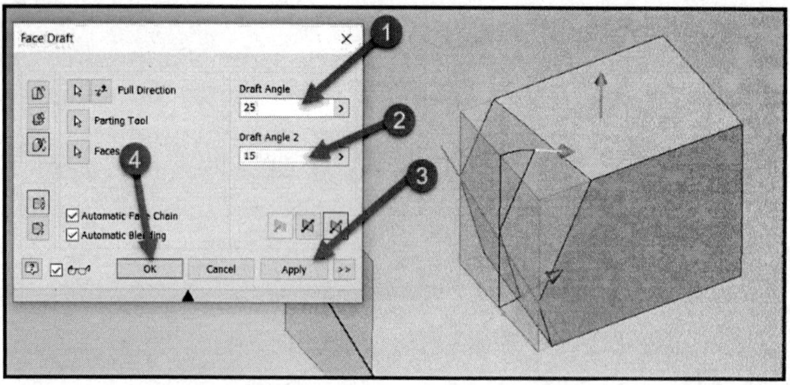

Thread

A screw thread is a cone wrapped around a cylinder. And has a cone in the form of a helix, the former of which is called a straight thread and the latter a thin thread. A thread is a ridge of uniform section in the form of a helix on the internal or external surface of a cylinder or it could be described as a sloping plane curled around a cylinder.

External threads are on bolts or screws.

Internal threads are on nuts.

Step 1: First, make a sketch for revolving.

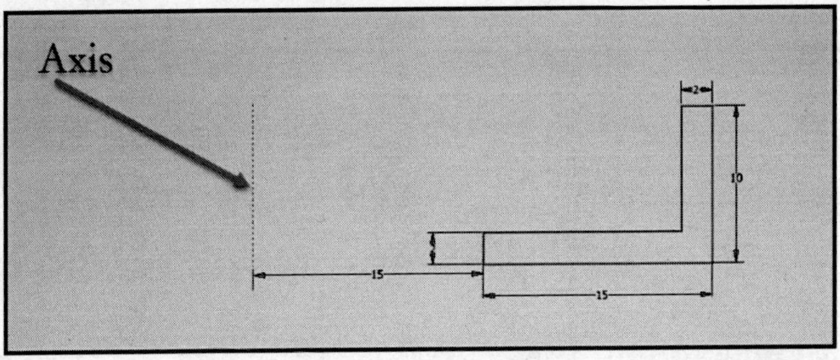

Step 2: Now, Revolve the sketch with the help of the Revolve tool.

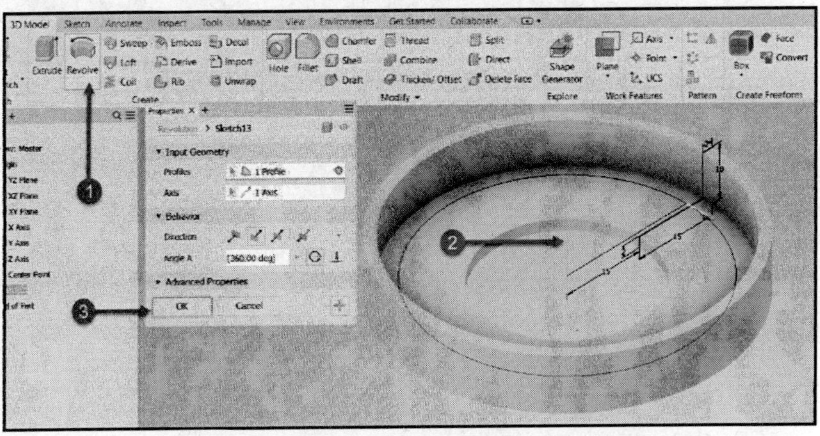

Step 3: By clicking the thread tool. Select the face where to thread.

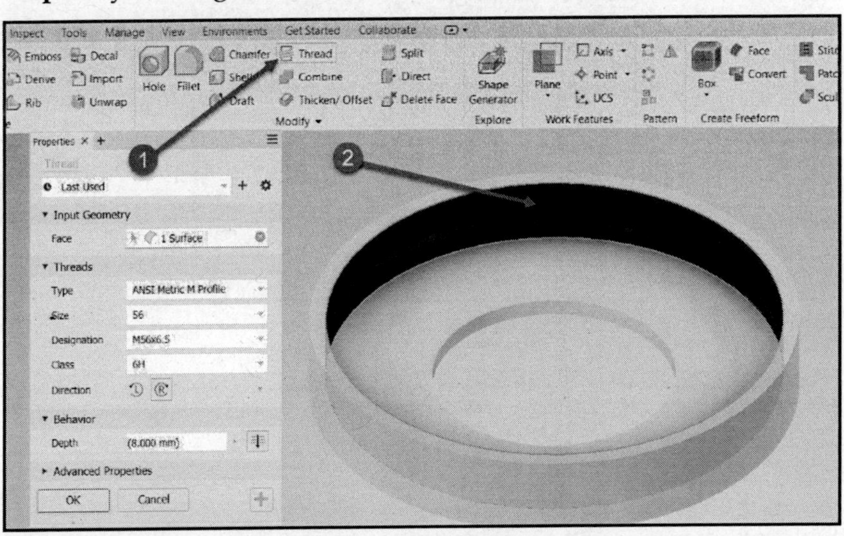

Step 4: Specify all the details in the thread tool window. And then click on OK.

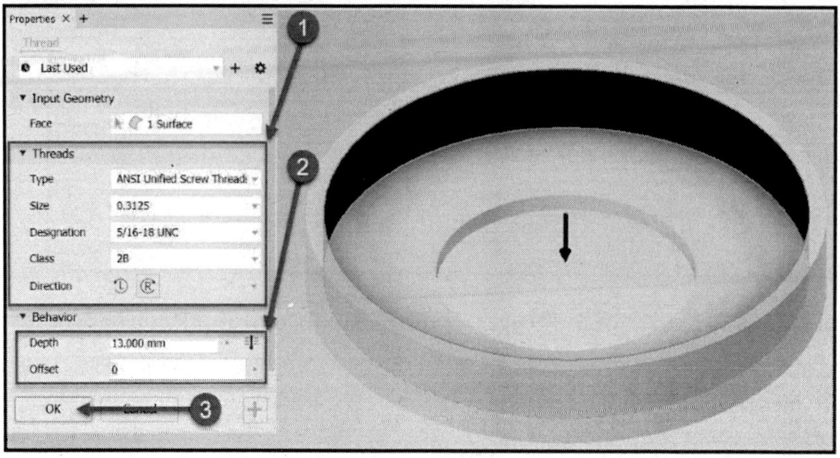

Combine

Merging two solid bodies, cutting from one body to another, and or two bodies intersecting each other. And to keep only the intersect part and remove the remaining part, we use the Combine tool.

Step 1: Create a Solid Box with Extrude Tool.

Step 2: Select the face of the body and click the "Start Sketch".

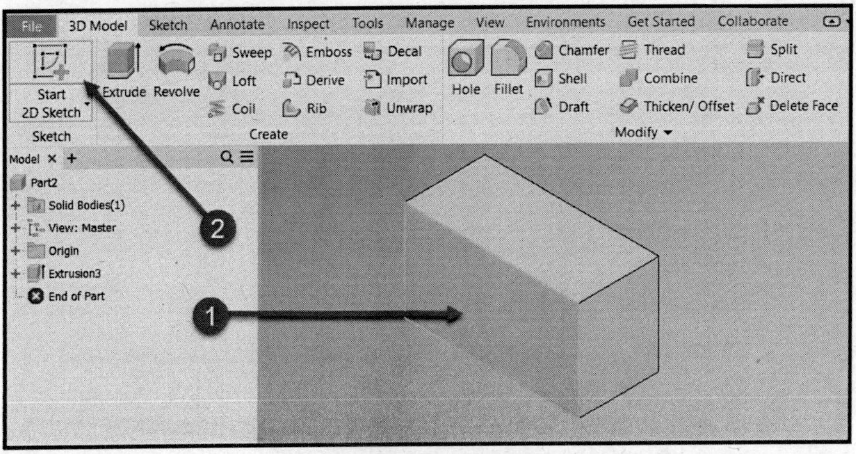

Step 3: Draw a circle and finish the sketch.

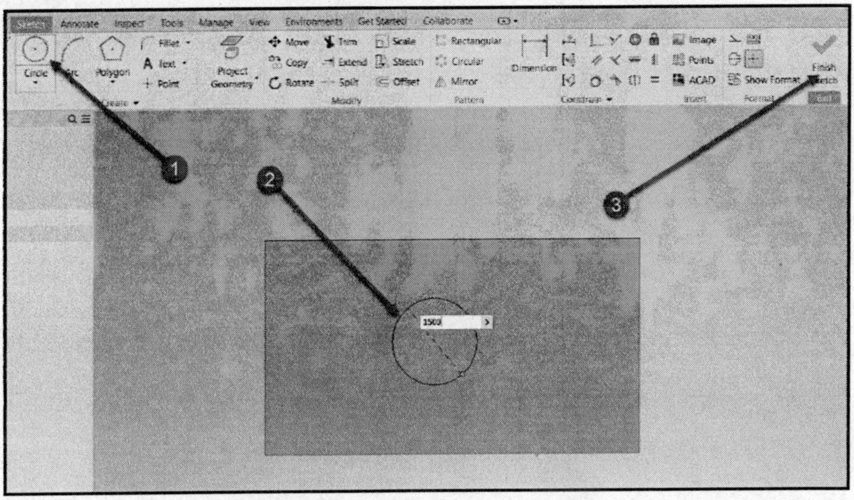

Step 4: Select the Symmetric option in the Extrude tool.. And make sure that the "new solid" option is selected in the output.

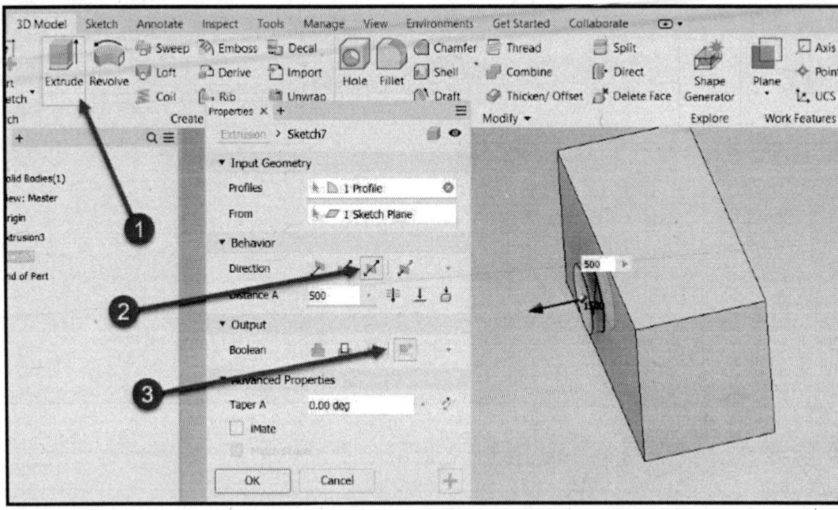

Step 5: Specify the distance and click the "OK" button.

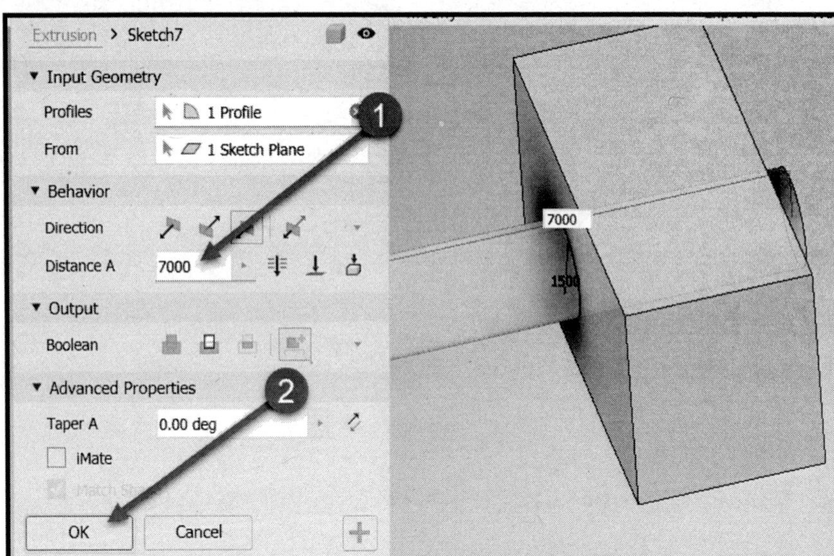

Step 6: Click the Combine Tool. After that, select the box for the base body and the cylinder for the tool bodies.

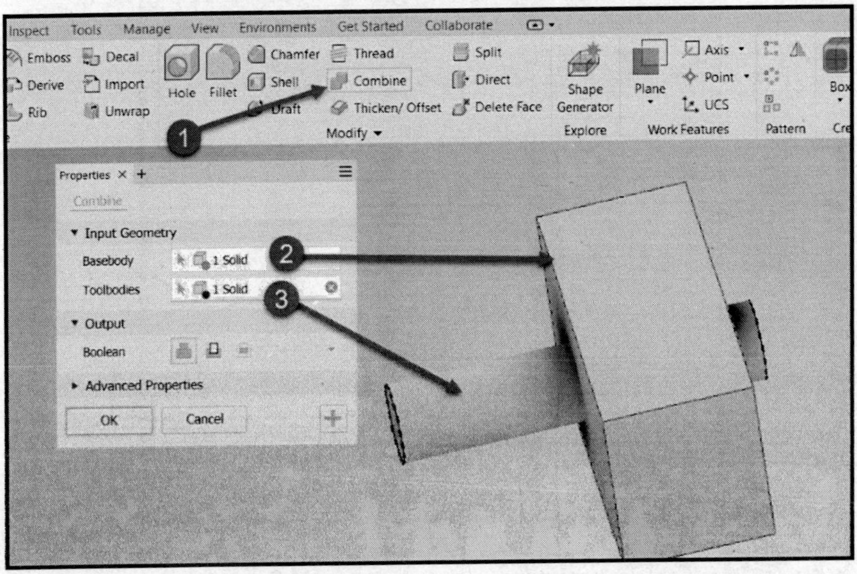

Step 7: After that, click subtract Boolean option and ok.

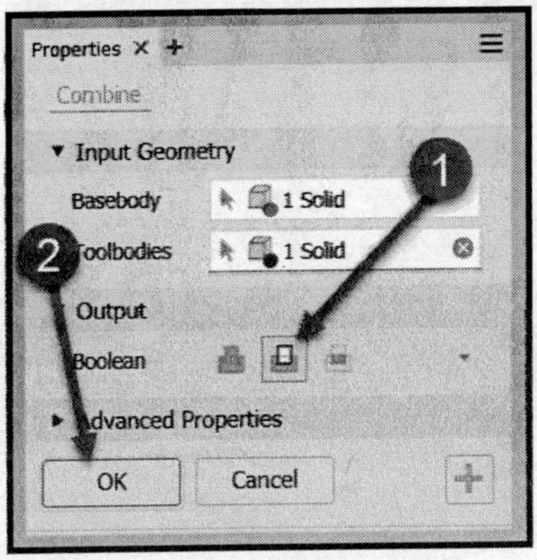

Thicken/offset

The Thicken/Offset command lets you add or remove thickness to faces of a part or a quilt, create an offset surface from a part face or surface, or create a new solid.

Step 1: First, make a sketch as given below.

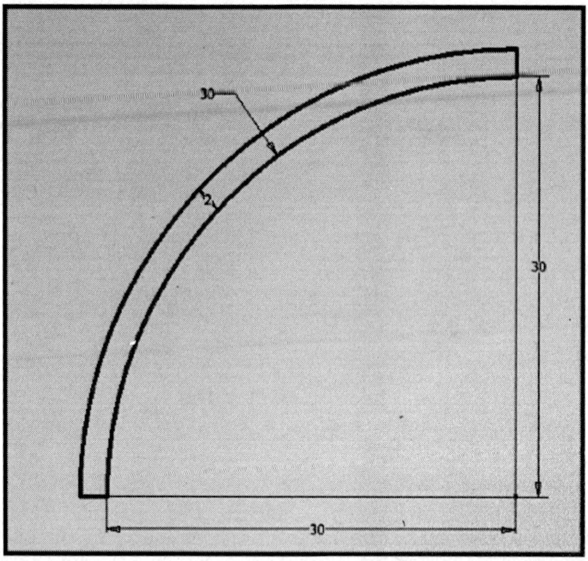

Step 2: Extrude the sketch.

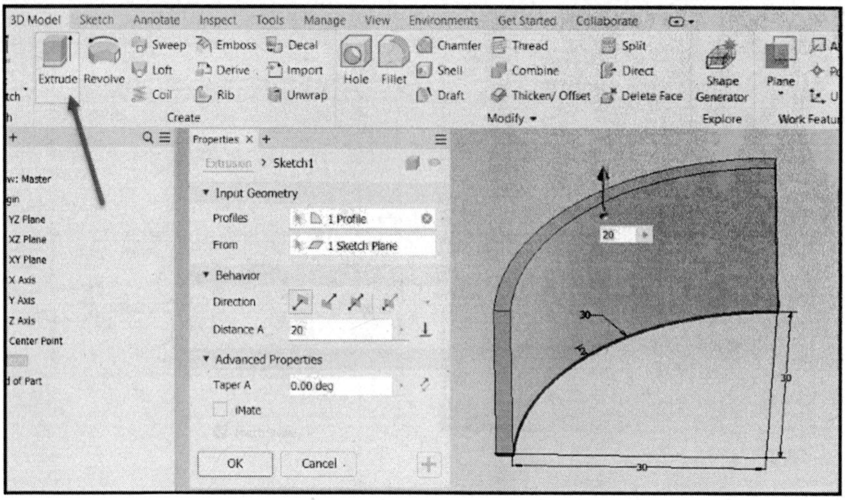

Step: Next, click on the thicken/offset tool. Then specify "thicken face" and "distance".

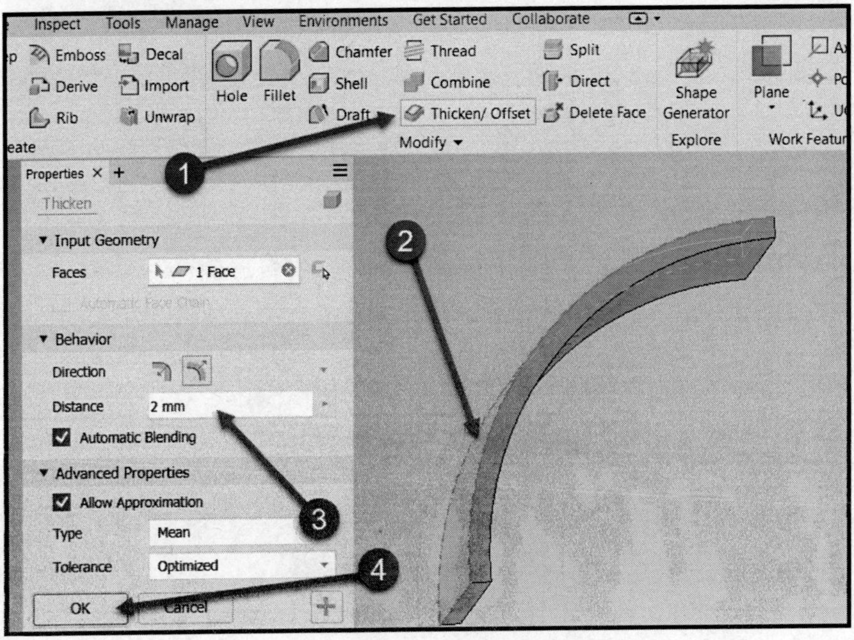

Split

It is used to divide / split an object. But to use it, it is necessary to have a surface or plane. Which will do the job of splitting.

Step 1: Make a cylinder.

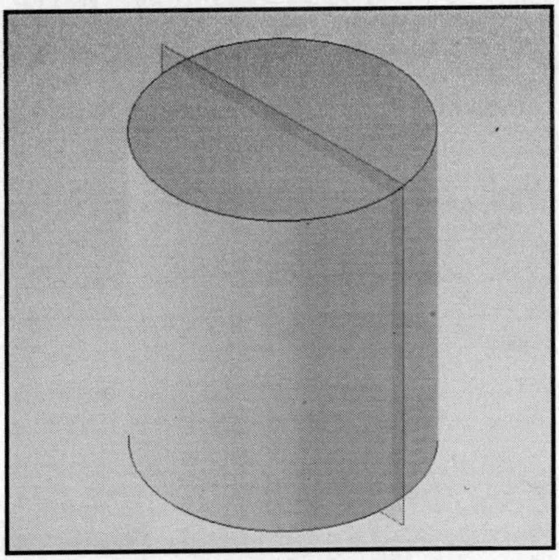

Step 2: Select the plane between the cylinders and start a sketch on it.

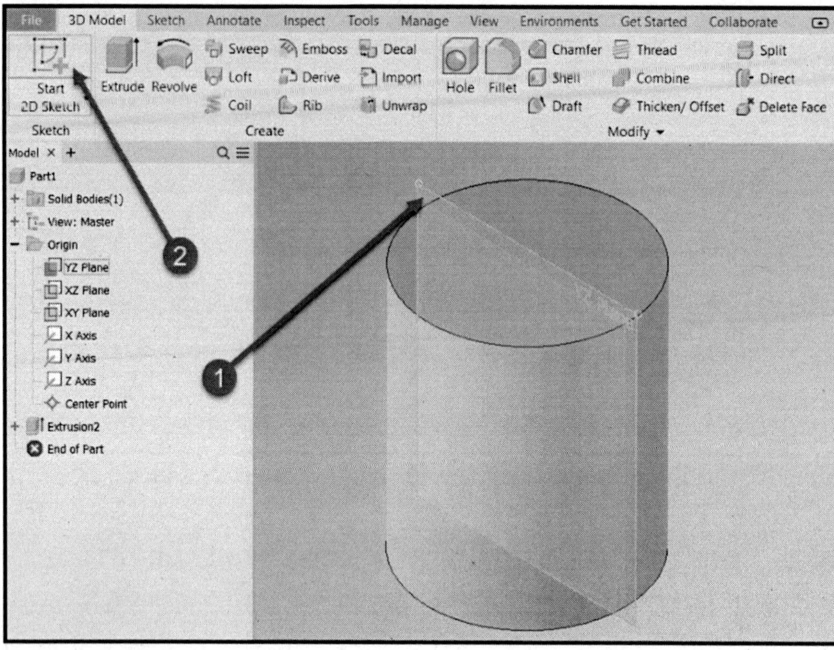

Step 3: Make a spline on selected plane then click on finish.

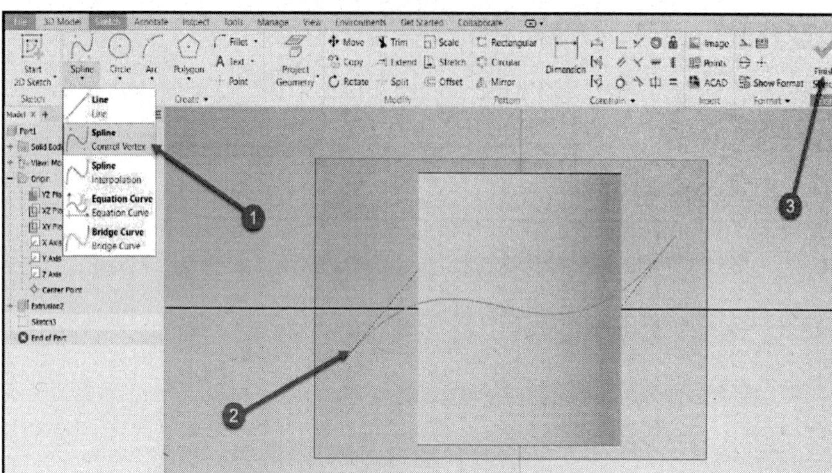

Step 4: Select spline and click extrude tool. Then click on extrude icon on extrude tab for surface extrude as given below.

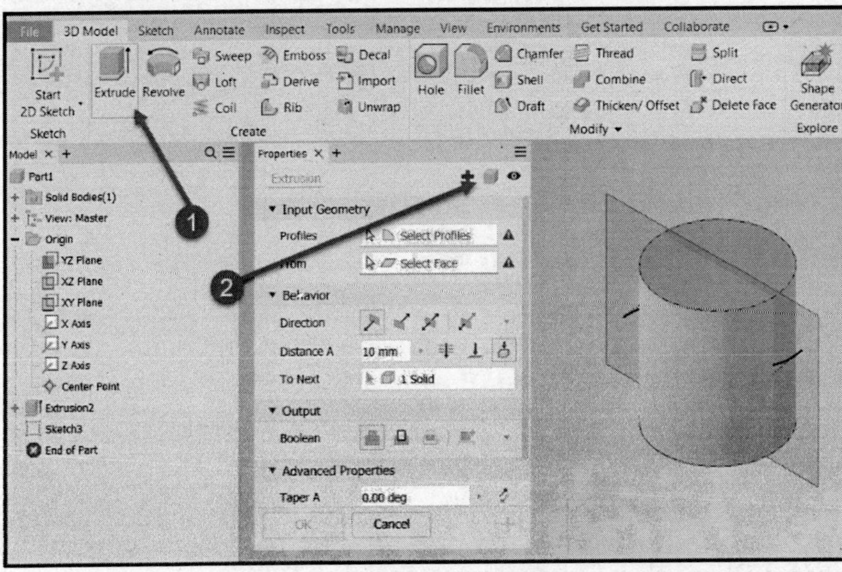

Step 5: Select spline and middle direction option.

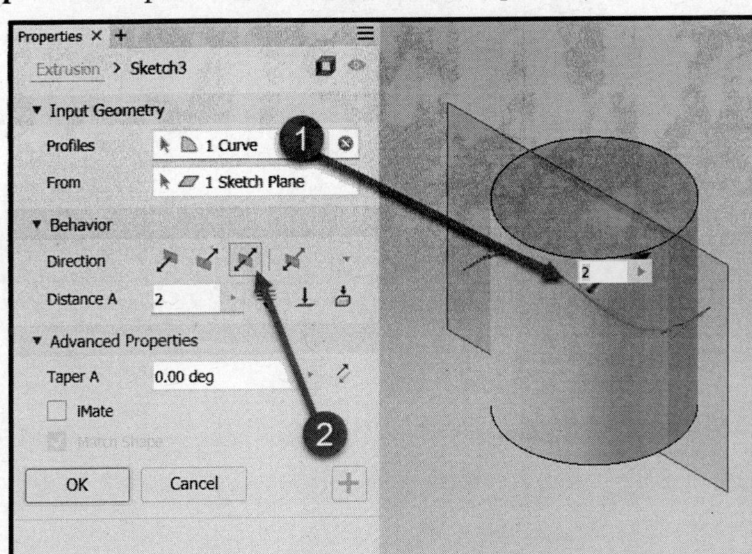

Step 6: After that, specify extrude distance and click "OK button".

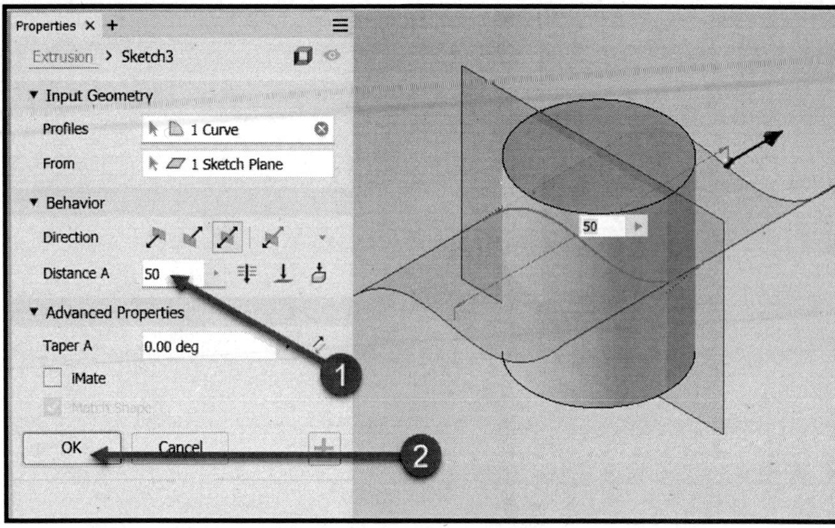

Step 7: First, Click on Split tool. Secondly, select spline surface as you created. Then select Cylinder body and click "OK".

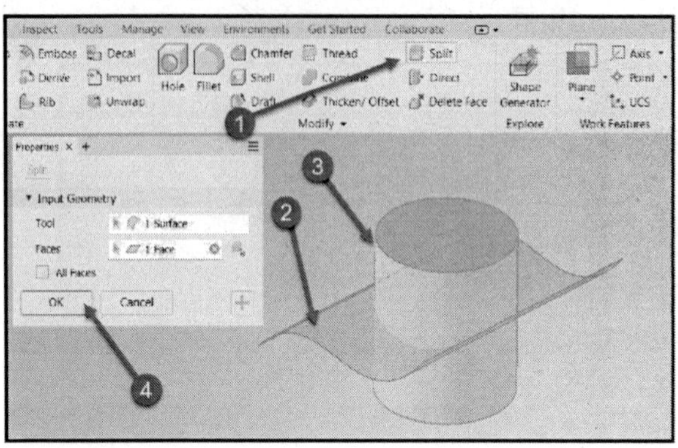

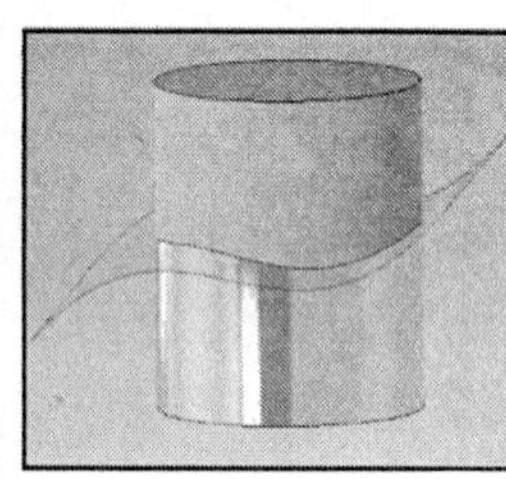

Direct

"Direct" tool is used for basic tool. such as, move, scale, divide, rotate, etc.

Step 1: Click on "Direct tool".

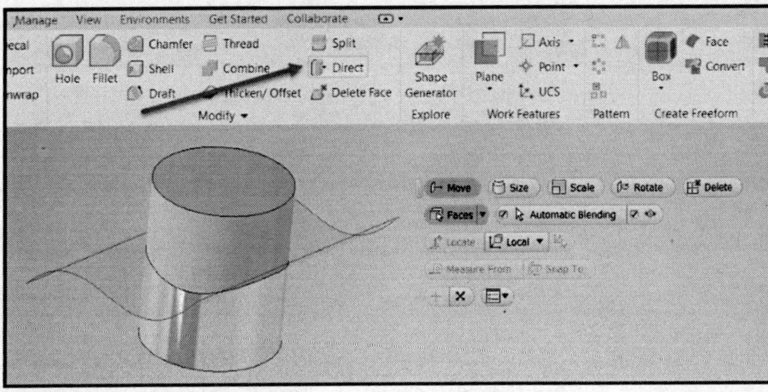

Step 2: Then, click on "move option and select faces option. After that, drag Axis. As given below on image.

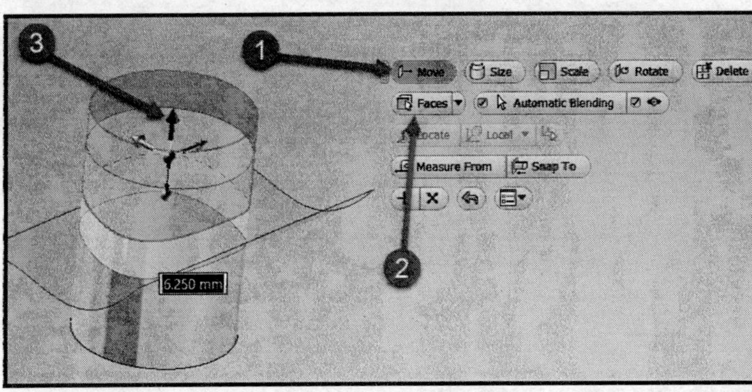

Step 3: If you want to increases Size. Same as, click on "Size option and drag Axis.

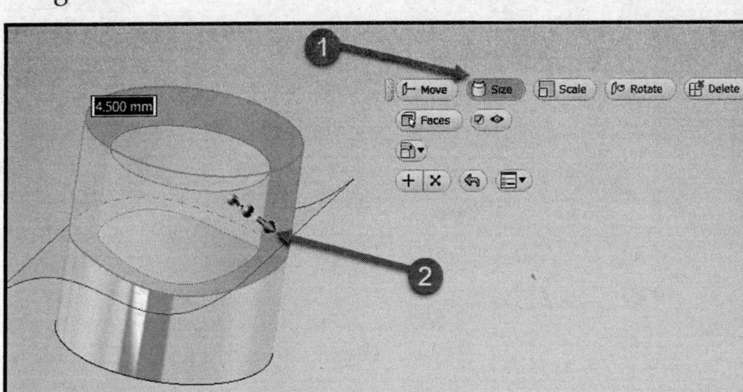

Step 4: Select scale option and specify scale as you want.

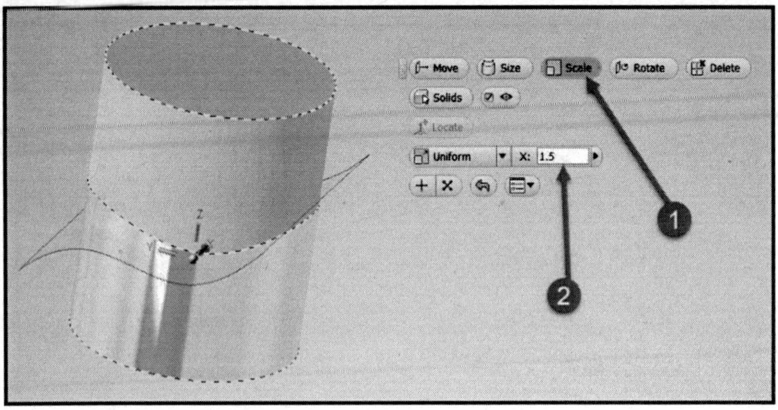

Step 5: Select rotate and select rotate axis.

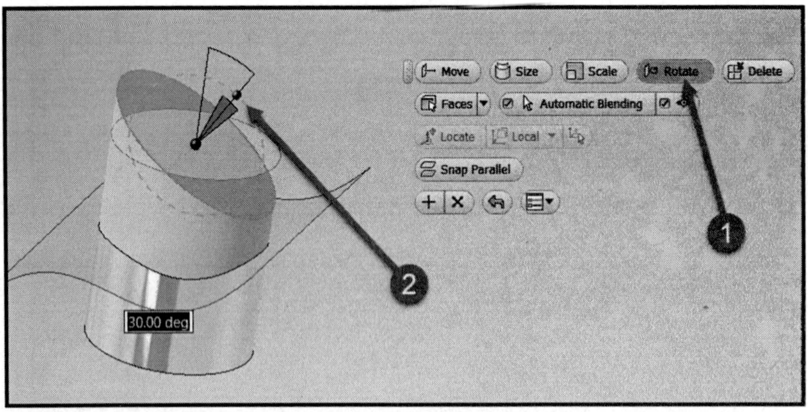

Step 6: Select delete option and select object as you want to delete.

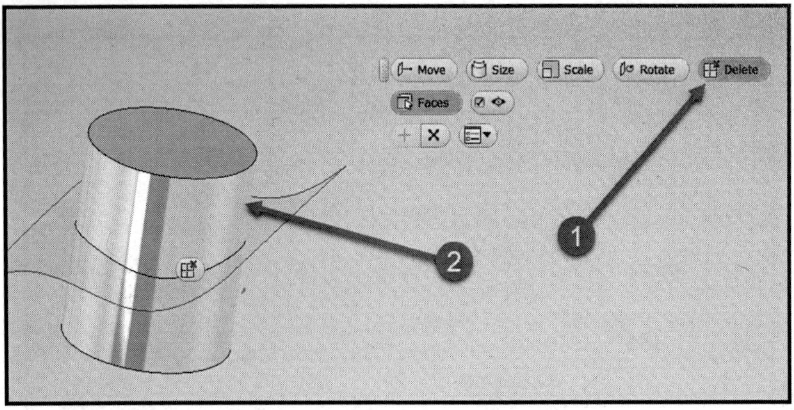

Delete face

This tool is used to remove the face of the object. This tool is like a shell tool.

Step 1: Click on "Delete face" tool and select object's face.

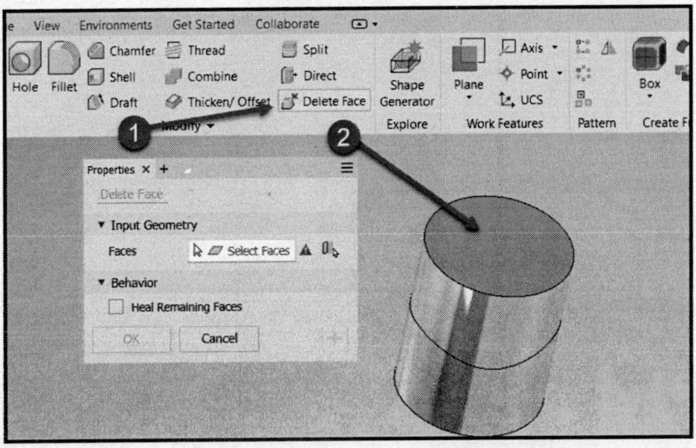

Step 2: After that selection face click "ok" option.

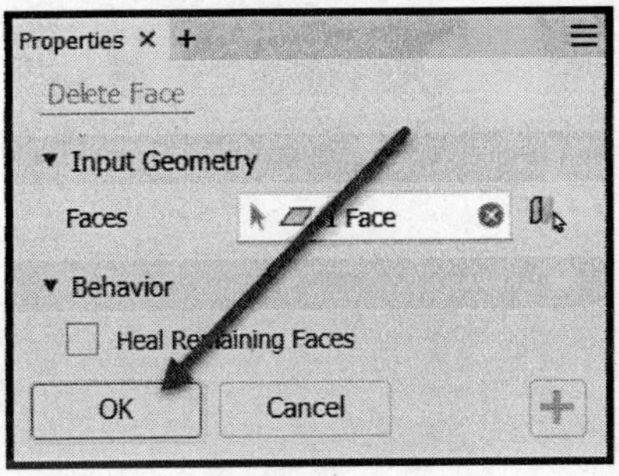

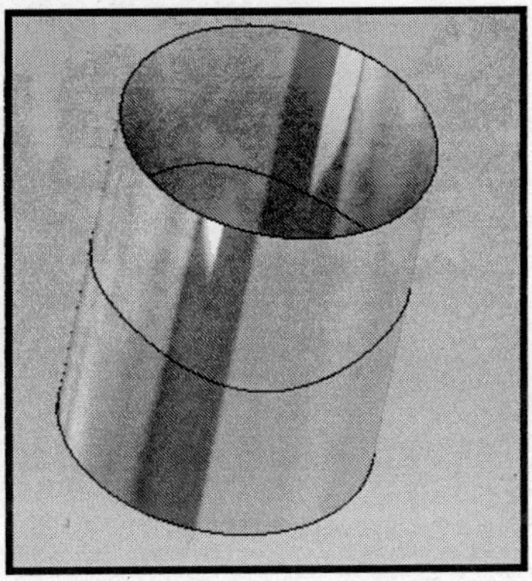

Move bodies

If you want to move an object. So, use this tool.

Step 1: First, make a rectangular plate as given below.

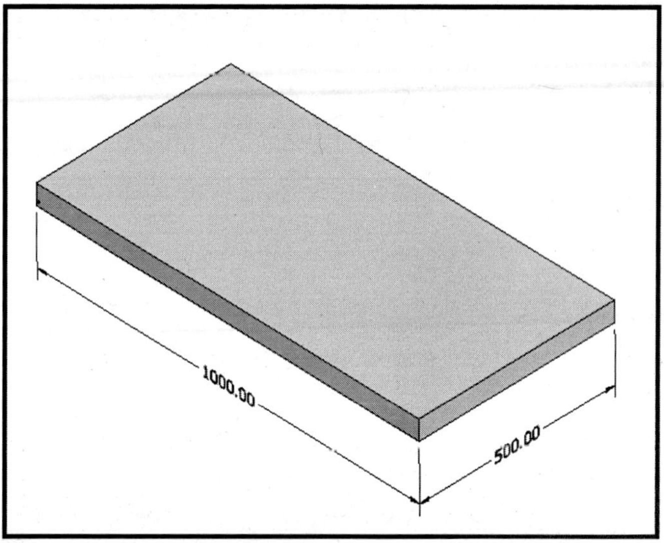

Step 2: After that, make a small cylinder through extrude. Make sure is it unmerge.

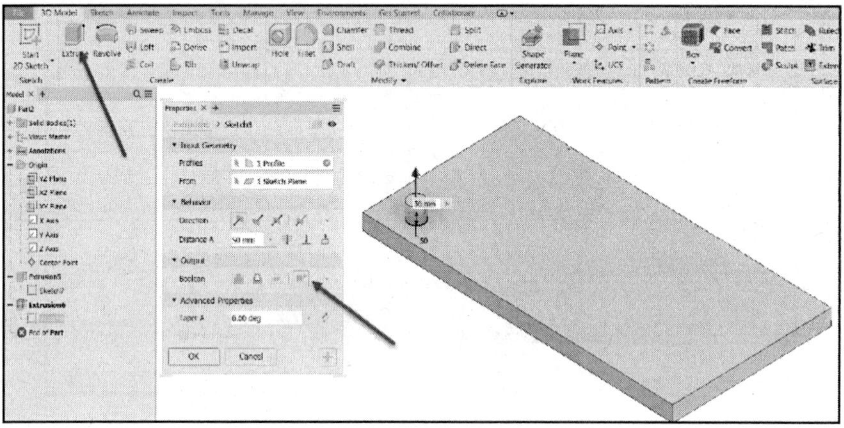

Step 3: Click on "move bodies" tool. Then select cylinder object.

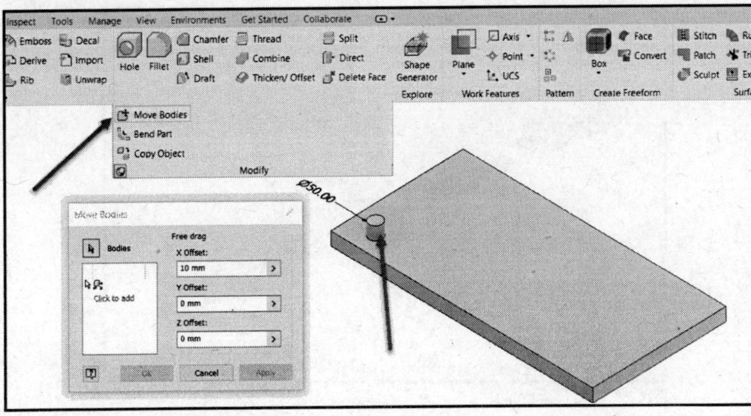

Step 4: After that, specify move distance as you want. Then click "apply and ok" button.

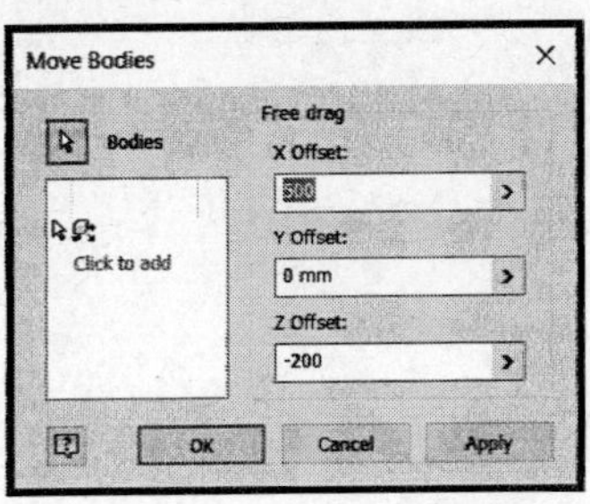

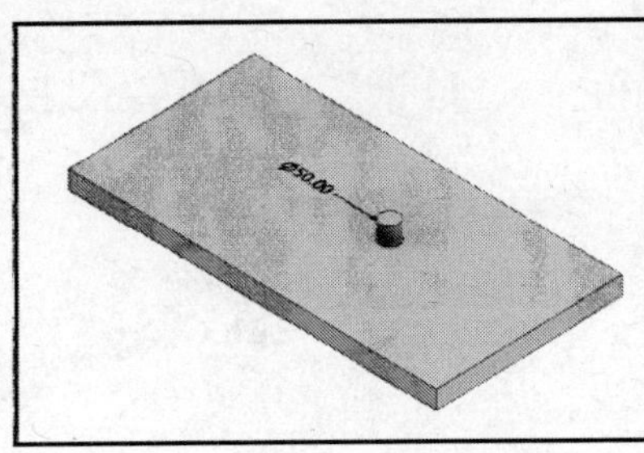

Bend Part

It is used to Bend an object. For this, it is necessary to draw a sketch line on the face of the object. Which indicates the bend position?

Step 1: First of all, make a T-Shape angle as given below.

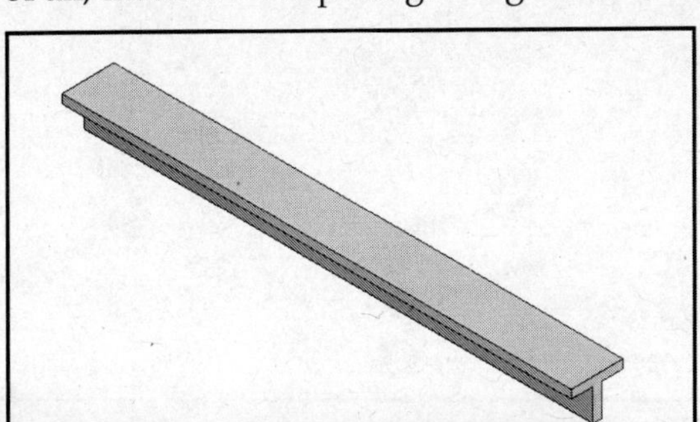

Step 2: Create a line on top face of the t-shape.

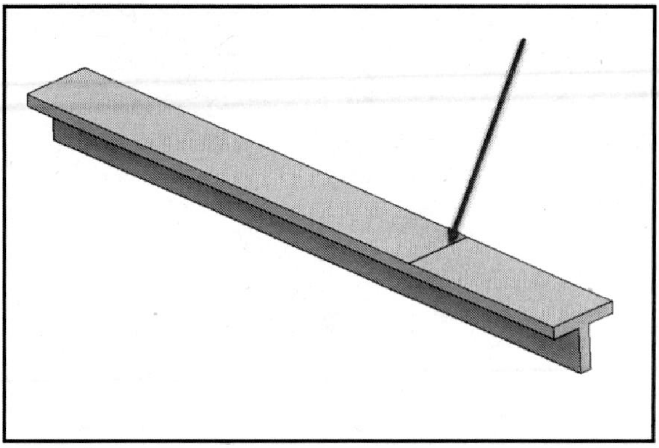

Step 3: Click on the "Bend Part" tool. After that, select bend line.

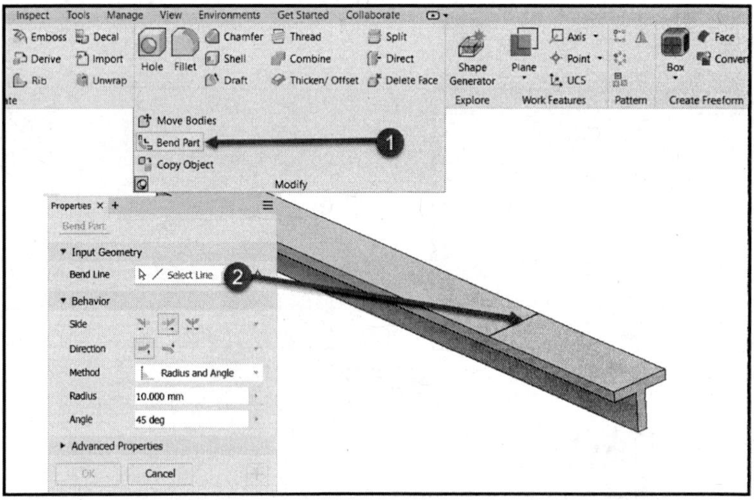

Step 4: Specify bend side, method, radius and angle then click "ok".

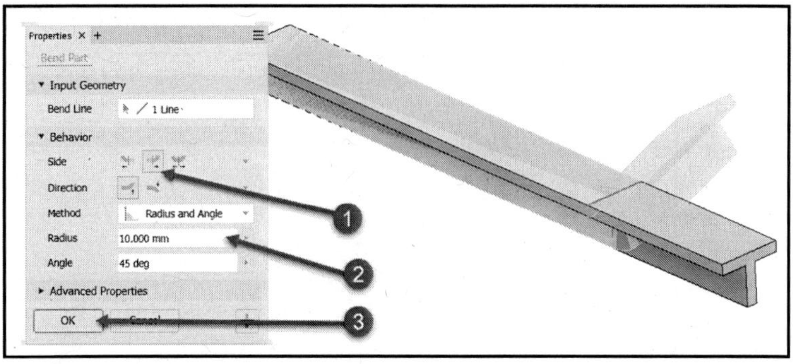

Copy Object

It is used to copy an object's face.

Step 1: Click on the "Copy Object" tool. Then select face of the object. Which you want to copy.

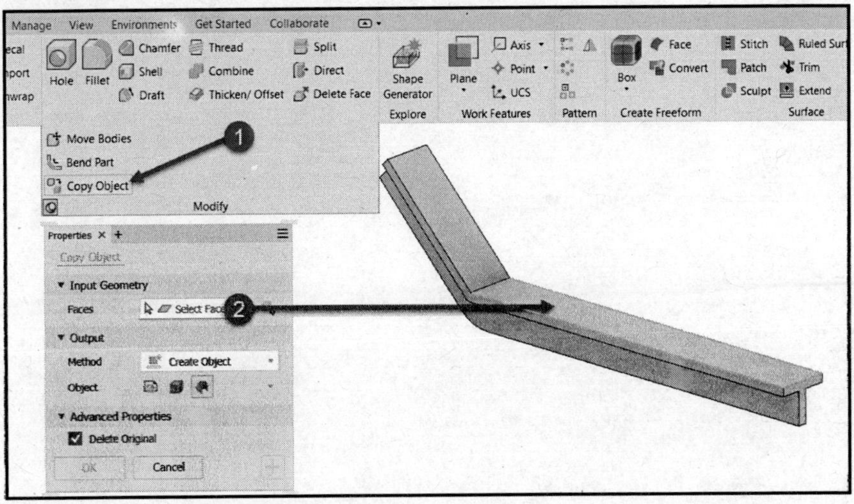

Step 2: Select face and click **"ok"**.

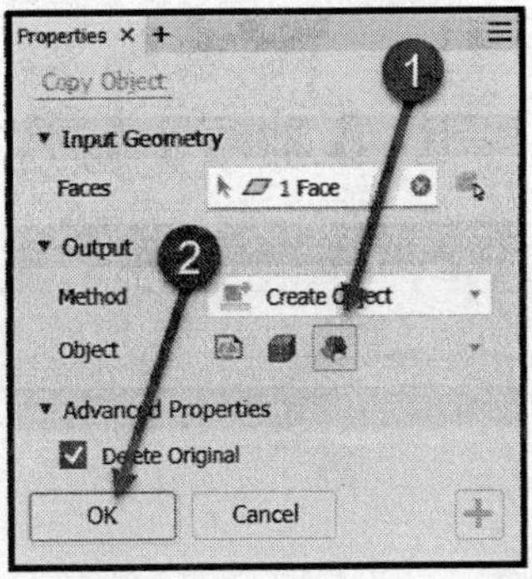

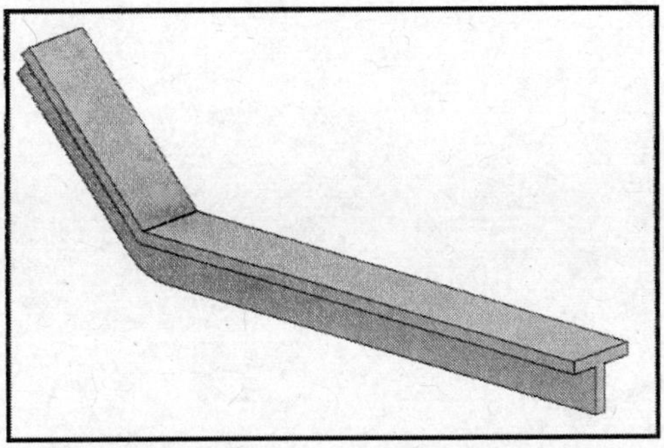

CHAPTER 6
Work Features

Plane

To make any sketch, a plane is required. But we only get 3 planes in the starting. If we have to make a separate plane. Which we need for the sketch. So, we can make a plane with the plane tool. there are many options, as given below.

Type 1 offset from plane:

Step 1: Click on the "plane" tool.

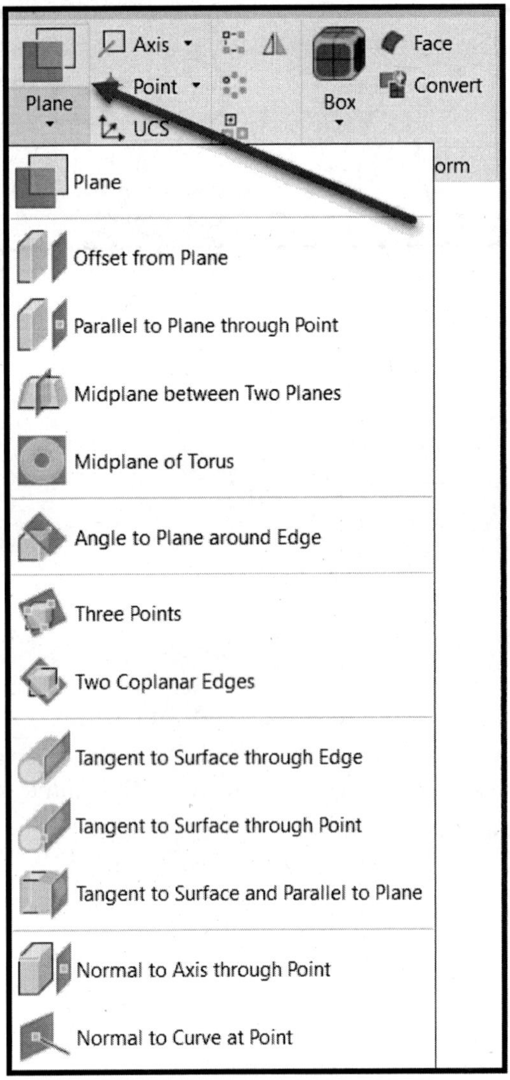

Step 2: First click on "offset from plane" option. Then select the required face & define the distance. Then click "ok".

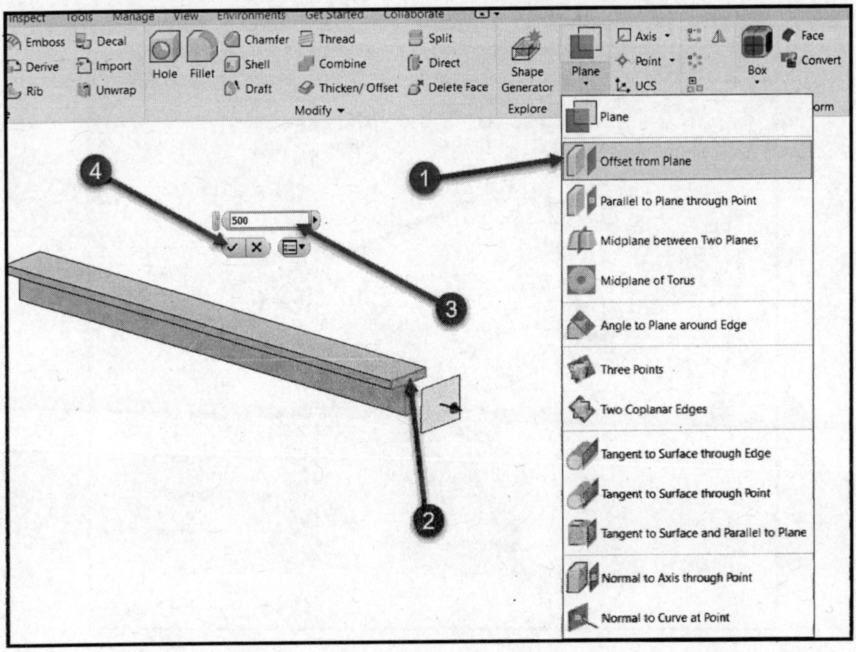

Type 2: Parallel to plane through point: Click on "Parallel to plane through point" Option. Then select the required face & point.

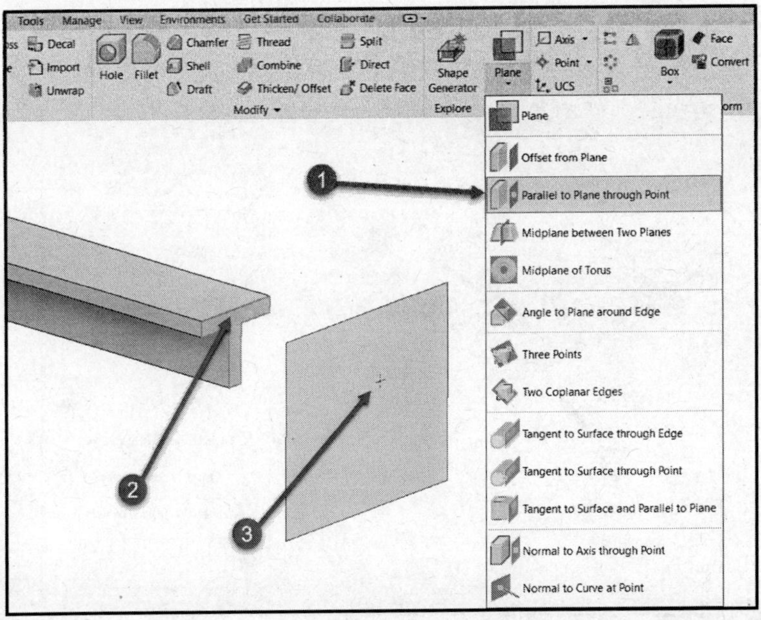

Type 3: Midplane between two planes: Click on "Midplane between two planes" option. Then select the required two faces, in between which a plane to be created.

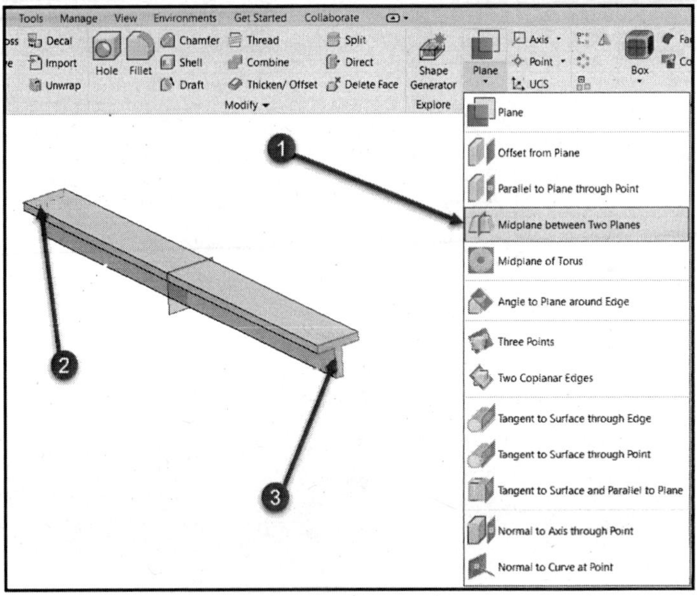

Type 4: Angle to plane around edge: Click on "Angle to plane around edge" option. Then select a face & an edge. Then mention the angle required for plane.

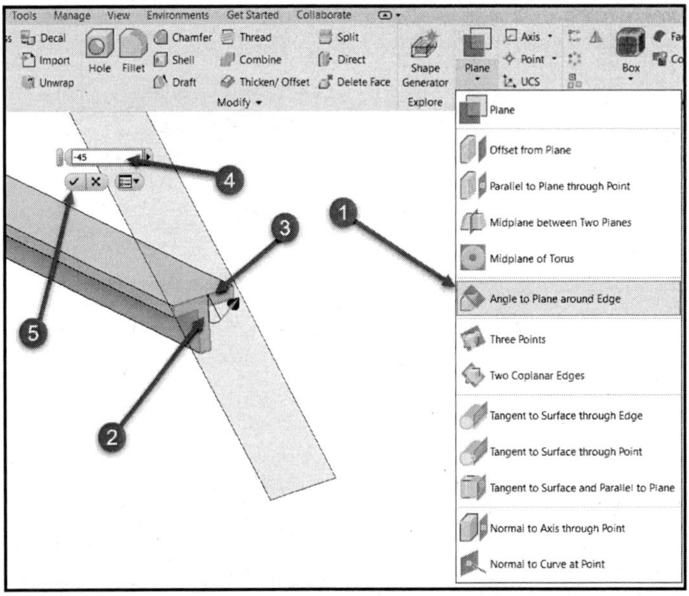

Type 5: Three points: Click on "Three points" option & then select the 3 points.

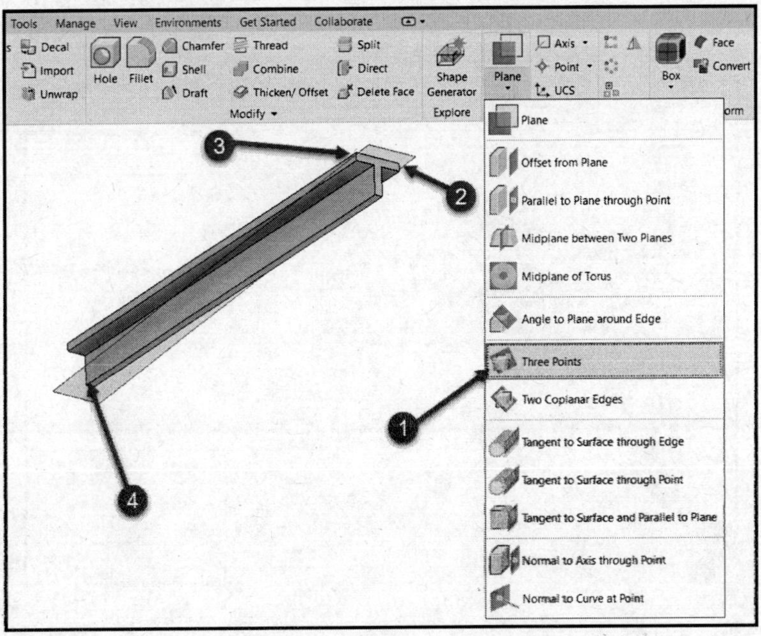

Type 6: Two coplanar edges: Click "Two coplanar edges" tool. Then, Select two colinear edges.

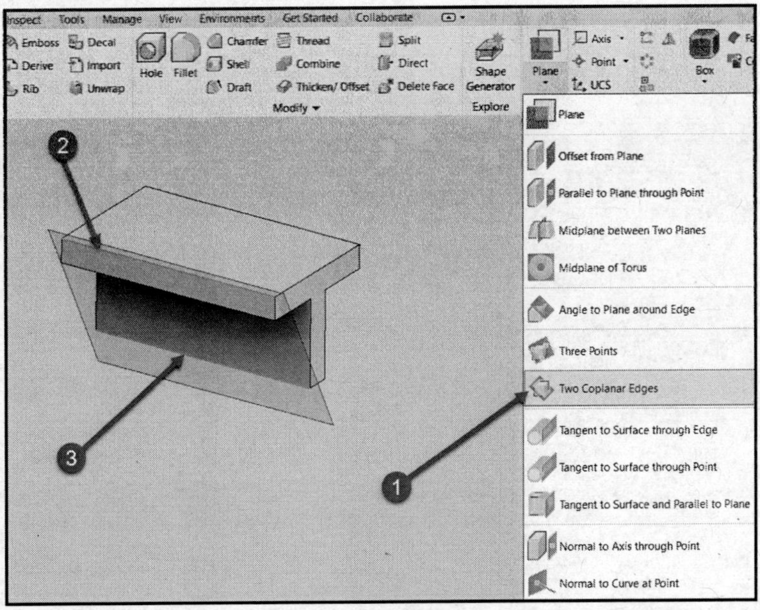

Type 7: Tangent to surface through edge: Click "Tangent to surface through edge" option. Then, select cylinder surface and edges. As given below.

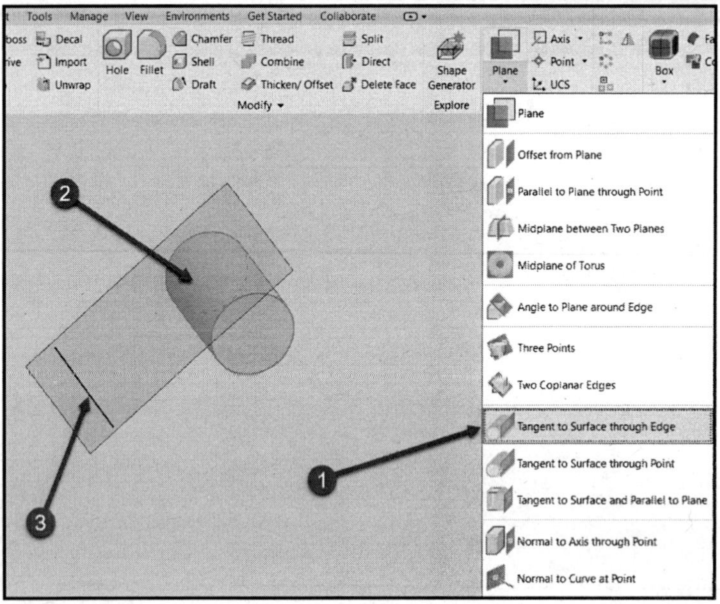

Type 8: Tangent to surface through point: Select point and surface as you want for the "Tangent to surface through point" option.

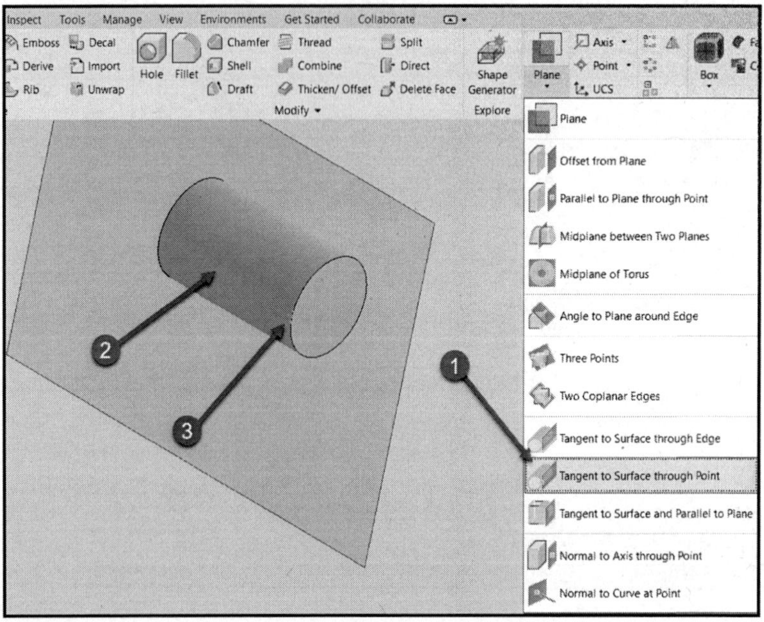

Type 9: Tangent to surface and parallel to plane: If you want to create "Tangent to surface and parallel to plane" plane. So, click flat face and select curve surface. As given below.

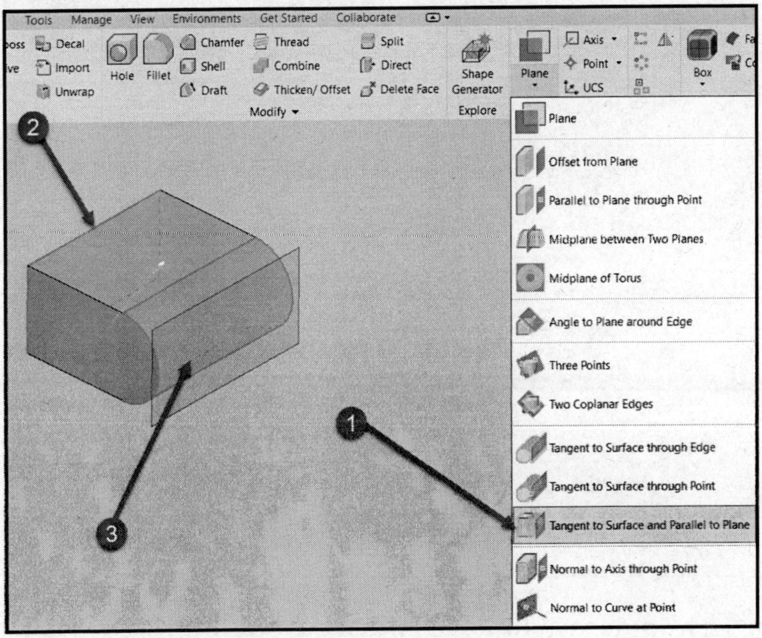

Type 10: Normal to Axis through Point: First, select edge then point.

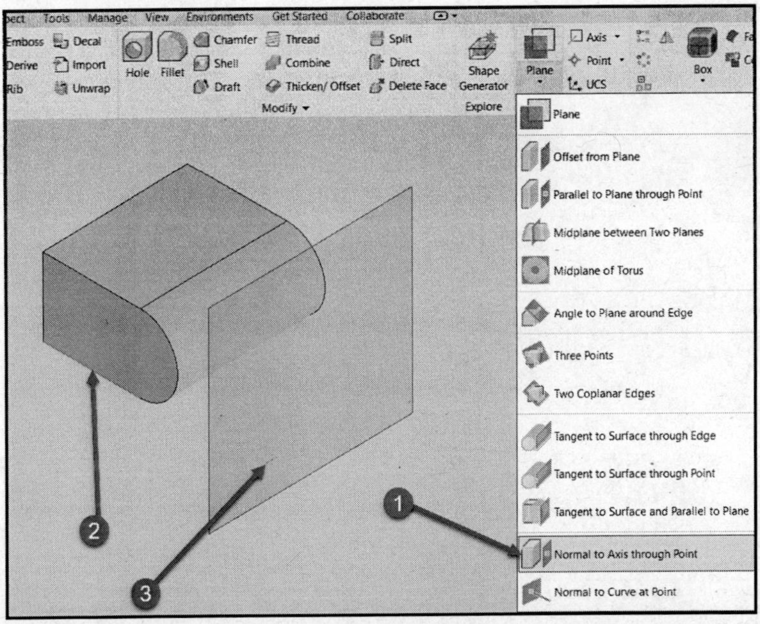

Type 11: Normal to curve at point: select any line then Click on the last point of the line.

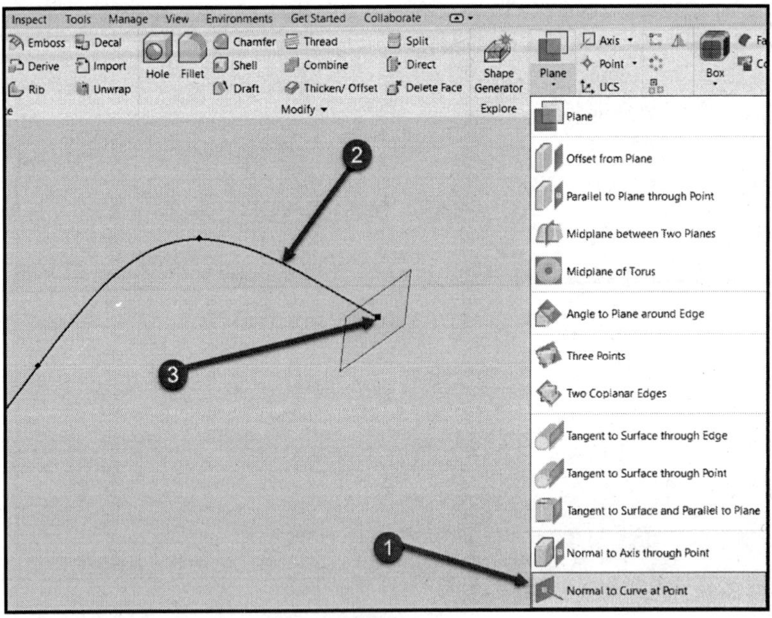

Type 12: Midplane of torus : first, make a torus then click "Midplane of torus" option.

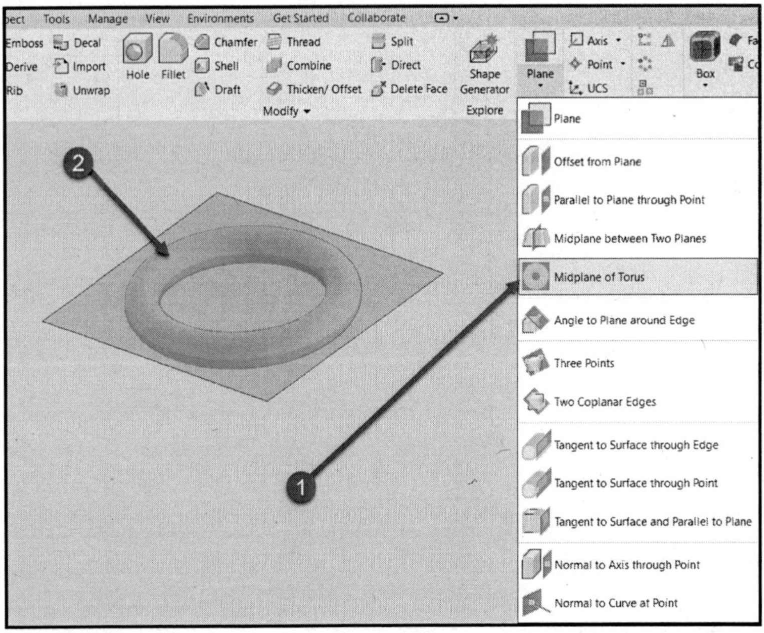

Axis

It is used to make an additional Axis. There is a different type of axis in this.

Type 1: First, click on "Axis" option. Then, select torus object.

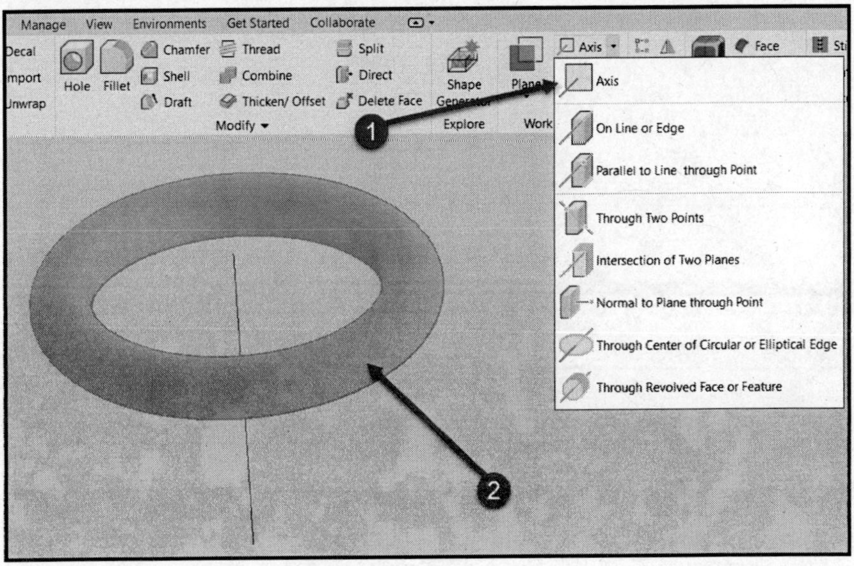

Type 2: First, click on "On line or edge" option. Then, select edge of the object.

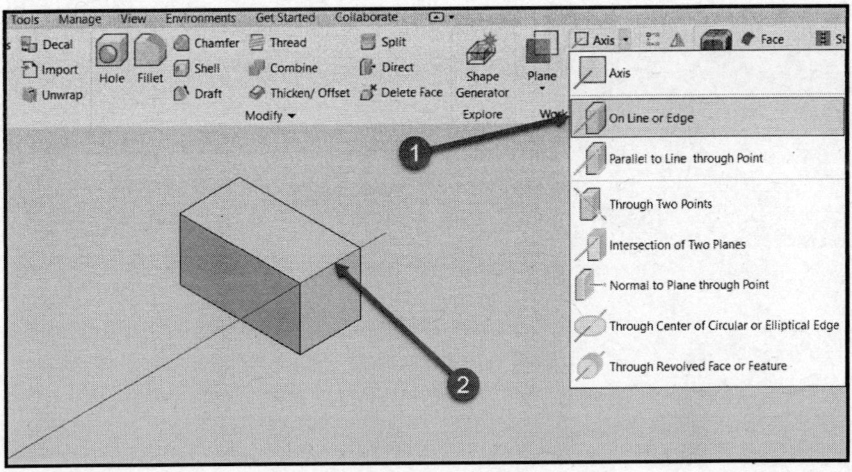

Type 3: First, click on "Parallel to Line through Point" option. Then, select torus object.

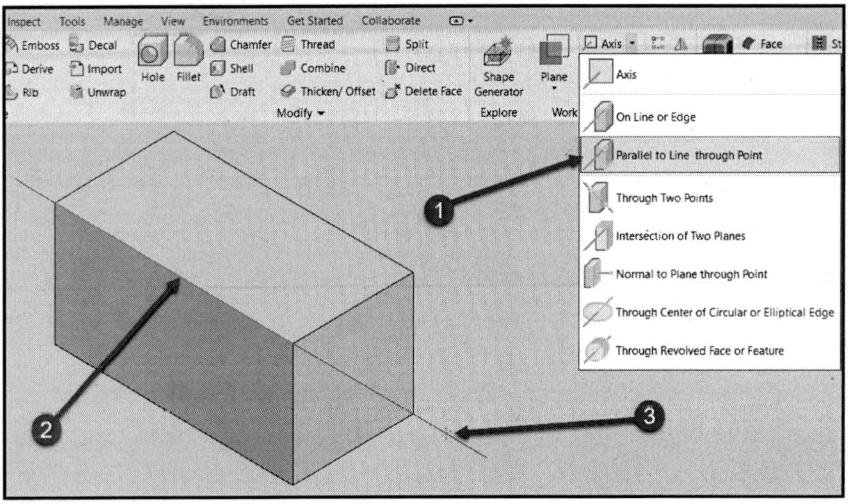

Type 4: First, click on "Through Two Points" option. Then, Select two points one by one.

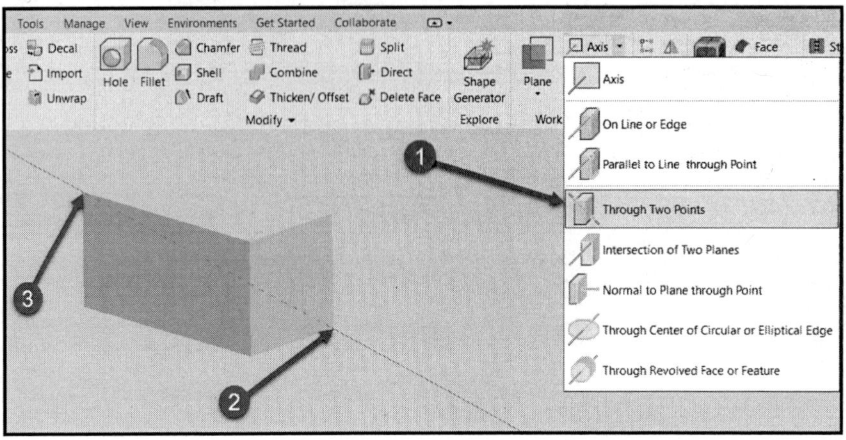

Type 5: First, click on "Intersection of Two Planes" option. Then, Select two planes one by one.

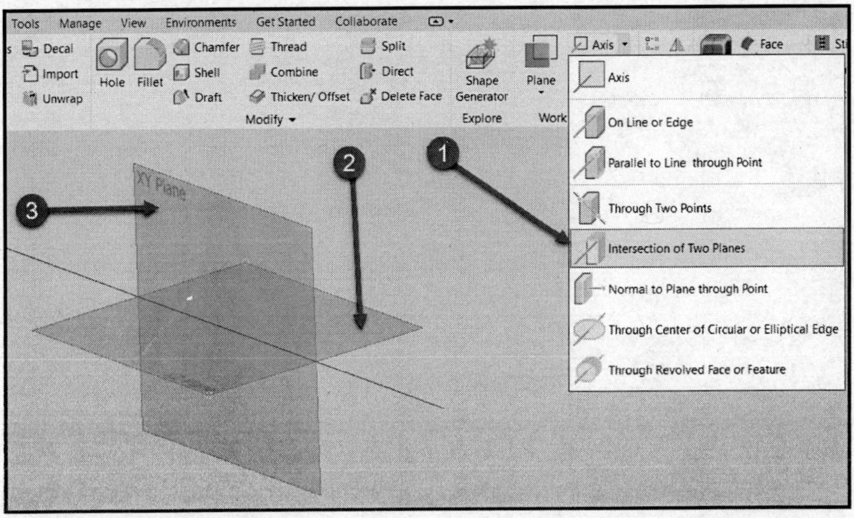

Type 6: First, click on "Normal to Plane through Point" option. Then, Select one face and a point.

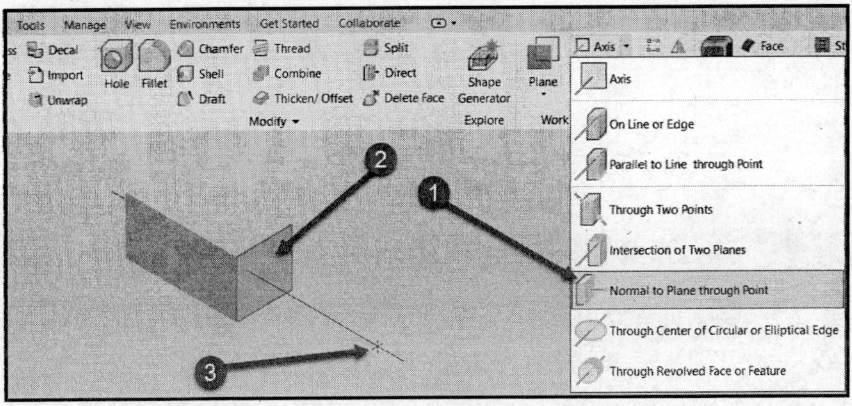

Type 7: First, click on "Through Center of Circular or Elliptical Edge" option. Then, Select Cylinder's circular edge.

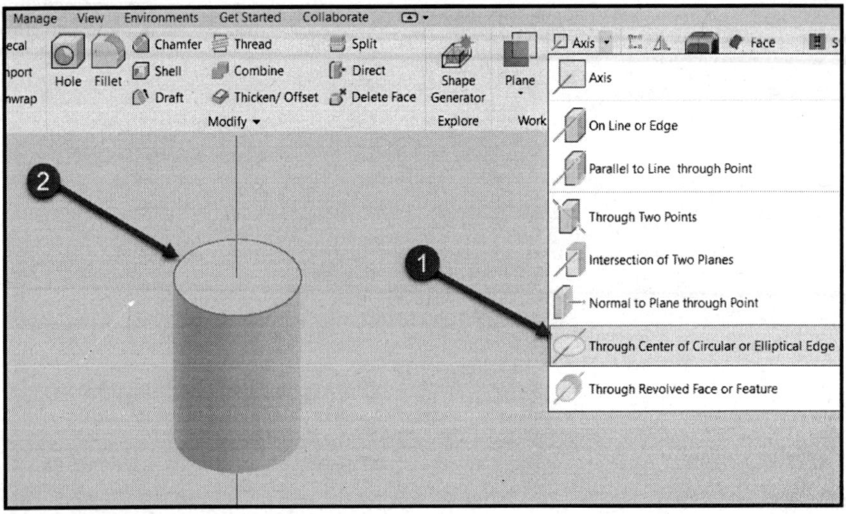

Type 8: First, click on "Through Revolved Face or Feature" option. Then, Select Cylinder's circular face.

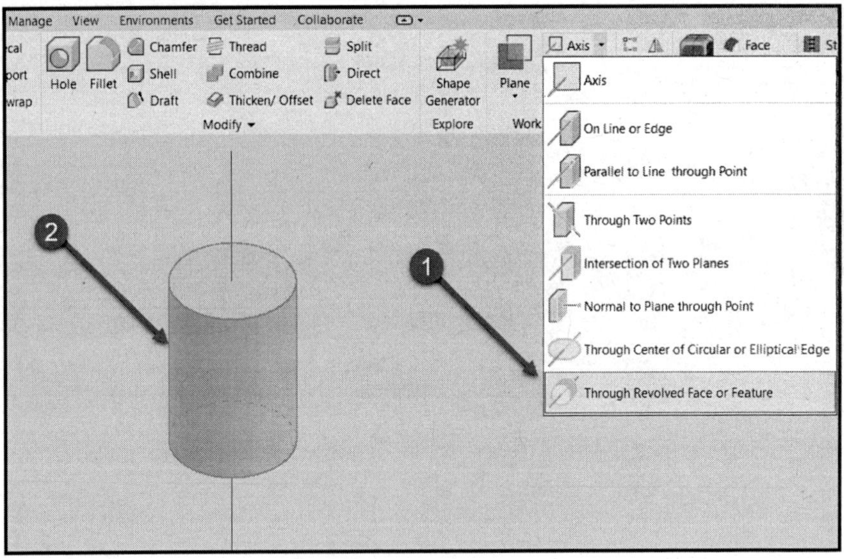

Point

It is used to make a point. There is different type of point in this.

Type 1: First, click on "Point" option. Then, select line and select curve's face, that you have created. As given below image.

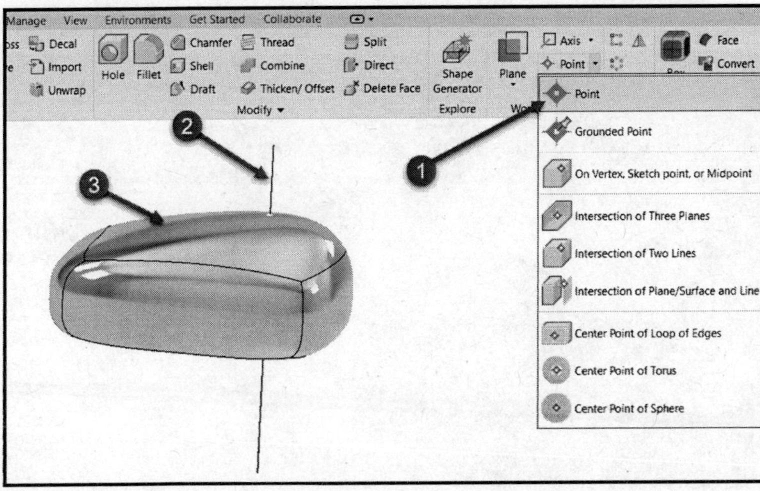

Type 2: First, click on "Grounded Point" option. Then, Select any corner point of the box. After that, you can move the point, through axis.

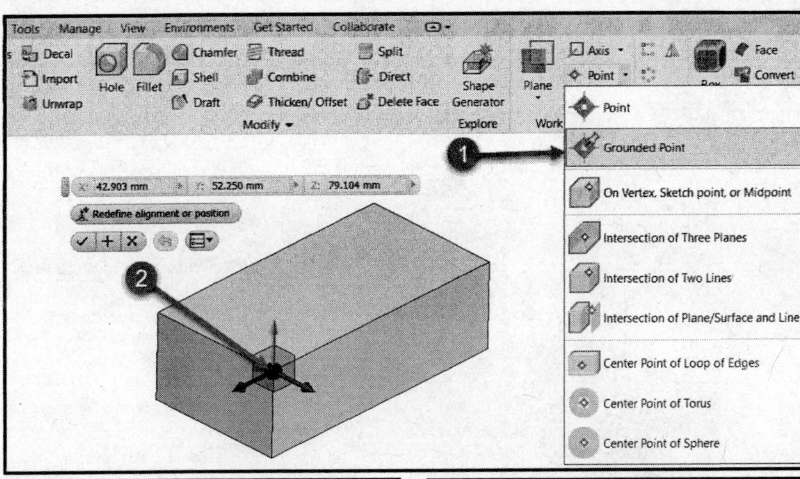

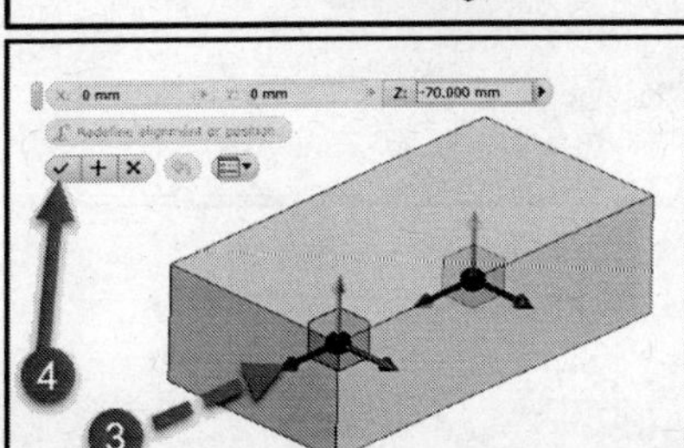

Type 3: First, click on "On Vertex, Sketch point, or Midpoint" option. Then, Click on the vertex of the box.

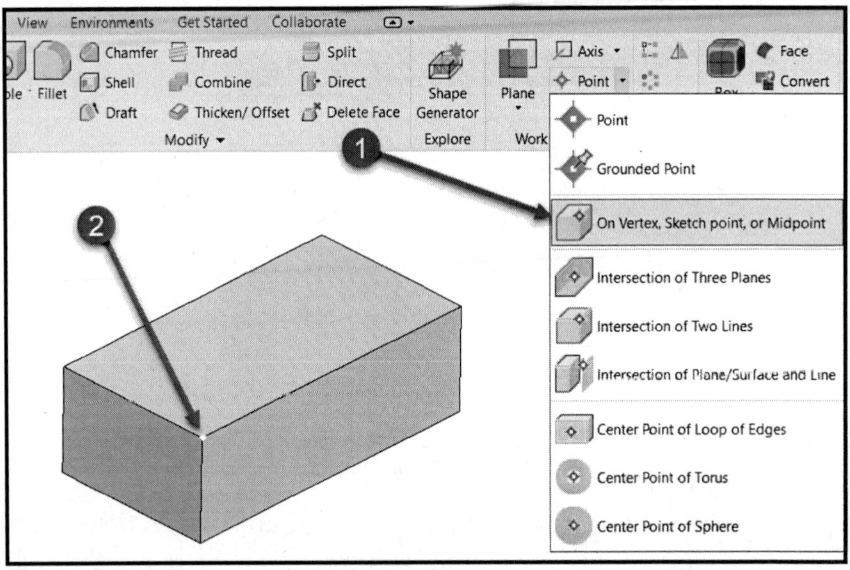

Type 4: First, click on "Intersection of Three Planes" option. Then, Select three planes one by one. Which are intersecting each other.

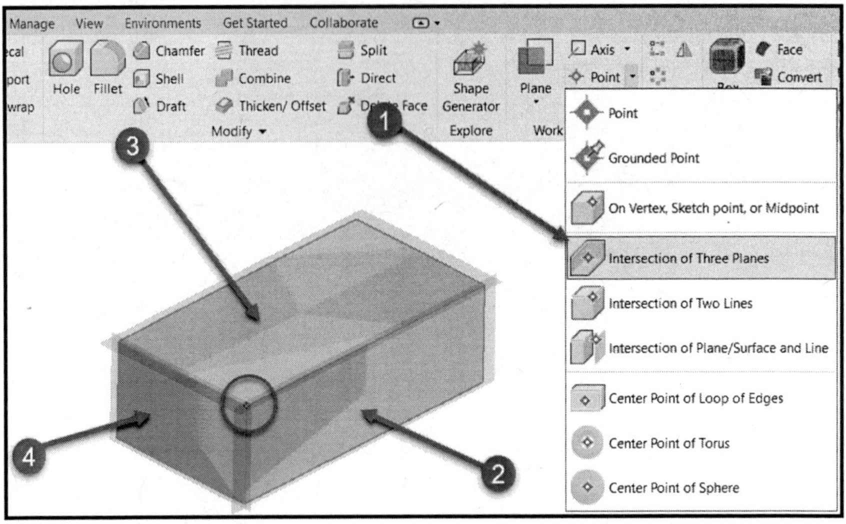

Type 5: First, click on "Intersection of Two Lines" option. Then, Select three planes one by one. Which are intersecting each other.

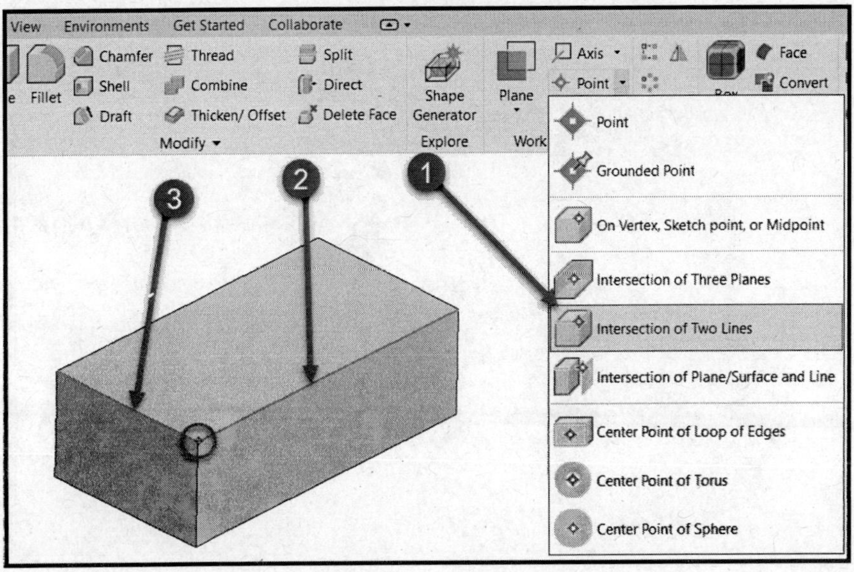

Type 6: First, click on "Intersection of Planes/Surface and Line" option. Then, select the box's face and axis as you created.

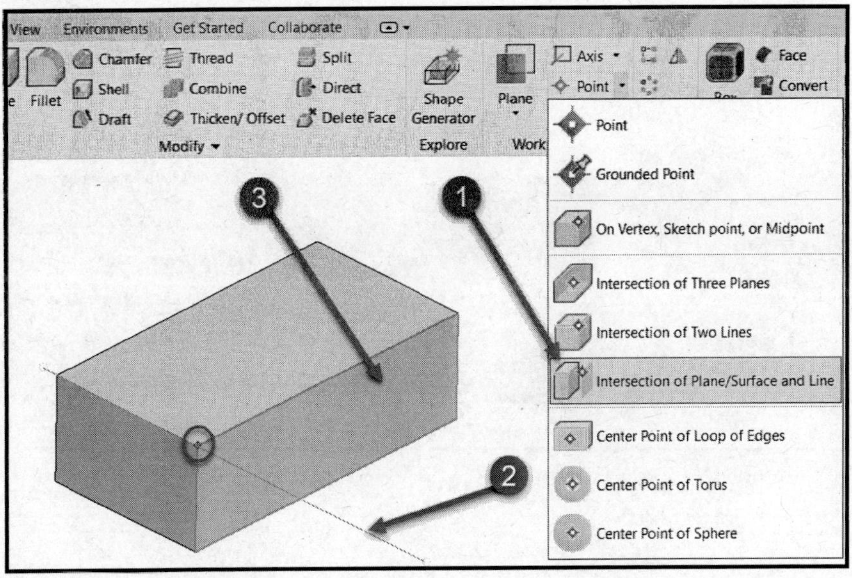

Type 7: First, click on "Center Point of Loop of Edges" option. Then, select the box's face.

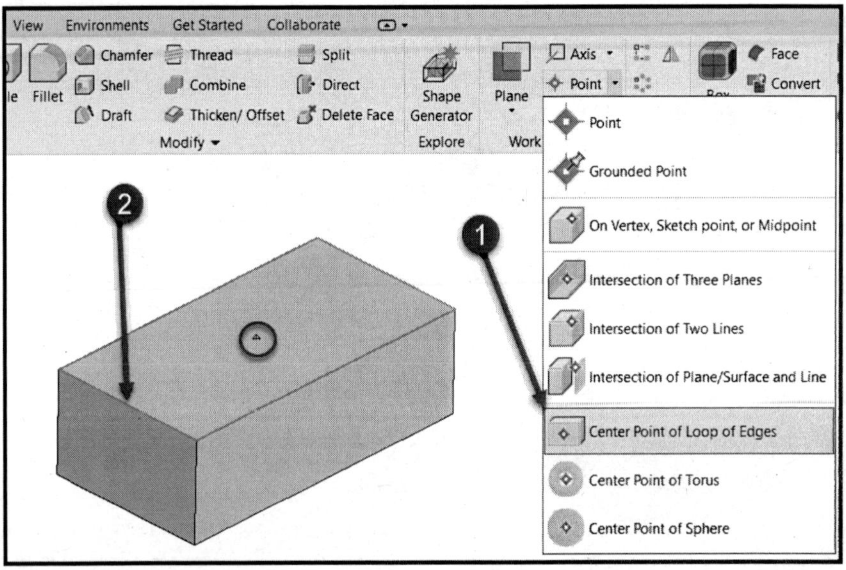

Type 8: First, click on "Center Point of Torus" option. Then, select torus, that you have created.

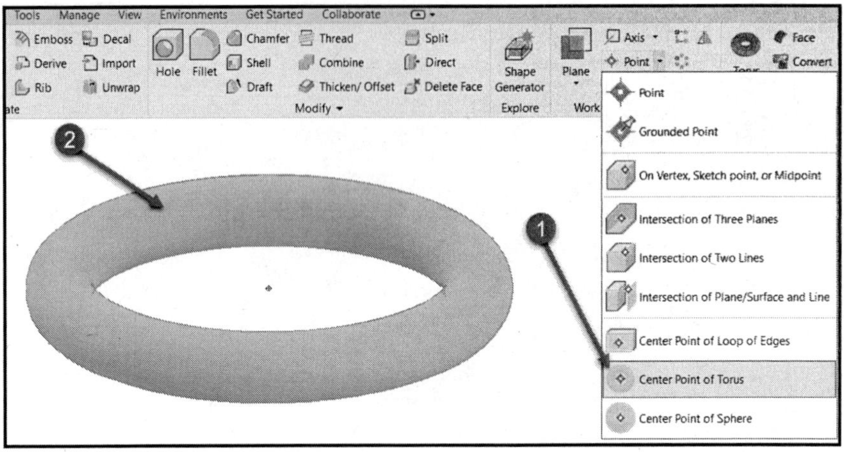

Type 9: First, click on "Center Point of Sphere" option. Then, select Sphere, that you have created.

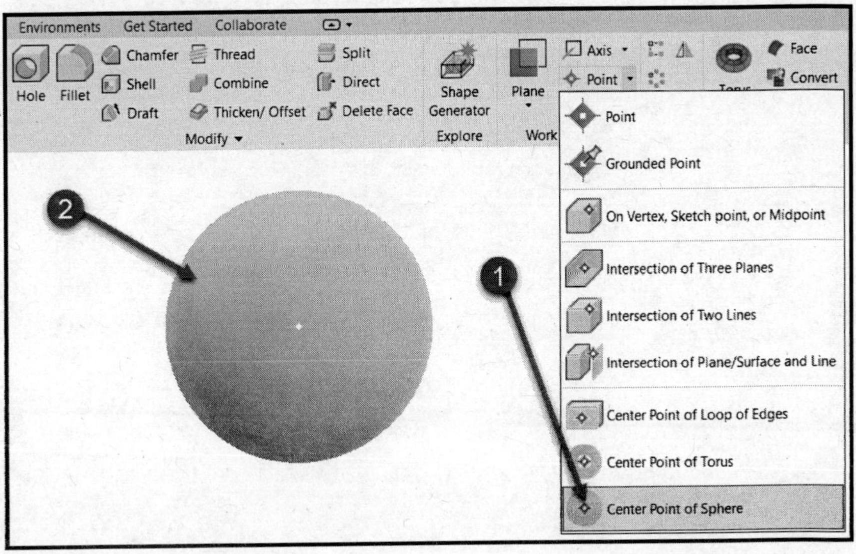

UCS

The full form of "UCS is "User Coordinate System". It is used to change the origin point.

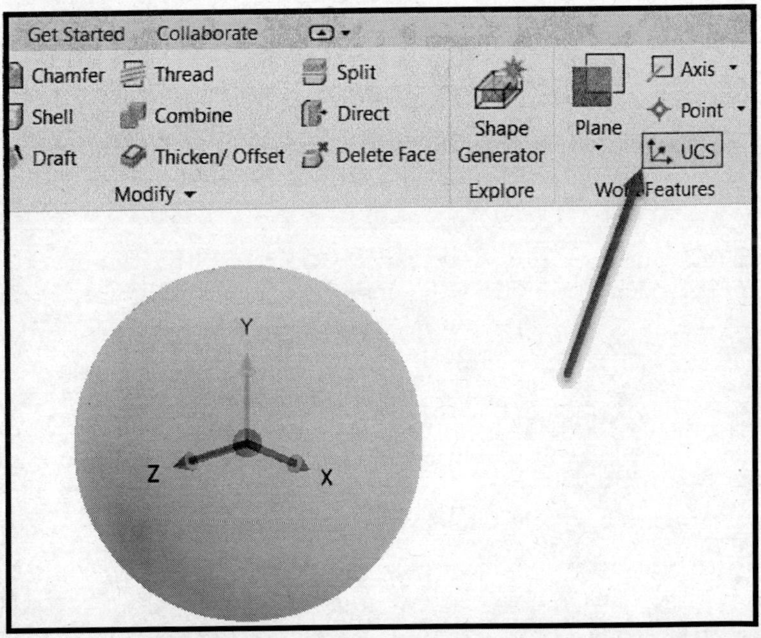

CHAPTER 7
Surface

Trim

Basically, it is used for surface option. To cut a surface object, use the trim tool.

Step 1: First, make a circle to 2D sketch After the sketch completed, close the sketch.

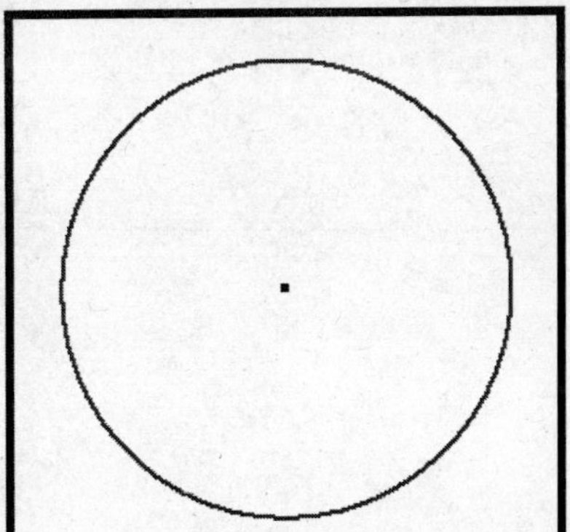

Step 2: Select circle and click "extrude" tool. After that, Click on Surface option in extrude tab and specify dimension.

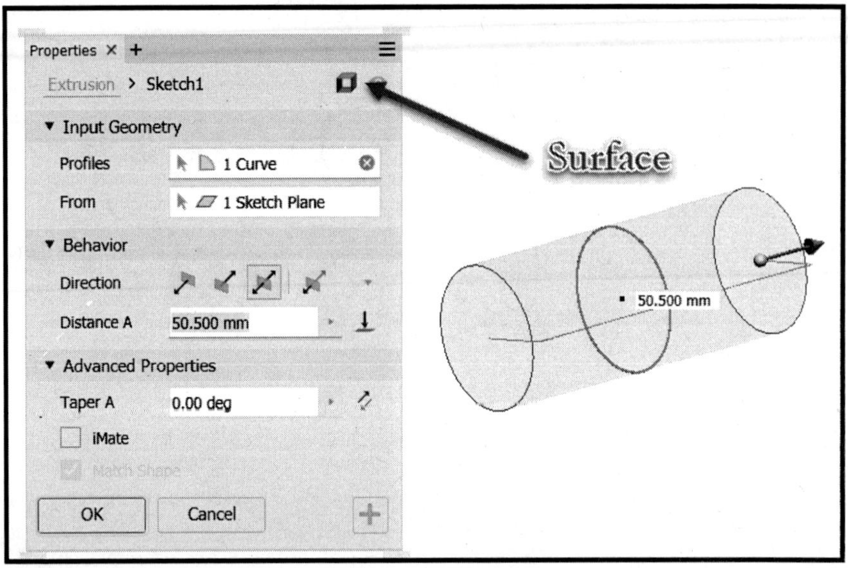

Step 3: Same As, again start 2D sketch on XY plane. Click the arc tool.

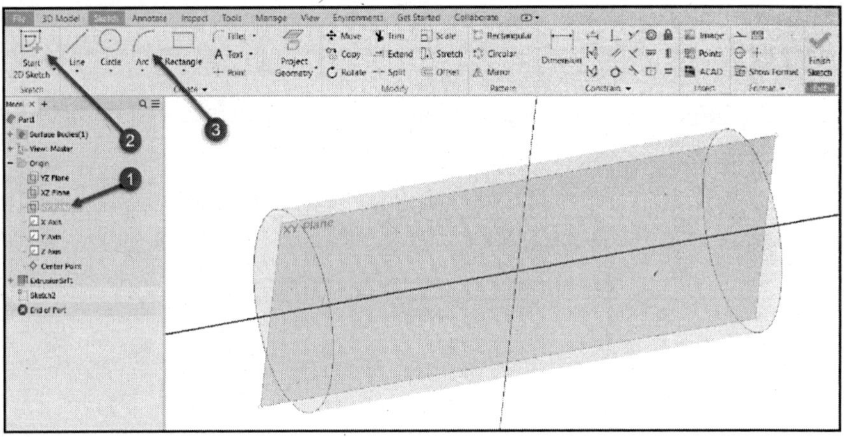

Step 4: Create arc on the plane. After that, Click "finish sketch" icon.

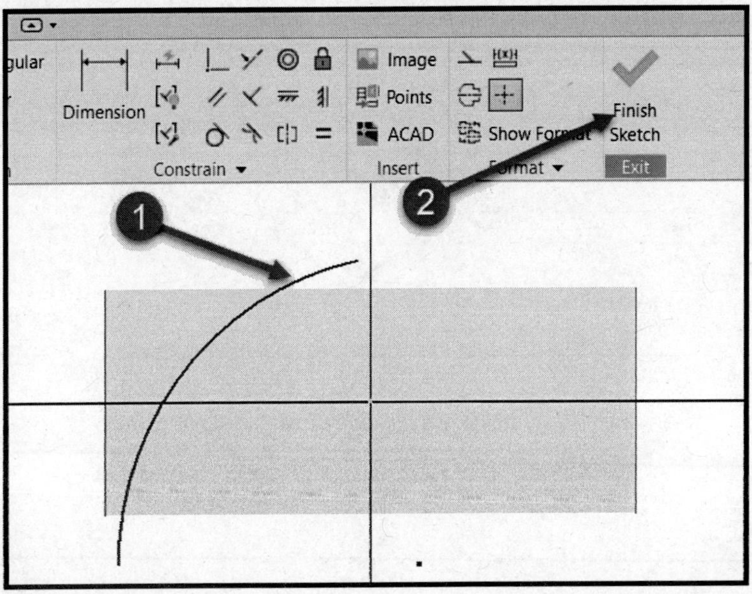

Step 5: Select the arc and use "extrude" tool for surface extrusion.

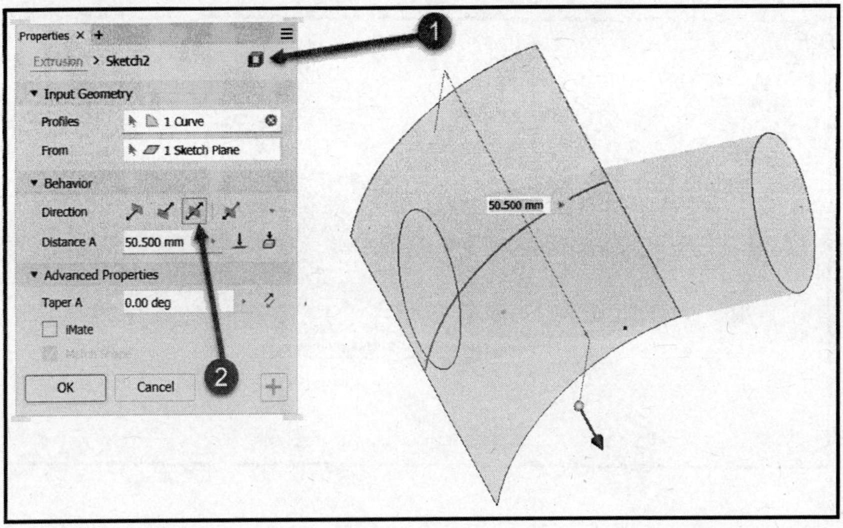

Step 6: Click "Trim" tool. Then click "cutting tool" icon in the "Trim surface" option. And select Arc surface as given below.

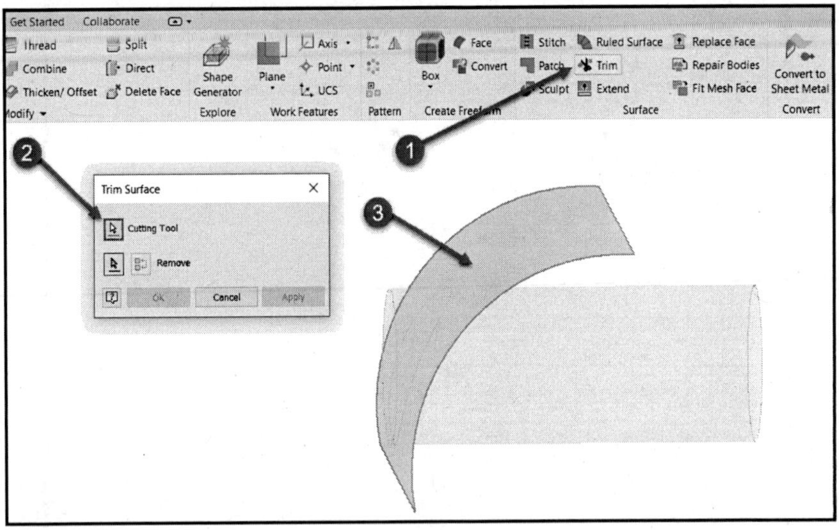

Step 7: Click "remove" icon in the "trim surface" option and select surface circle.

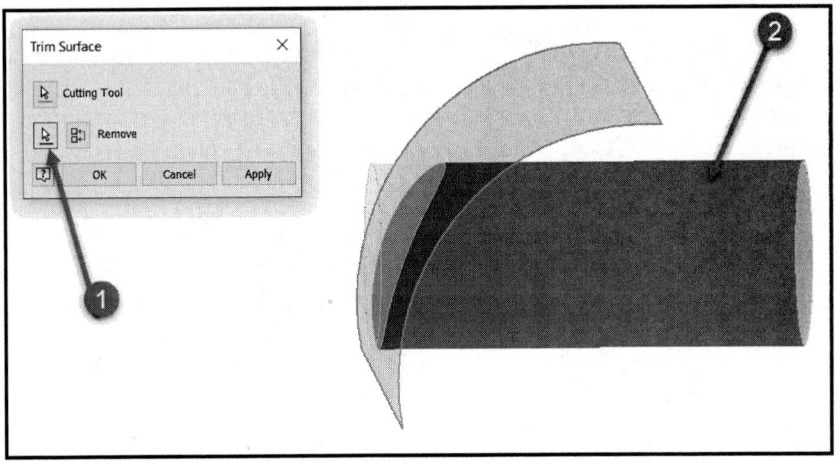

Step 8: Click "remove" in the "trim surface" option. After that, Click "apply" and "ok" button.

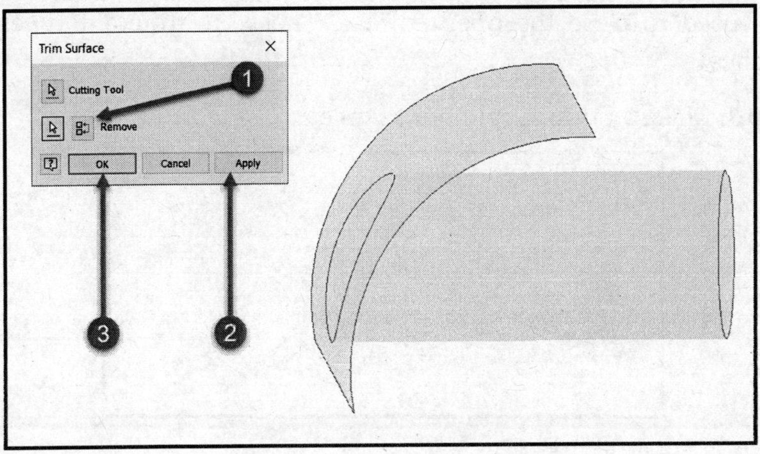

Step 9: Select "extrudesrf2" in Presentation tree. Simultaneously, click on the right button of the mouse. And Click on the "visibility" option. As given below.

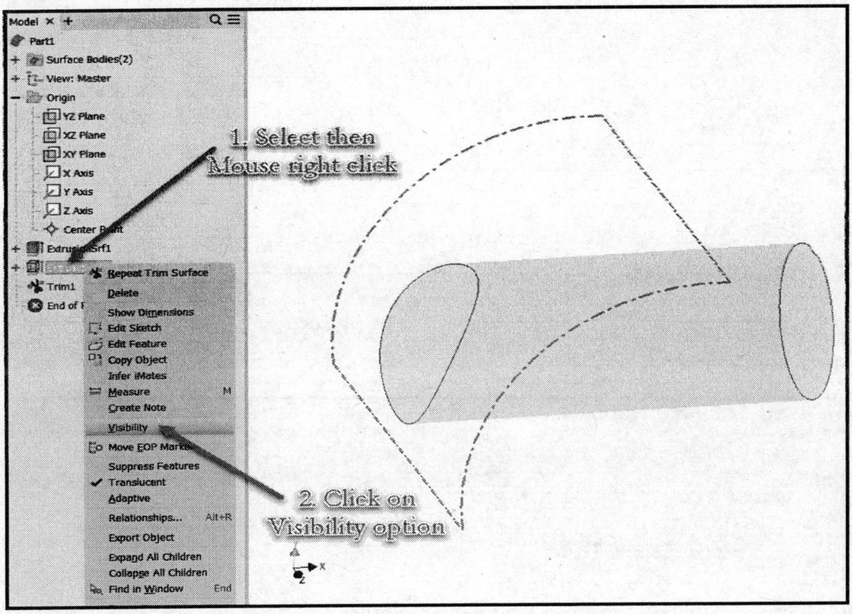

Patch

It is used to close the open surface. There are different types of patches.

Step 1: Make a Surface cylinder as given.

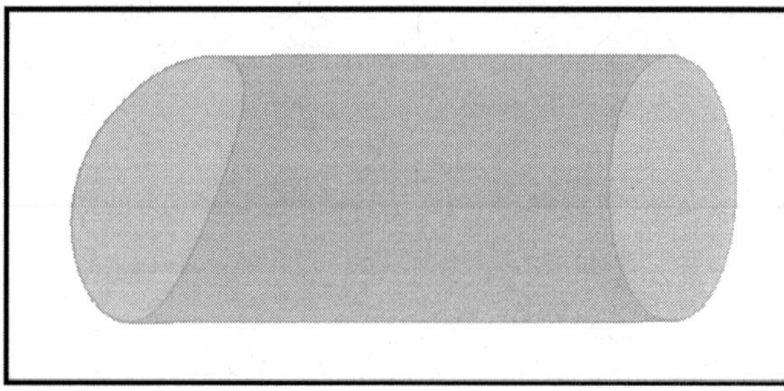

Step 2: Click the "patch" tool. And select edge of Surface cylinder.

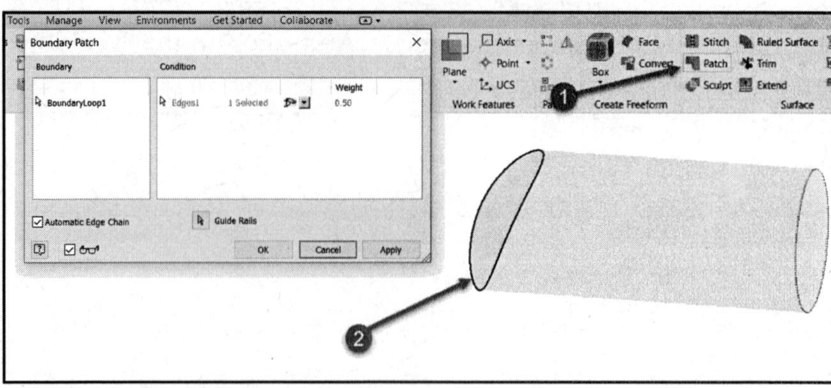

Step 3: Choose patch type and specify weight. Then Click "apply" and "ok" button.7859196533

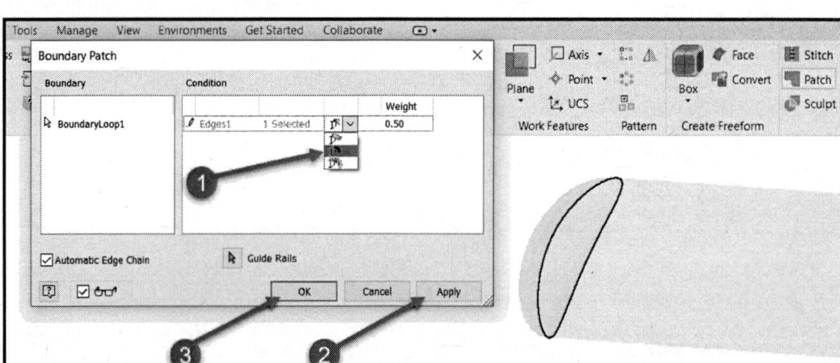

Stitch

It is used to join two surfaces. With this tool, different surfaces can be made into one surface.

Step 1: we have already created two different surfaces. as shown below. For such a surface, Used the "Extrude tool", "Patch tool" and "Trim tool".

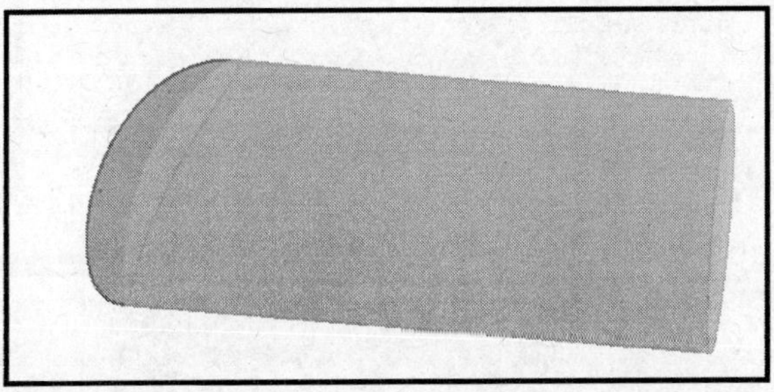

Step 2: Click the "Stitch" tool. Then select both surfaces. Click "Apply" and "Done" button. You can also specify tolerance.

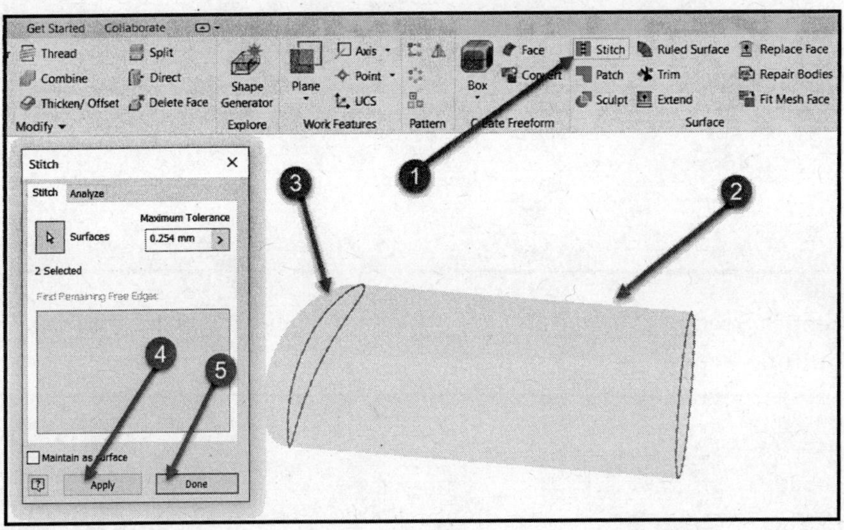

Ruled surface

It is used to extend the surface. By selecting the edges of the surface, you can increase the surface at any Angle.

Step 1: Like, the surface we used for the patch tool. We will make similar surface cylinders.

Step 2: Click the "ruled surface" tool. then select ruled type to ruled surface window and select edge of surface cylinder.

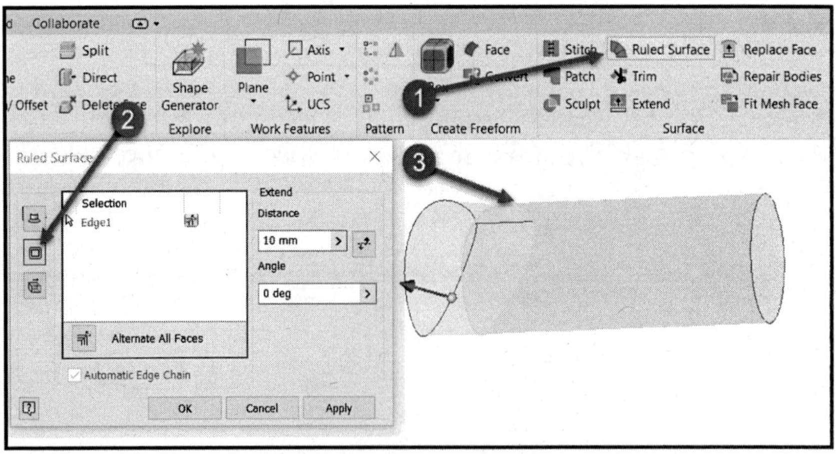

Step 3: Specify distance and angle. After that, click "apply" and "ok" button.

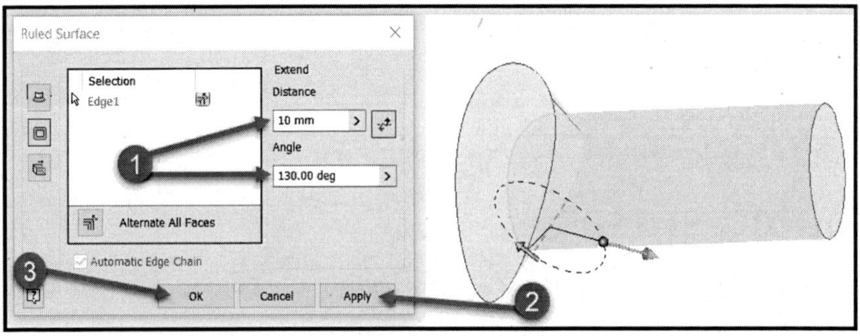

Extend

It is used to expand the surface. By selecting the edges of the surface, you can extend it forward in the direction of the surface itself.

Step 1: Click on the "Expand" tool. Then click on the "Edges" icon of the window. And then, select the edge of the surface cylinder.

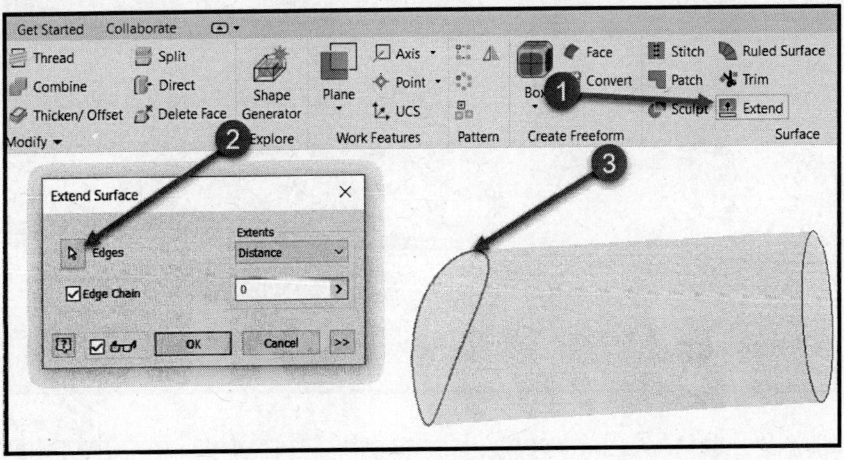

Step 2: Specify distance of extend. After that, Click "ok" button.

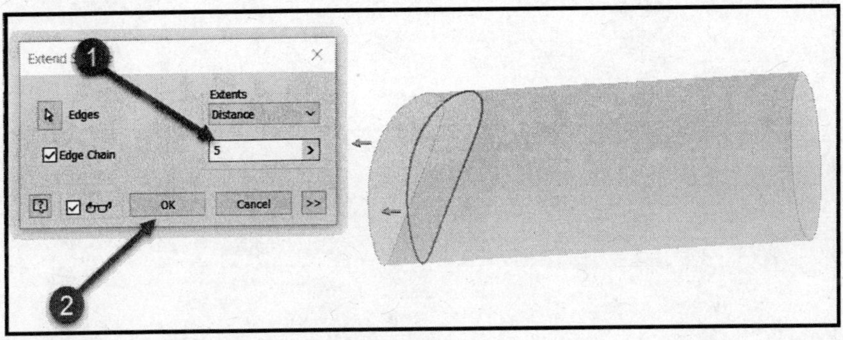

Sculpt

We used this tool to join two parts, cut one part, or extract the intersecting part into two parts.

Step 1: First, Make a sphere.

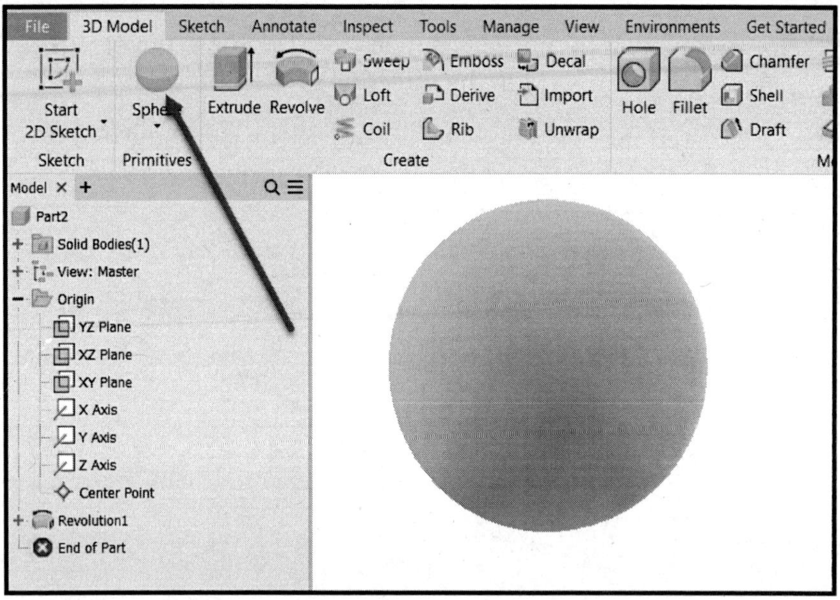

Step 2: Select XZ plane and Click the "start 2D sketch" button on the ribbon bar. Then, Click the "Arc" tool.

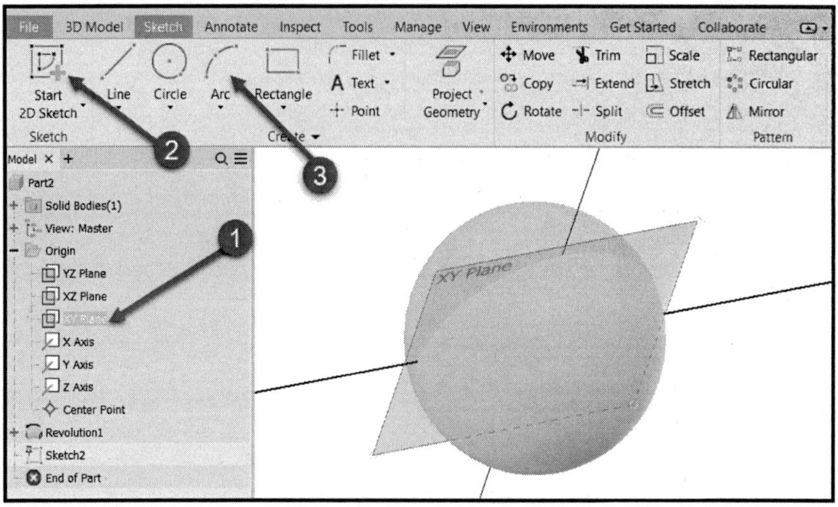

Step 3: Create arc as shown.

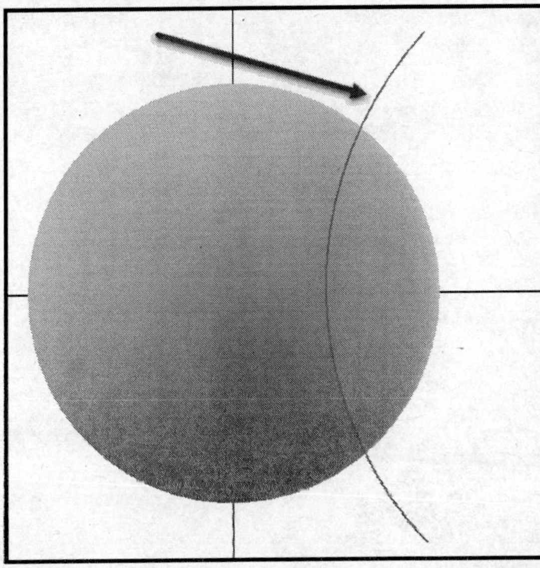

Step 4: Select arc and extrude it with the Extrude tool as given below.

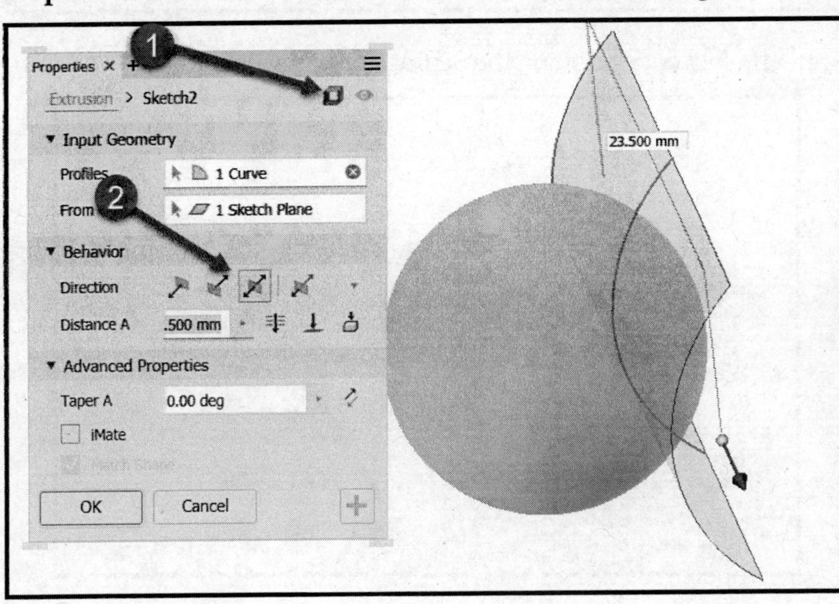

Step 5: Click the "Sculpt" tool and select Surface arc.

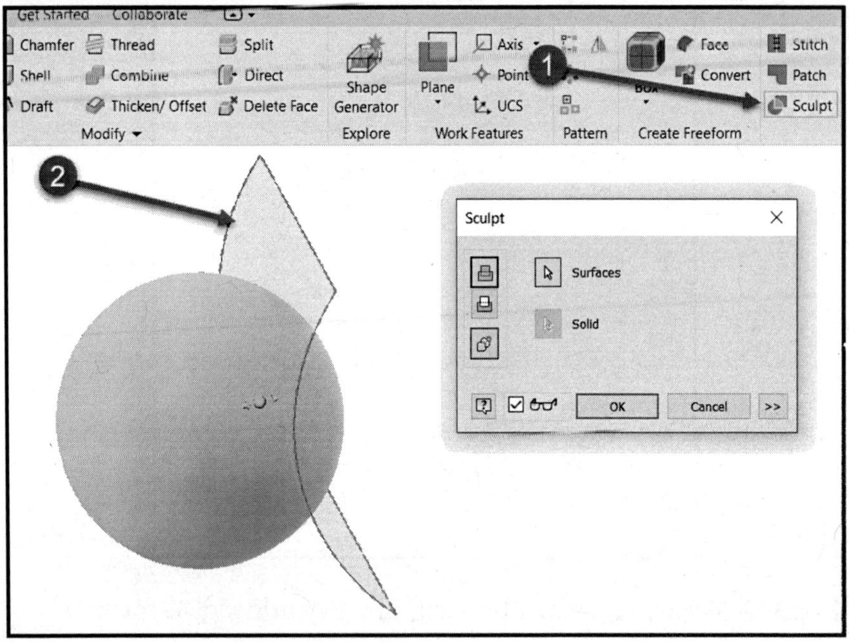

Step 6: Select cut option on the Sculpt window and click "ok" button.

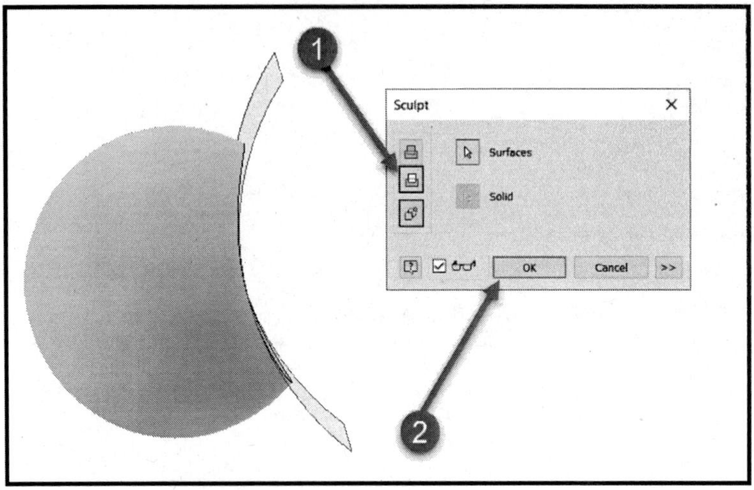

Replace face

It is used to replace the face. For this, we project the face on another face or surface.

Step 1: First of all, make a solid box and a surface as shown.

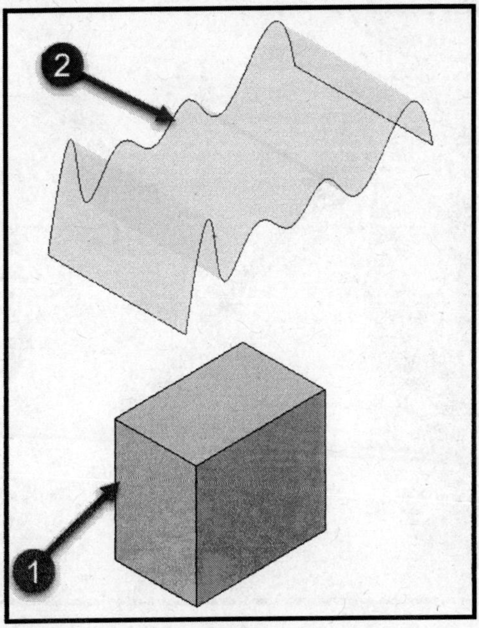

Step 2: Click the "Remove face" tool. Select the face of solid box.

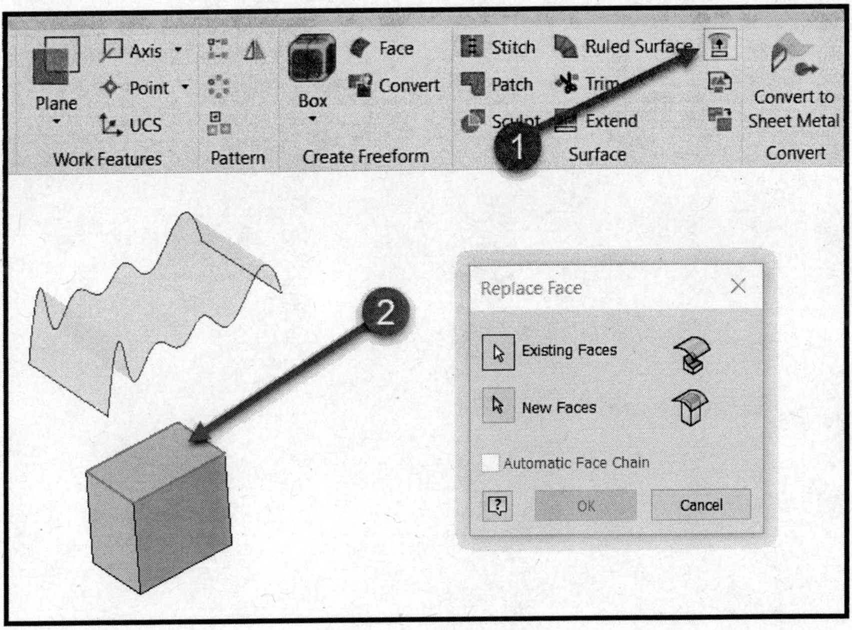

Step 3: Select surface that as created. Then click "ok" button.

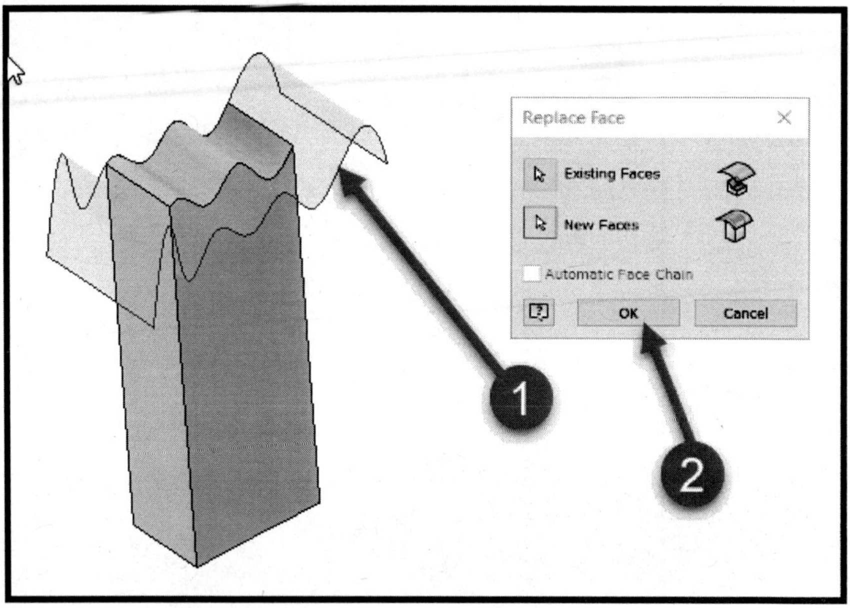

CHAPTER 8
Sheet Metal

How to open Sheet Metal option?

Step 1: If you want to open the sheet metal option. First, click the "Convert to Sheet Metal" icon on the ribbon bar.

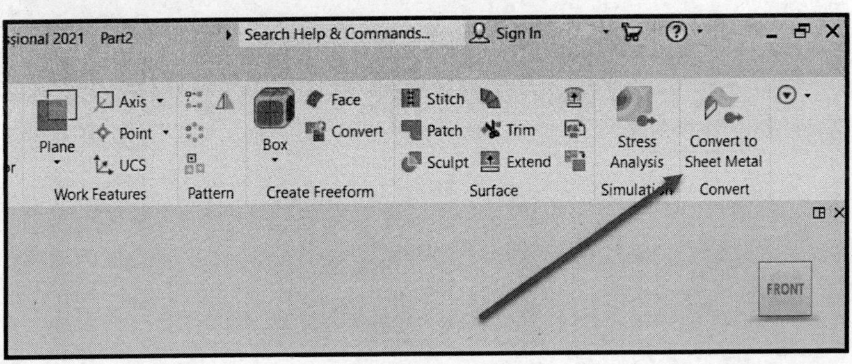

Step 2: Create a rectangle on the plane.

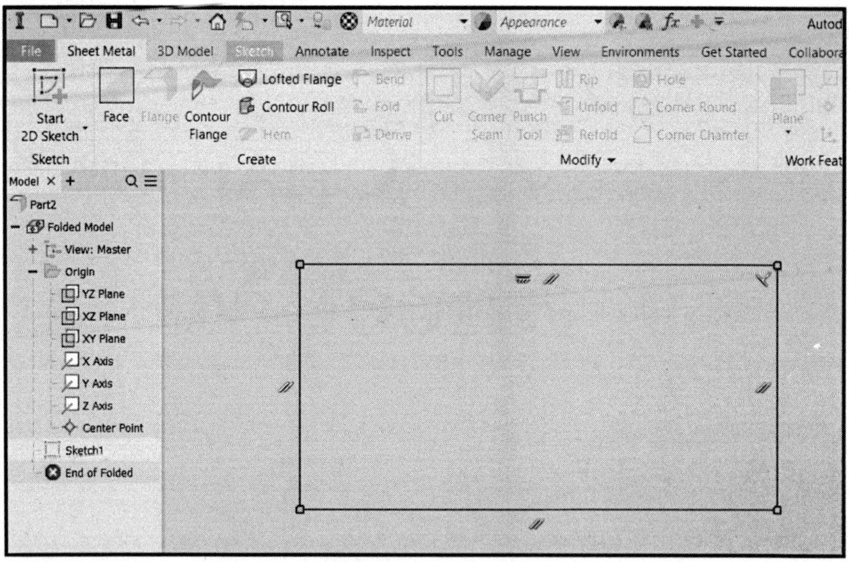

Step 3: Select rectangle that as created and click the "Face" tool.

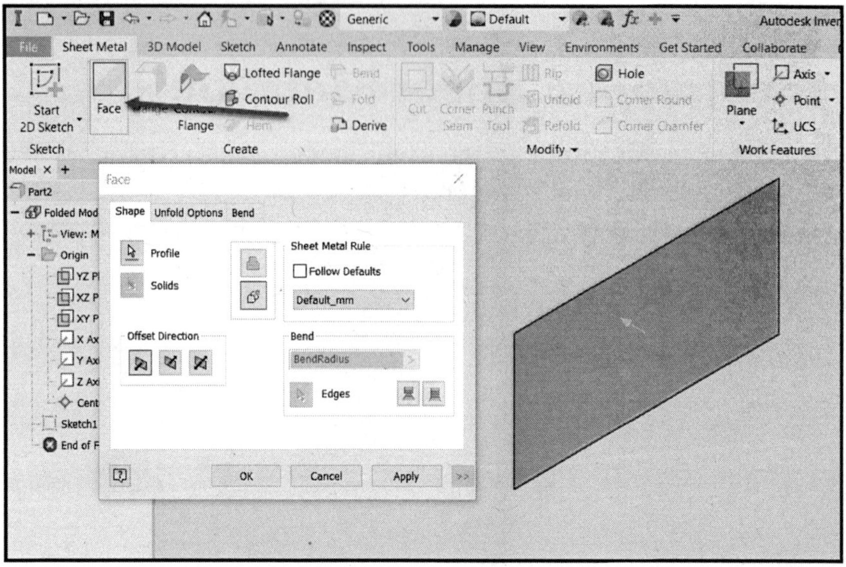

Step 4: Click bend tab on the face window and select "tear" option from the relief shape. After that, click "apply" and "ok" button.

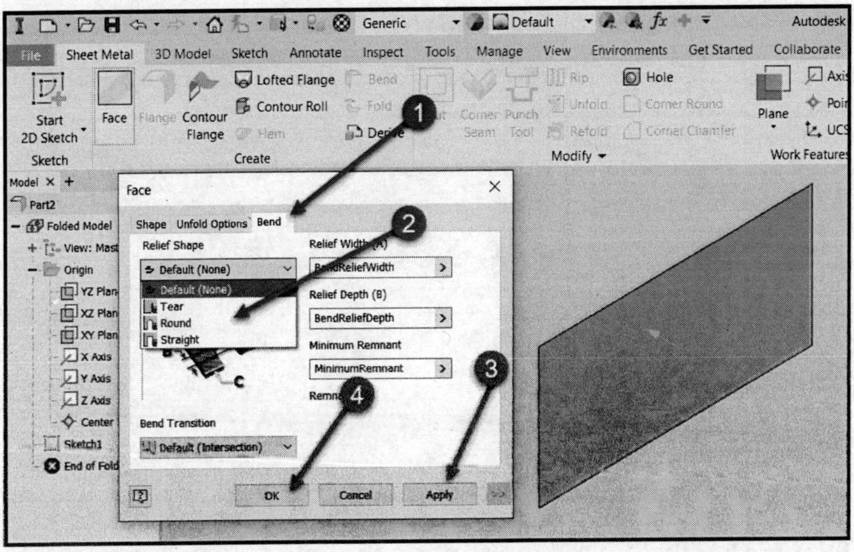

How to change sheet thickness and material?

It is used to change the thickness of the sheet.

Step 1: First, click "sheet metal defaults" tool.

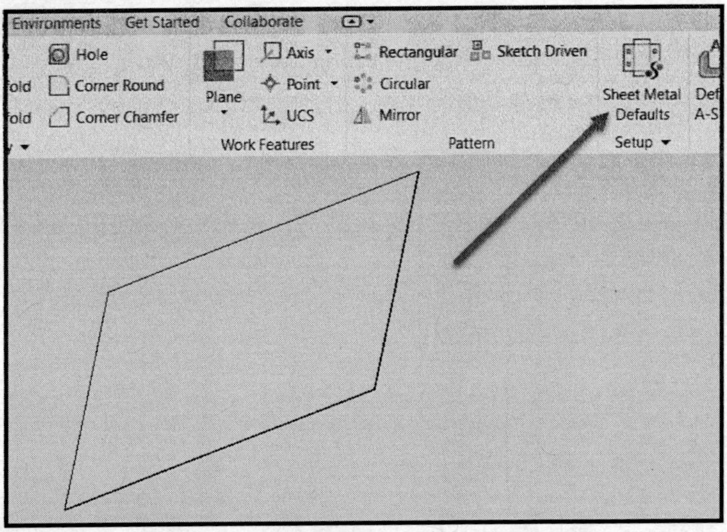

Step 2: First of all, Uncheck the box "Use Thickness from Rule". Then change thickness and material.

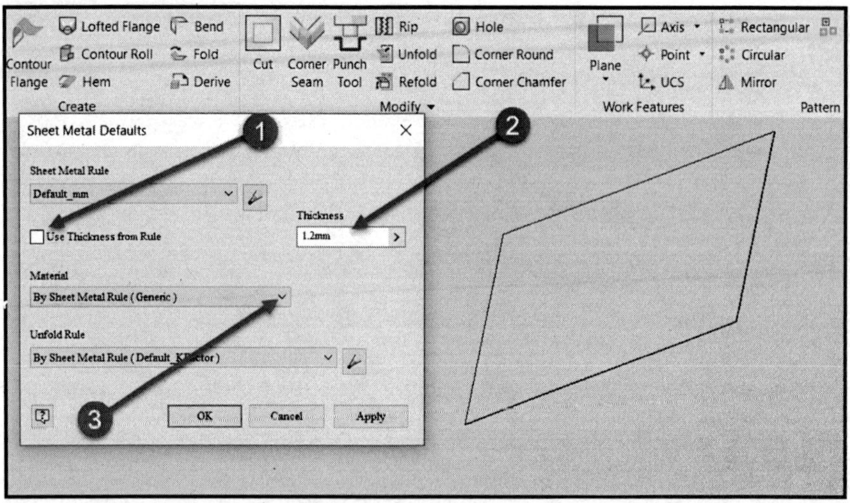

Step 3: After that, click "apply" and "ok" button.

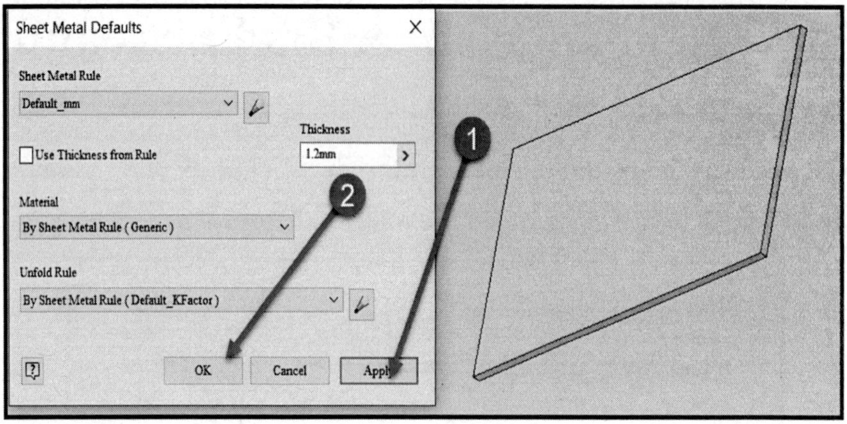

Note: If you want to change the unit of thickness. So, they can also do it, as shown.

Step 1: First, click "sheet metal defaults" tool.

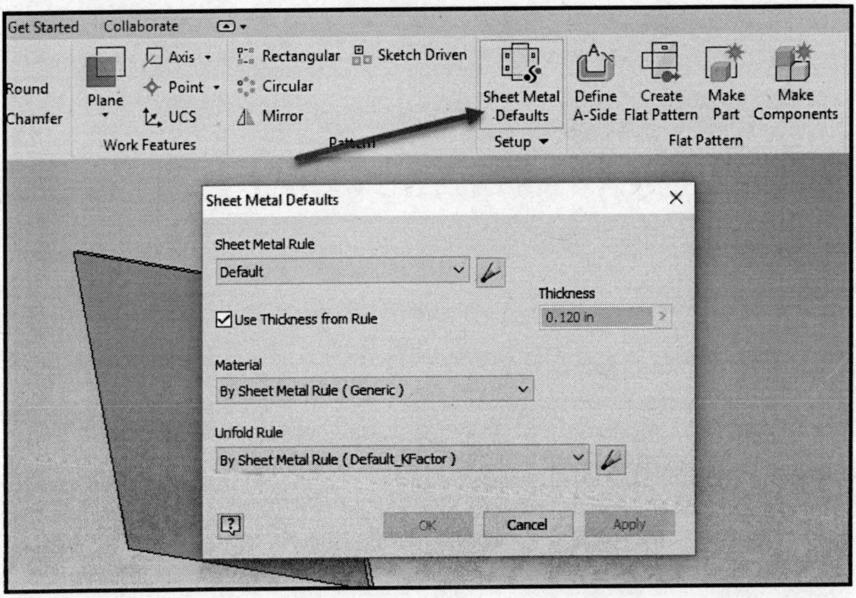

Step 2: First of all, Uncheck the box "Use Thickness from Rule". Then change "Sheet metal rule" and change the thickness.

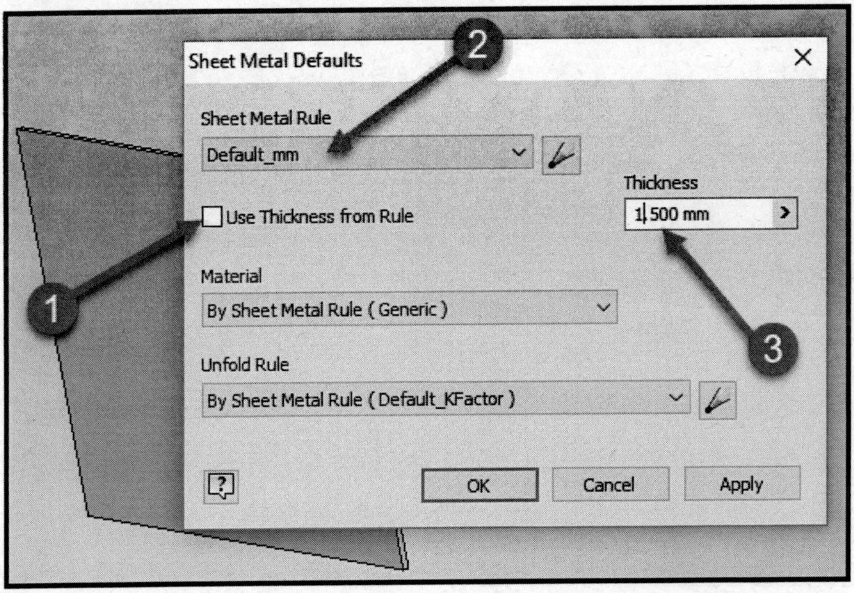

Step 3: Change the material then click "apply" and "ok" button.

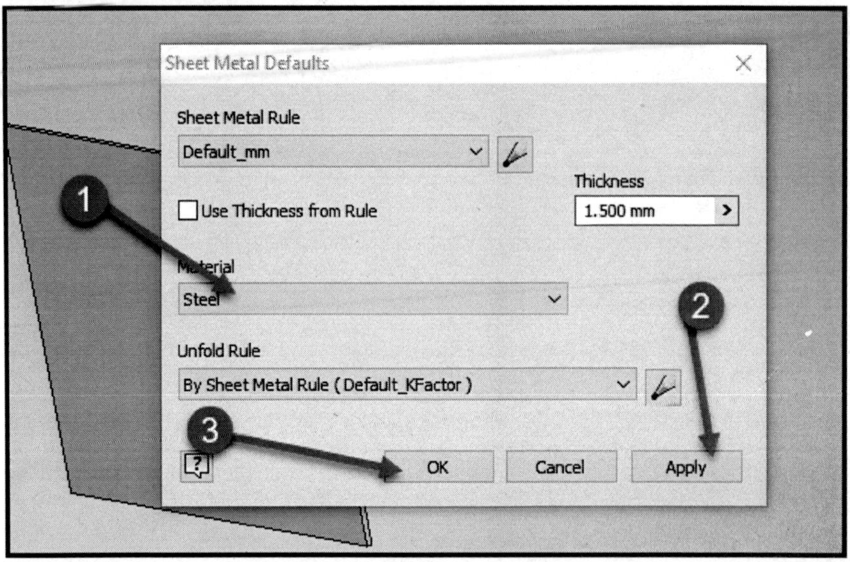

Flange

It is used to make the band wall of the sheet.

Step 1: First, Create a rectangle in the sketch.

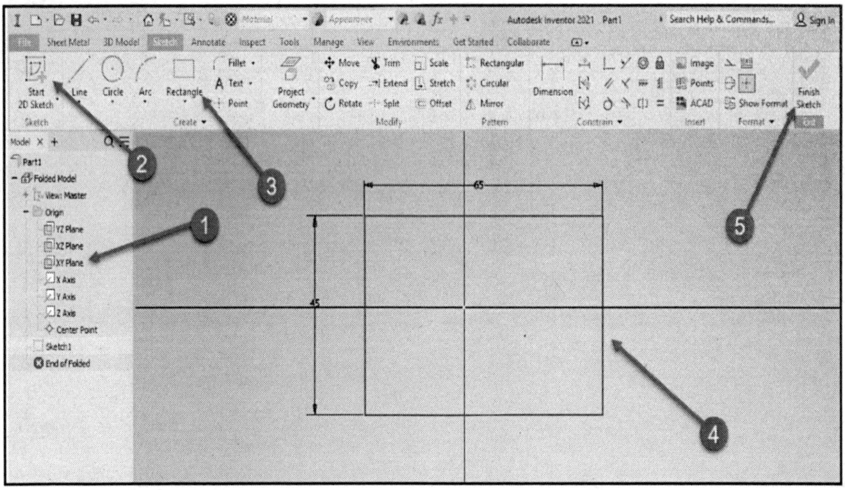

Step 2: Convert the rectangle into a sheet with the "Face" tool.

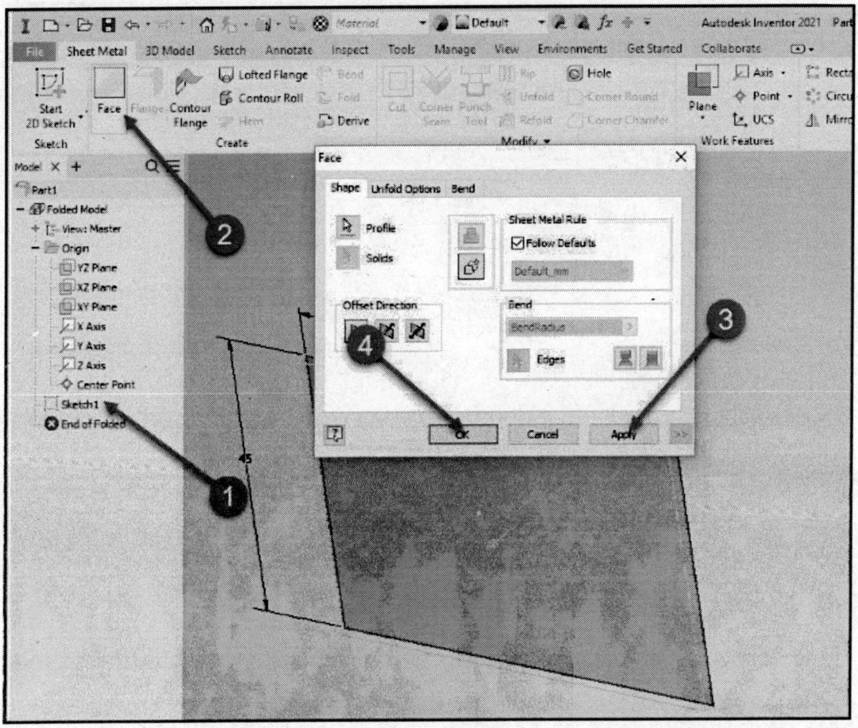

Step 3: Select the edge of the sheet and click "Flange Tool".

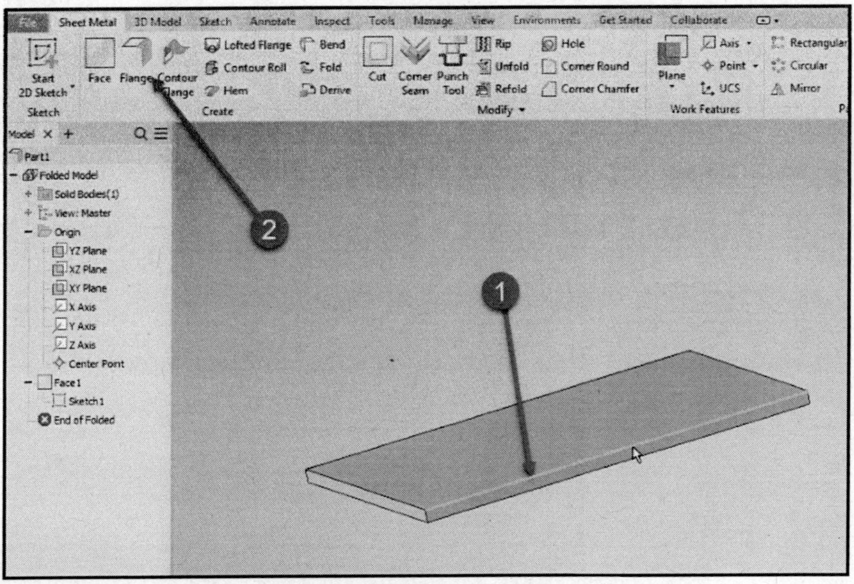

Step 4: Specify band type, band position and angle.

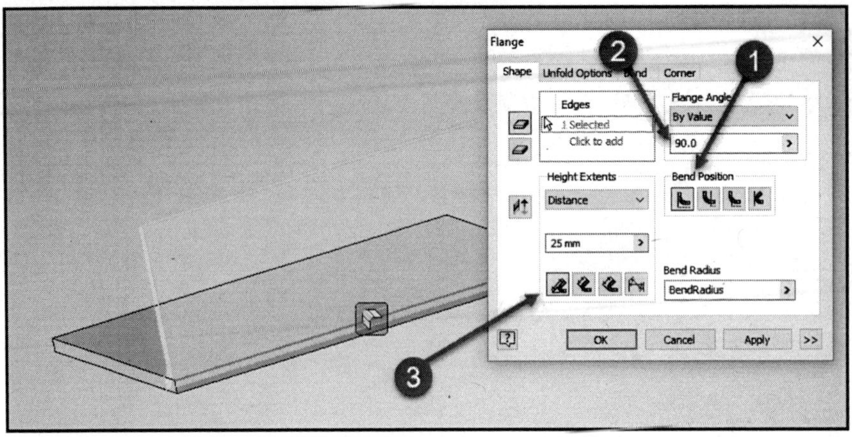

Step 5: Specify distance. Then click "apply" and "ok" button.

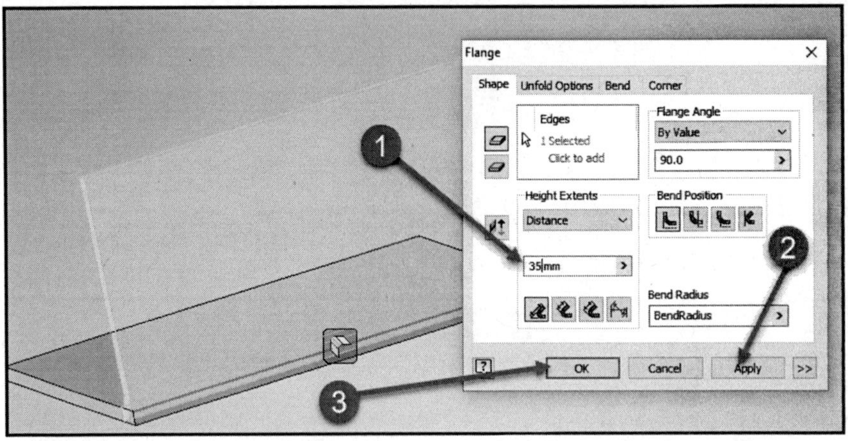

Contour Flange

It is used to make various types of the flange. Such as L-shape, C-shape, and zig-zag shape. In this, we make sketches for flanges. Then after that convert to "flange" with the "contour flange" tool.

Step 1: Make a sketch on the plane. As shown.

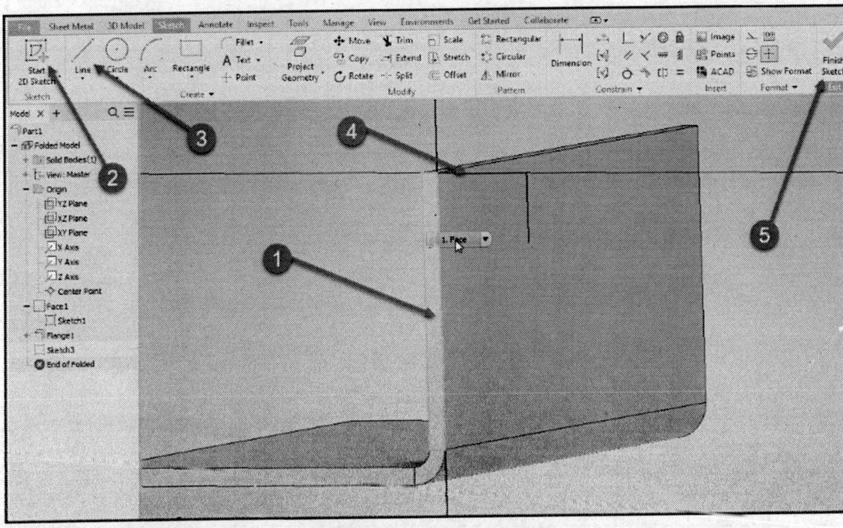

Step 2: Select sketch then click "Contour Flange" tool.

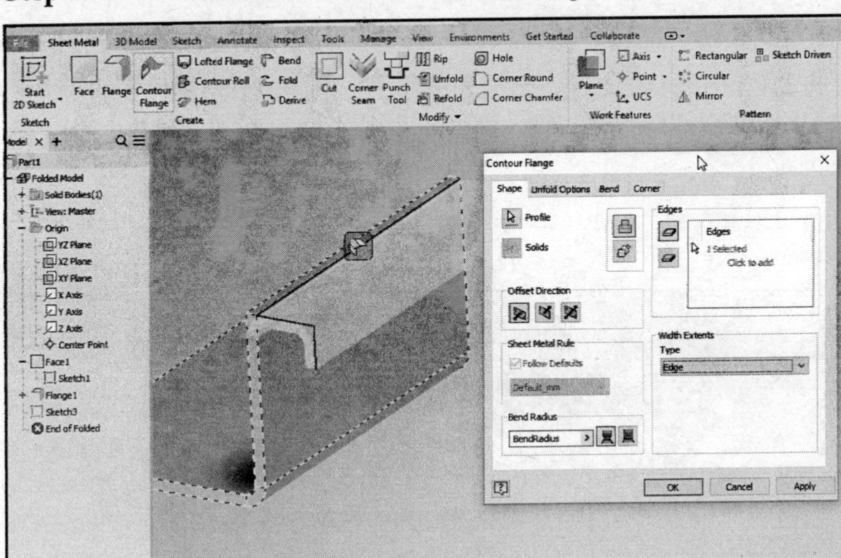

Step 3: Chose "Width Extents" type and specify Width. Then Click "Apply" and "Ok" button.

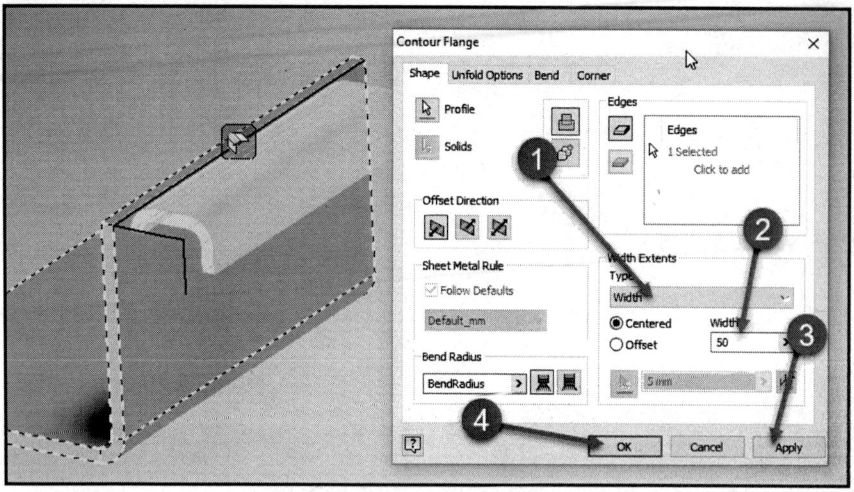

Lofted Flange

It is used to create a complex profile. There should be two sketches for the "lofted flange". For example, there is a rectangle and there is a circle.

Step 1: First, draw a rectangle on the XY plane and then finish the sketch.

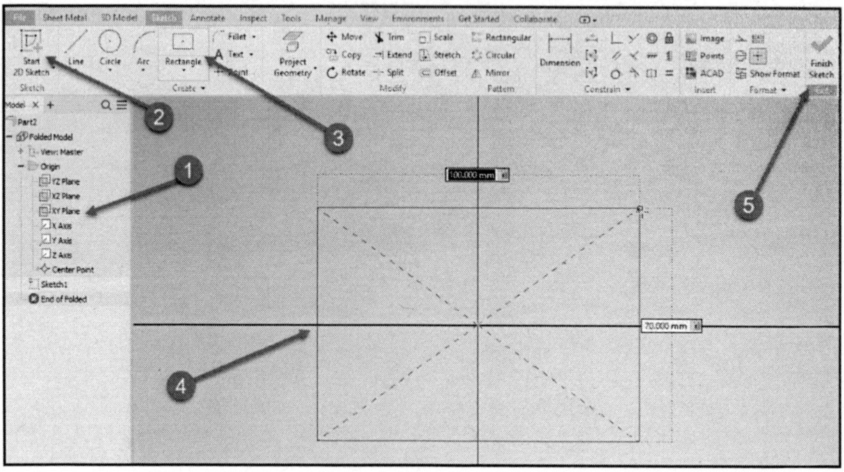

Step 2: Select the XY plane again and click on the "Offset from plane" option of the plane tool.

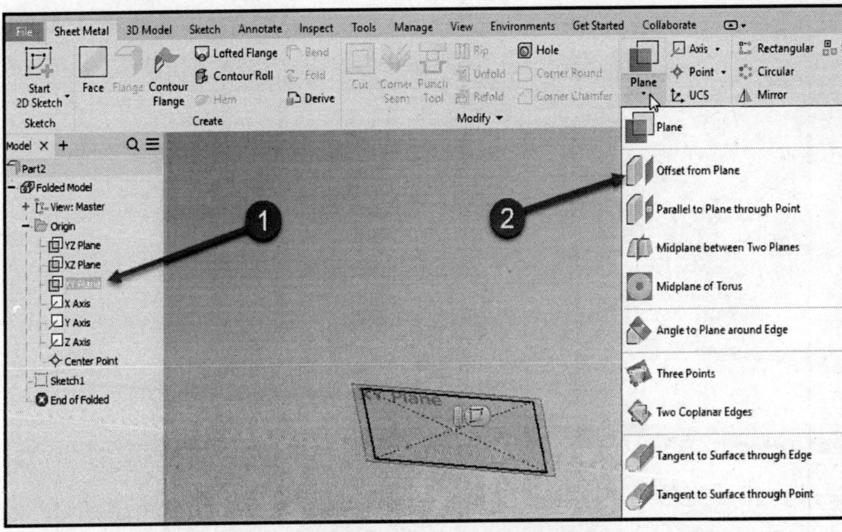

Step 3: Specify the plane offset distance.

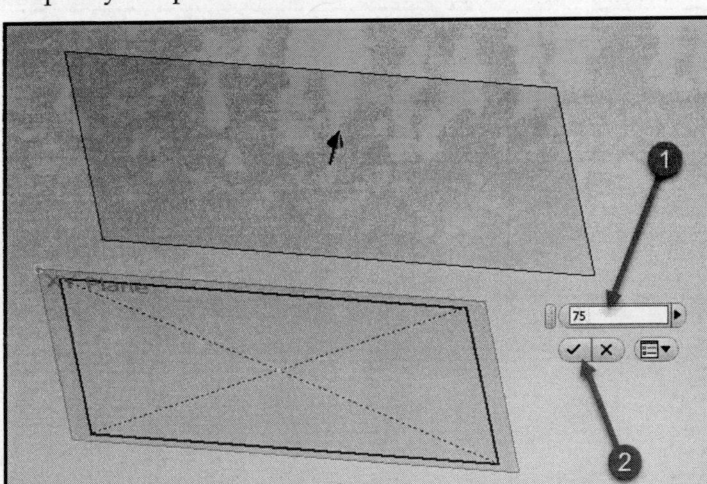

Step 4: The plane that has just been created. Draw a circle on that plane.

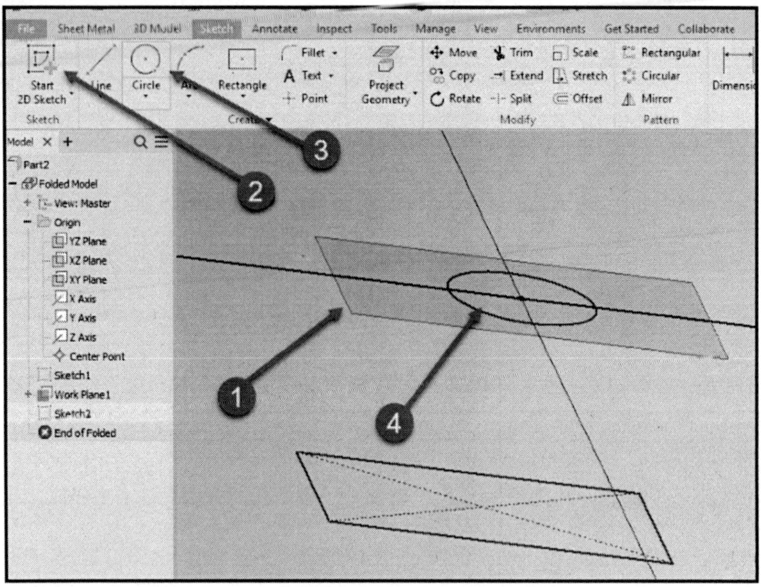

Step 5: Hide the plane that was created.

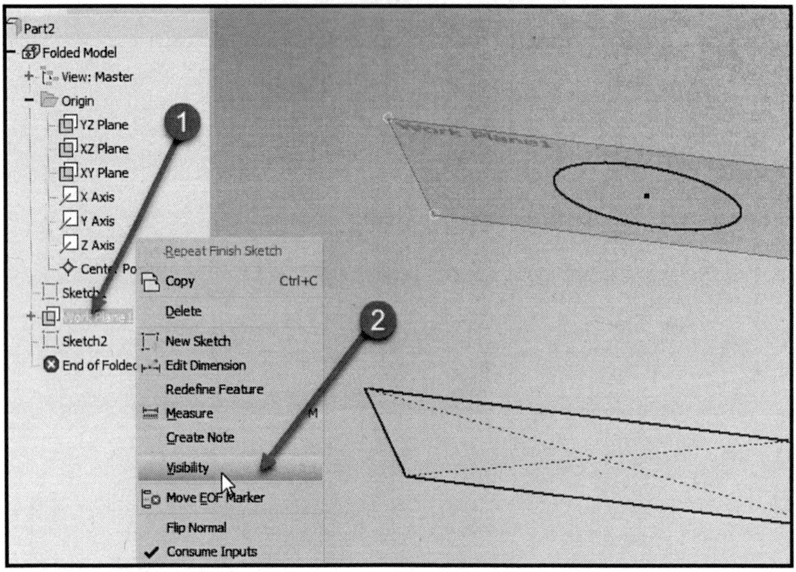

Step 6: Click the "lofted flange" tool. then select rectangle and circle.

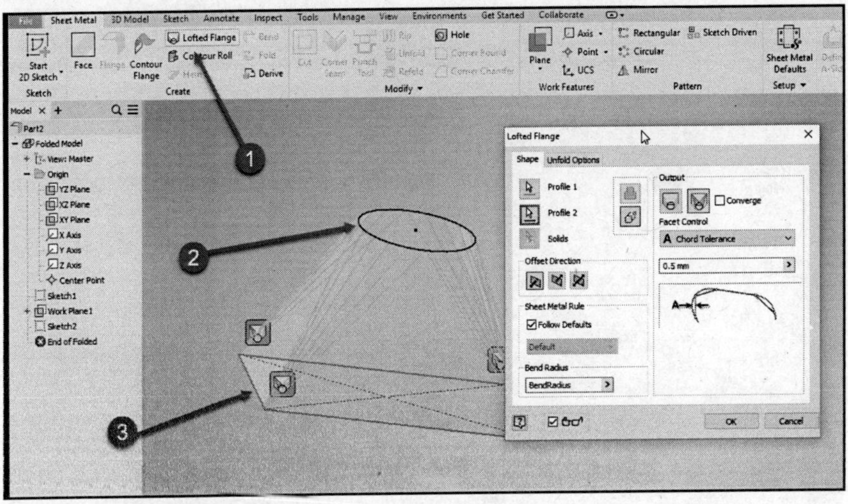

Step 7: Select "Facet distance" option and specify the distance, then click "ok" button.

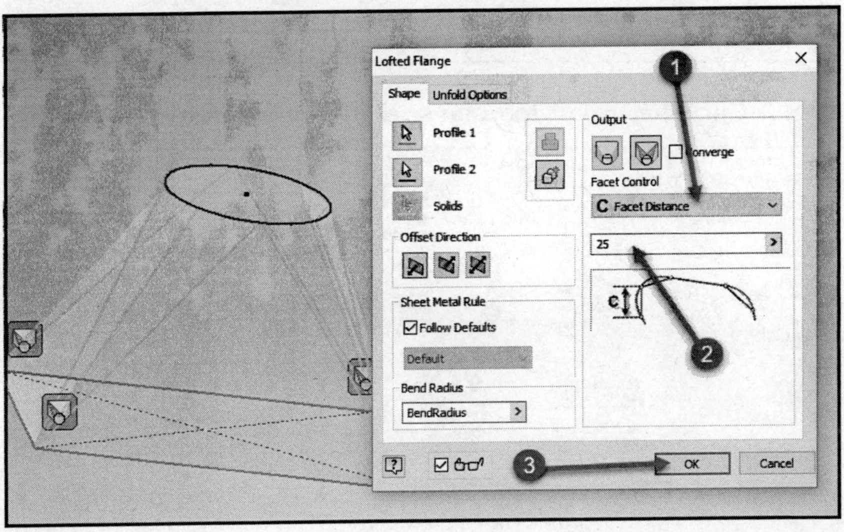

Hem

It is used to smooth out the sharpness of the sheet edge or to shape the edge into a U-shape flange.

Step 1: First, Select edge of the flange.

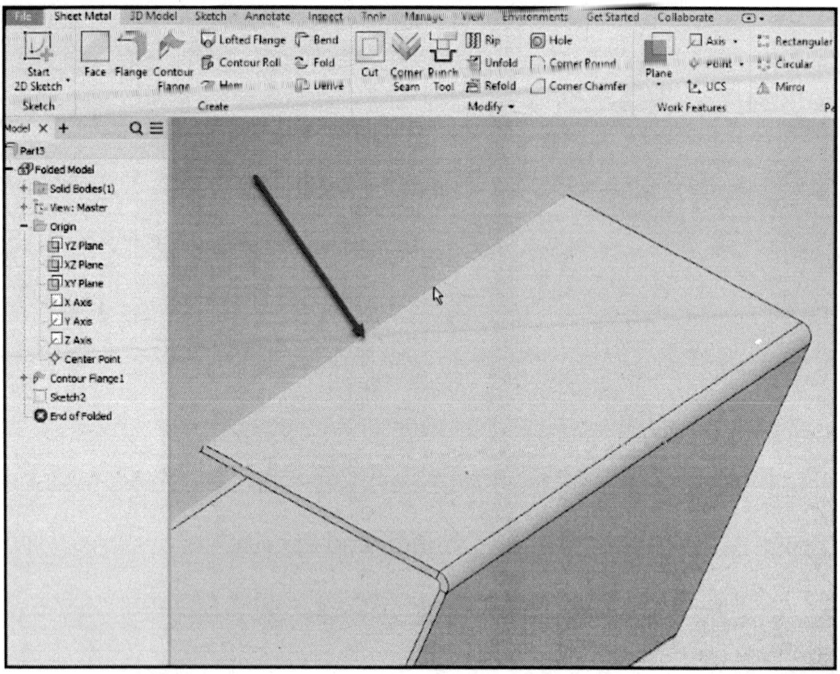

Step 2: Click the "Hem" tool and select the hem type on the hem tab.

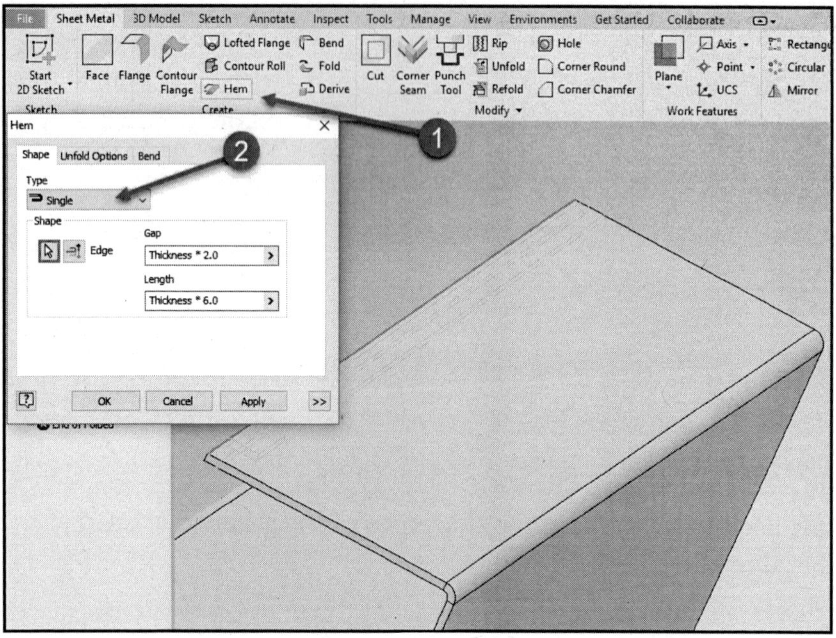

Step 3: Specify Gap and Length. Then click "apply" and "ok" button.

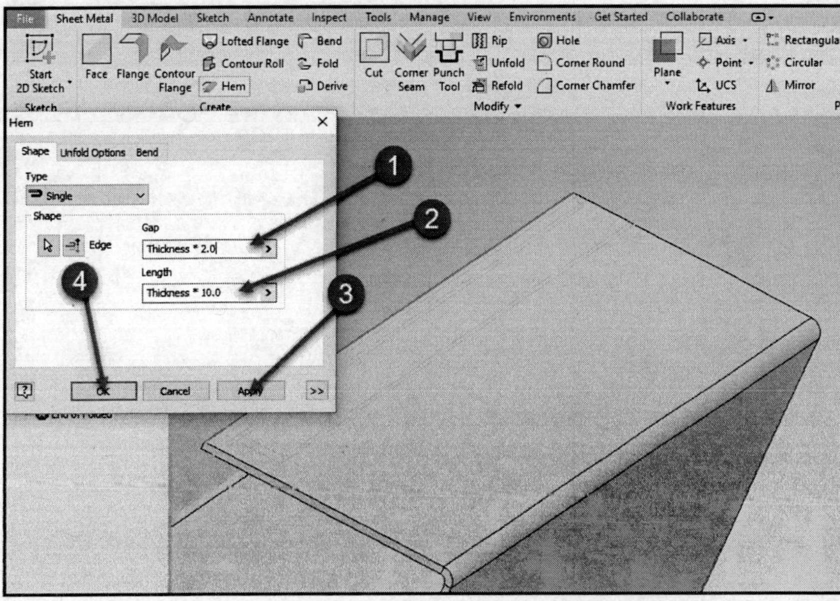

Bend

It is used to join two sheets with a bend. It is like a sloping bend.

Step 1: First, Make a sheet on the XY plane.

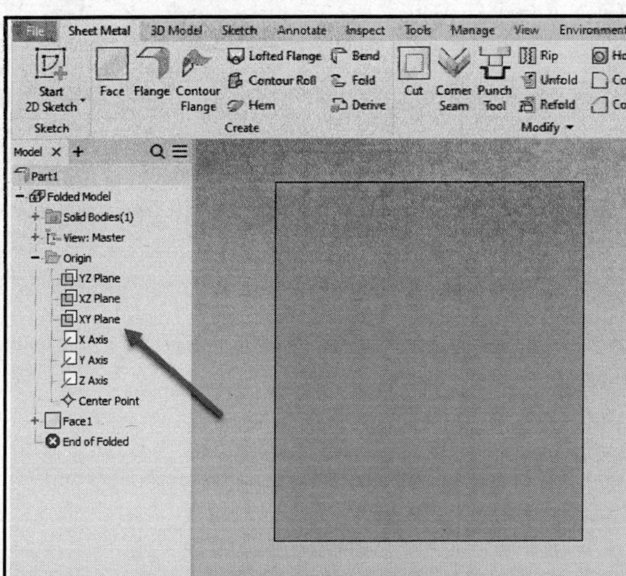

Step 2: Select XY plane after that click "offset from plane" tool.

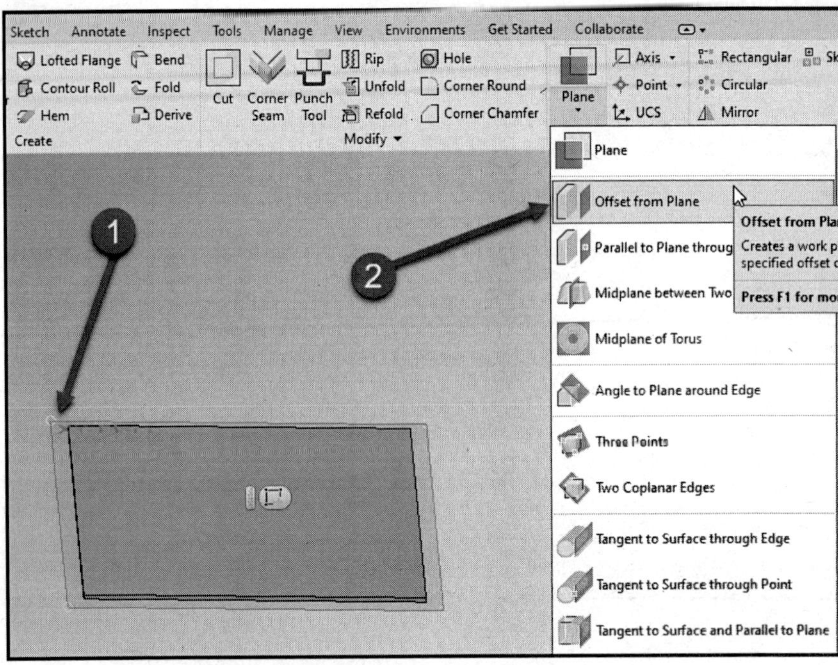

Step 3: Specify plane distance.

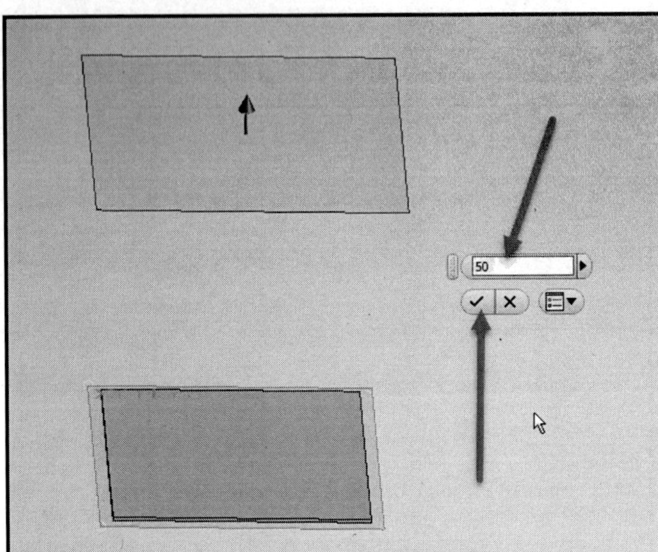

Step 4: The plane that has just been created. Draw a Rectangle on that plane.

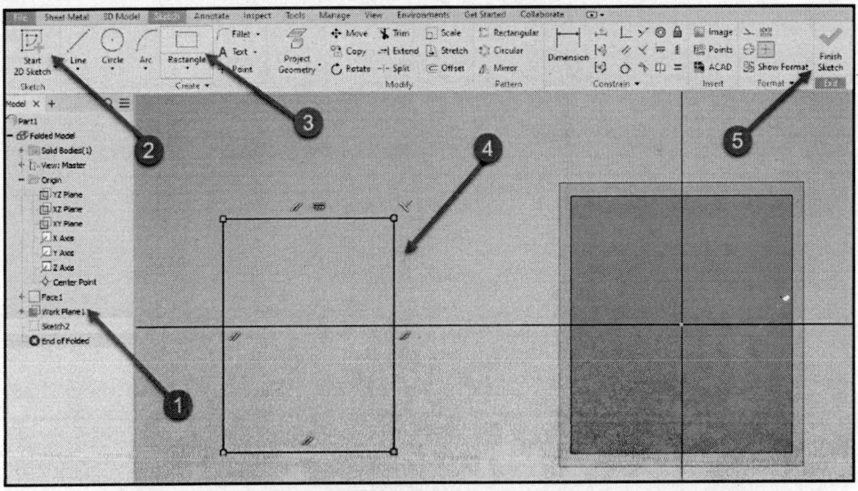

Step 5: Select the rectangle and convert it into a sheet by the "face" tool.

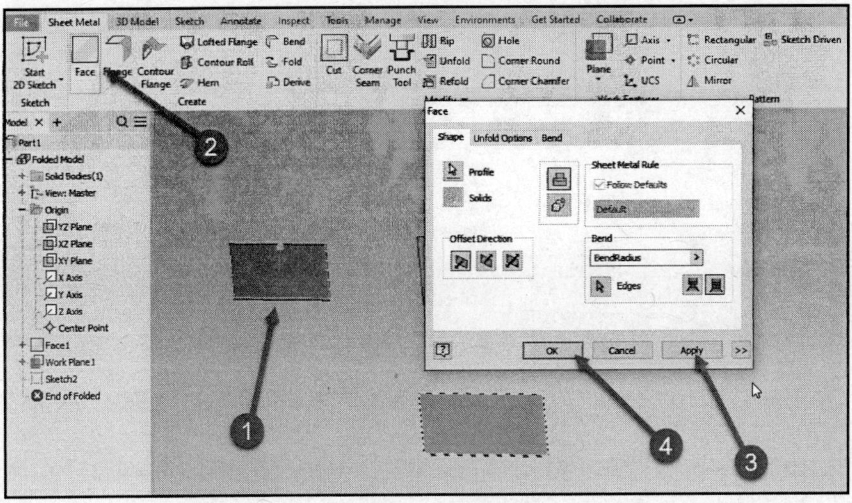

Step 6: Click the "Bend" tool. then Select Both edges one by one, As shown.

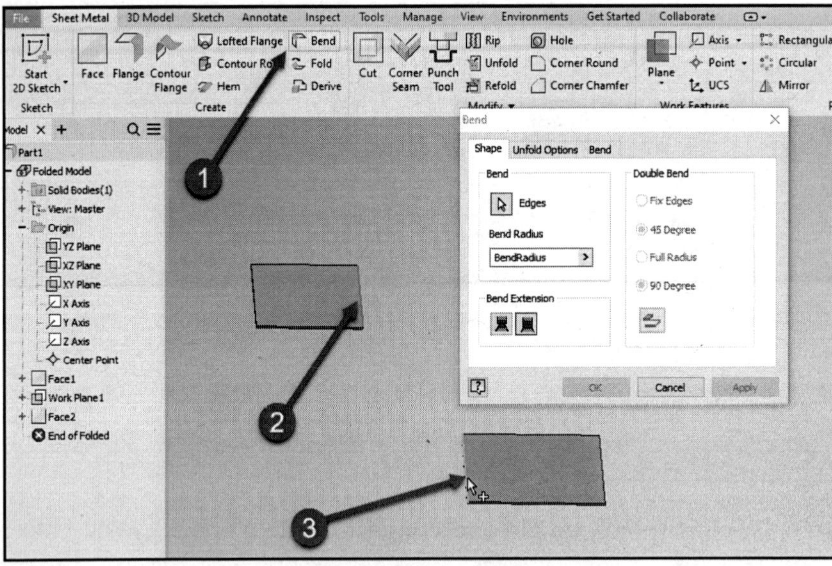

Step 7: Select type of "Double bend". Then click "apply" and "ok" button.

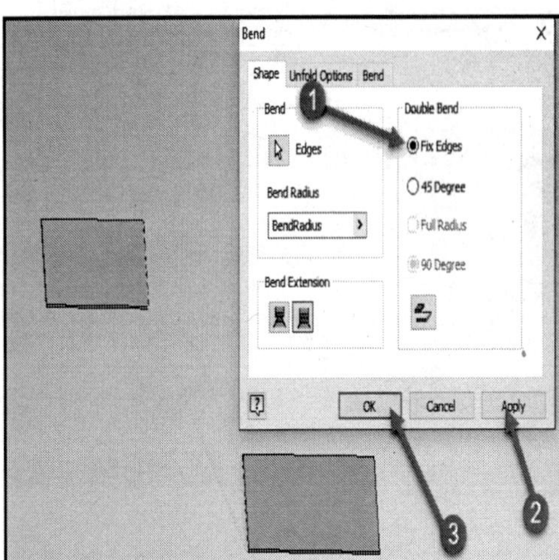

Fold

It is used to bend flat sheets.

Step 1: First, Make a sheet on XY plane.

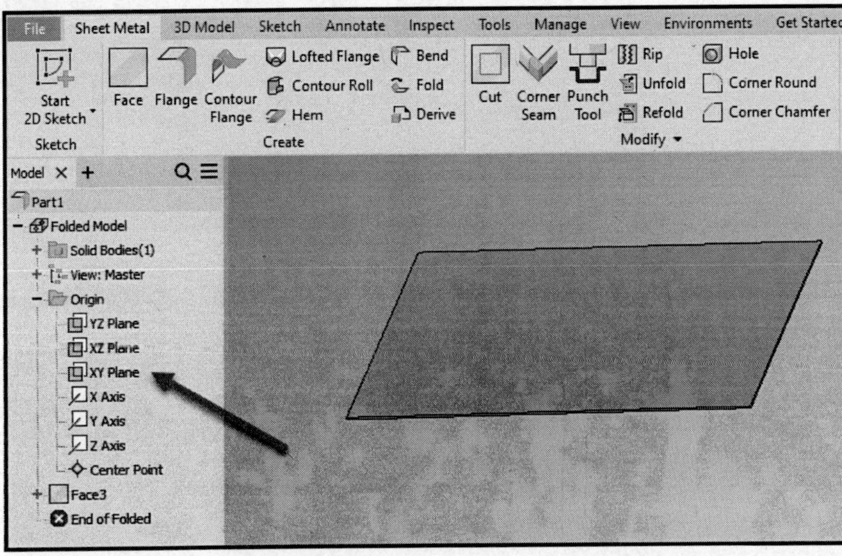

Step 2: After that, select face of the sheet and create a line.

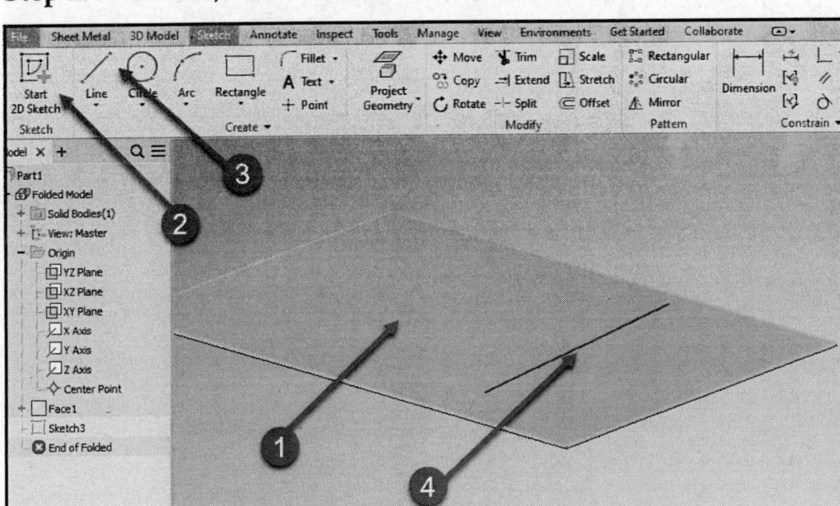

Step 3: First, select the line's point. Second, Select Sheet's edge. Then click Constrain tool.

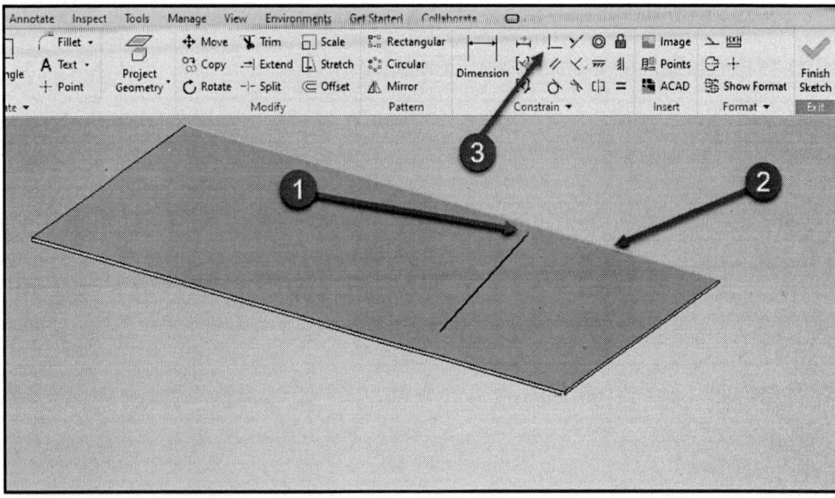

Step 4: Again, the same steps as you used above.

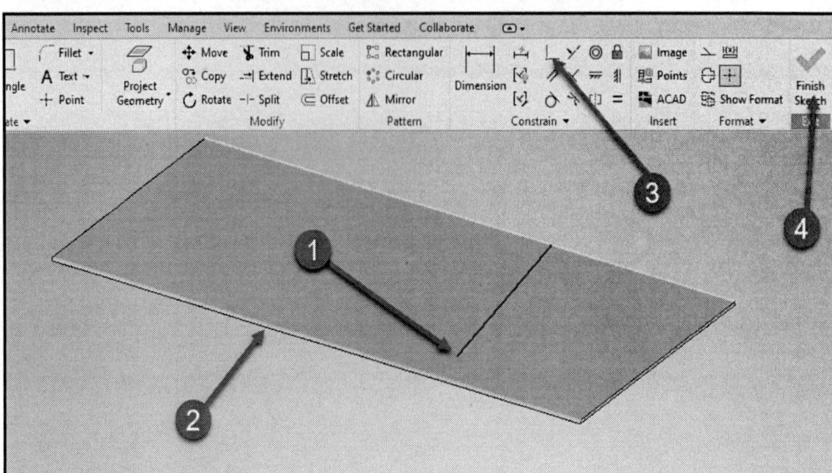

Step 5: Click the "Fold" tool and select the line that you created.

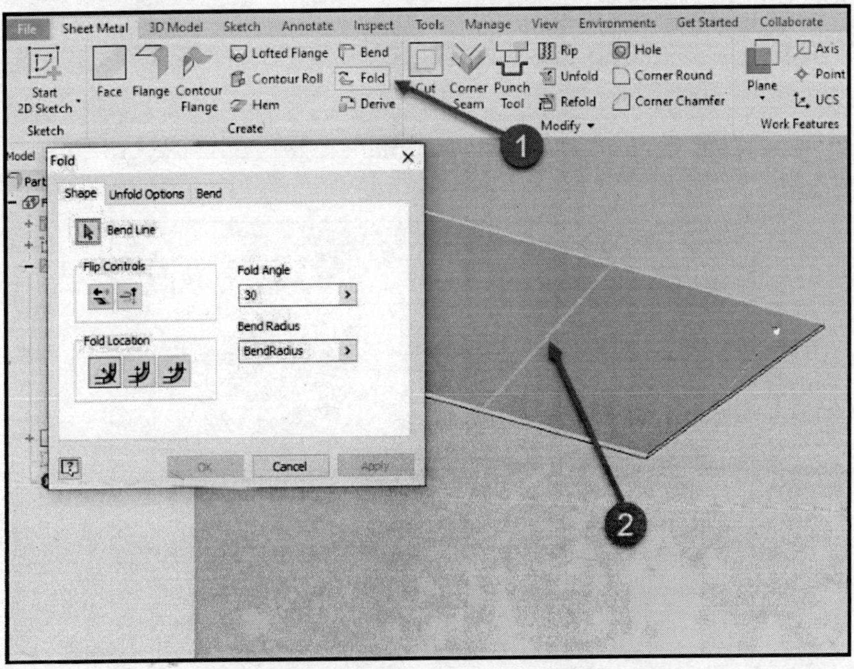

Step 6: Specify "fold angle" and select "Fold location" type. Then Click "Apply" and "Ok" button.

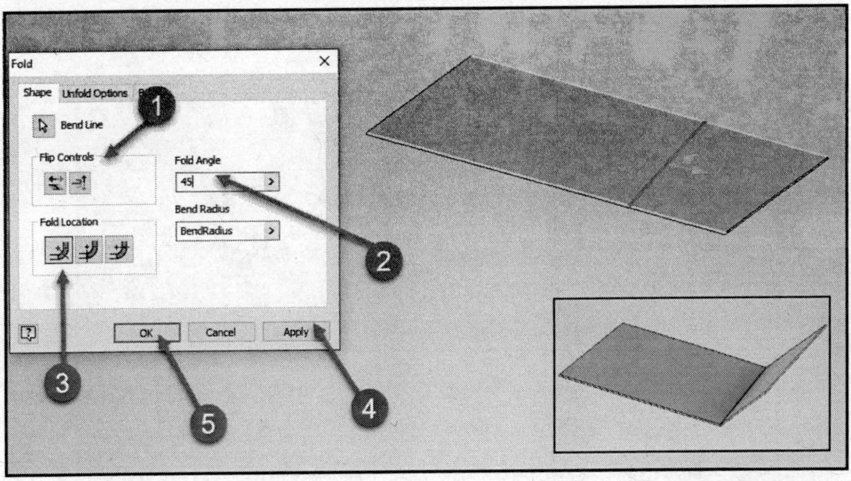

Contour Roll

This tool is similar to the Revolve tool. It is used to make a circular and arc-shaped sheet.

Step 1: First, make a sketch on XY plane with Axis line, As shown below.

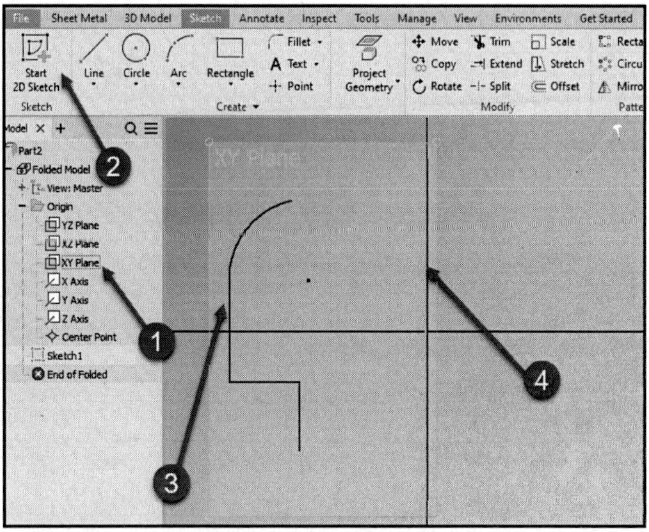

Step 2: Select Axis line. Then, Right-Click at the same time. And click the "centerline" option.

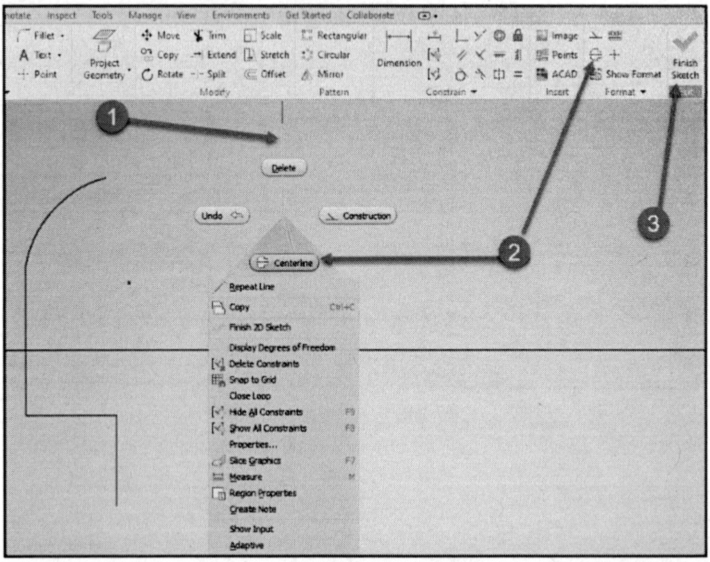

Step 3: Click the "contour roll" tool. then select profile and axis. After that, specify angle, click "apply" and "ok" button.

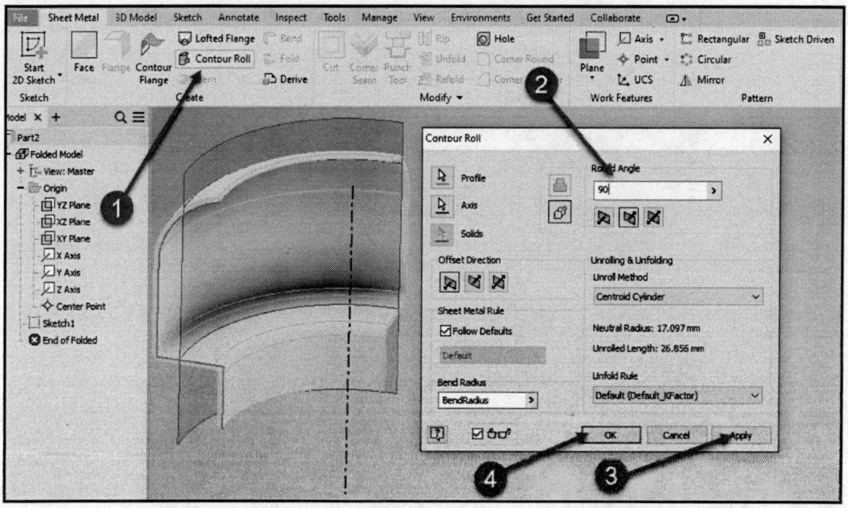

Cut

It is used to cut profile on sheet.

Step 1: First, make a rectangle on XY plane.

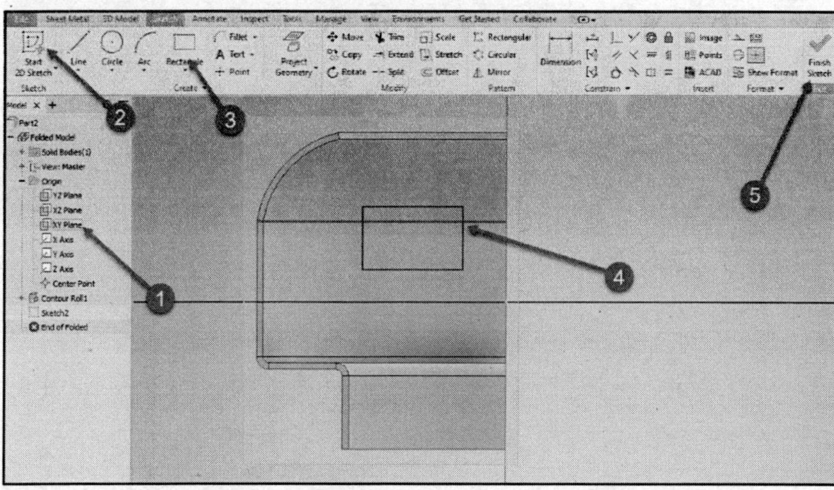

Step 2: Click the "Cut" tool and specify the cut direction.

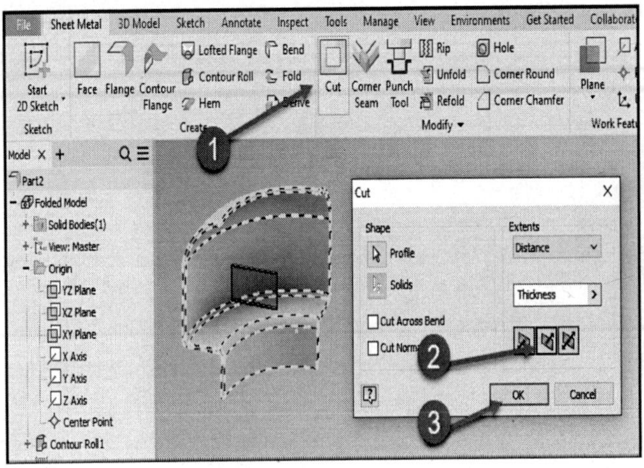

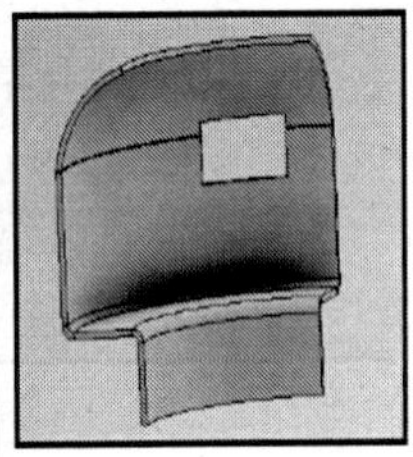

Corner seam

To cover the gap between two separate bends, the corner seam tool is used.

Step 1: First create a sheet.

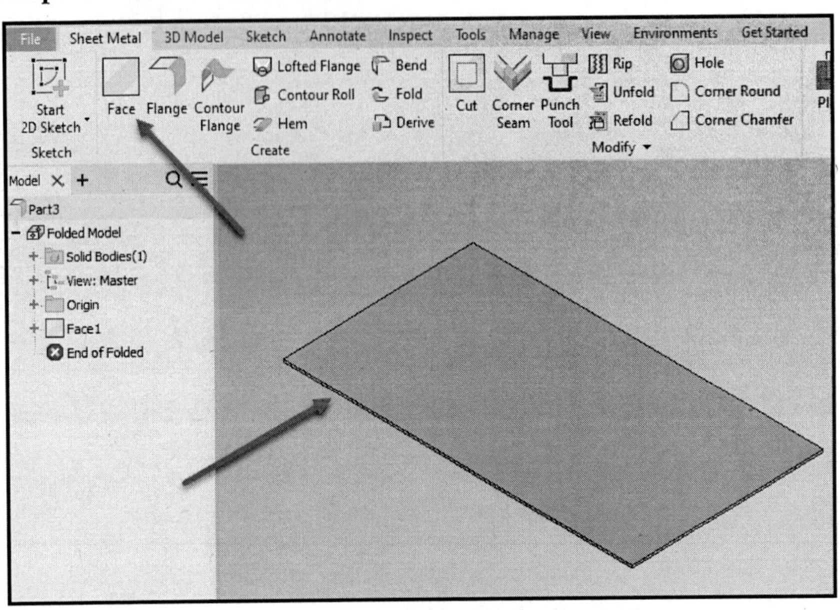

Step 2: Use flange tool and make to bend.

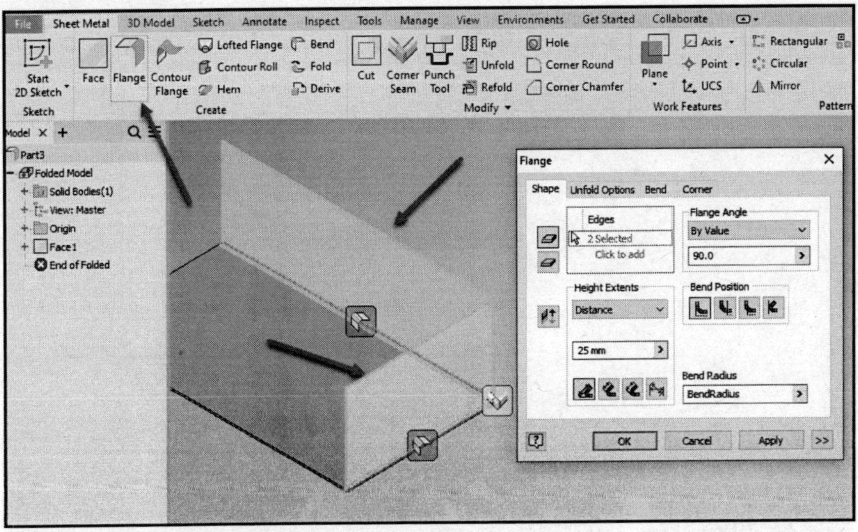

Step 3: Click the "Corner seam" tool. Then, Select "Seam" and "face/ edge distance" option.

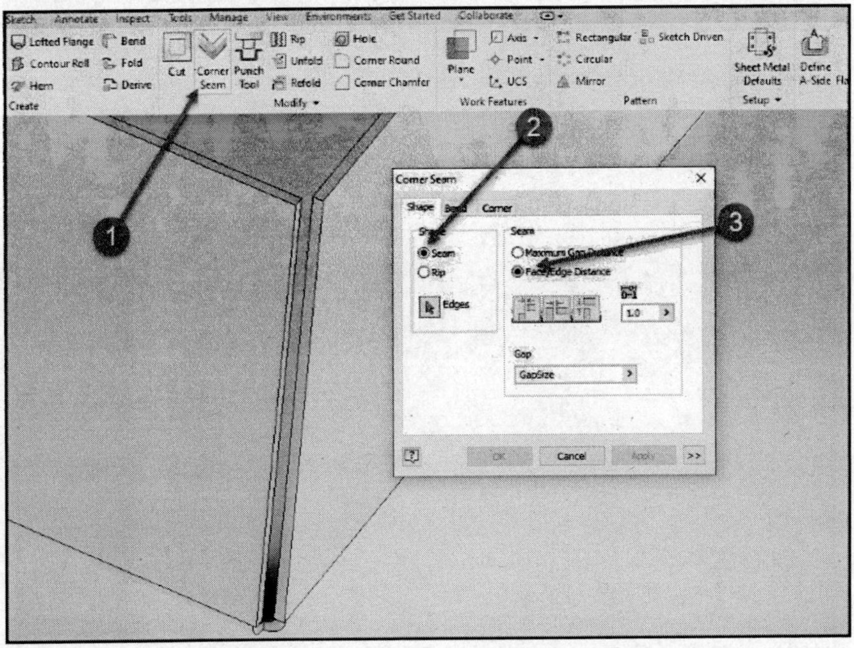

Step 4: Select bend corners. And select gap type and specify distance.

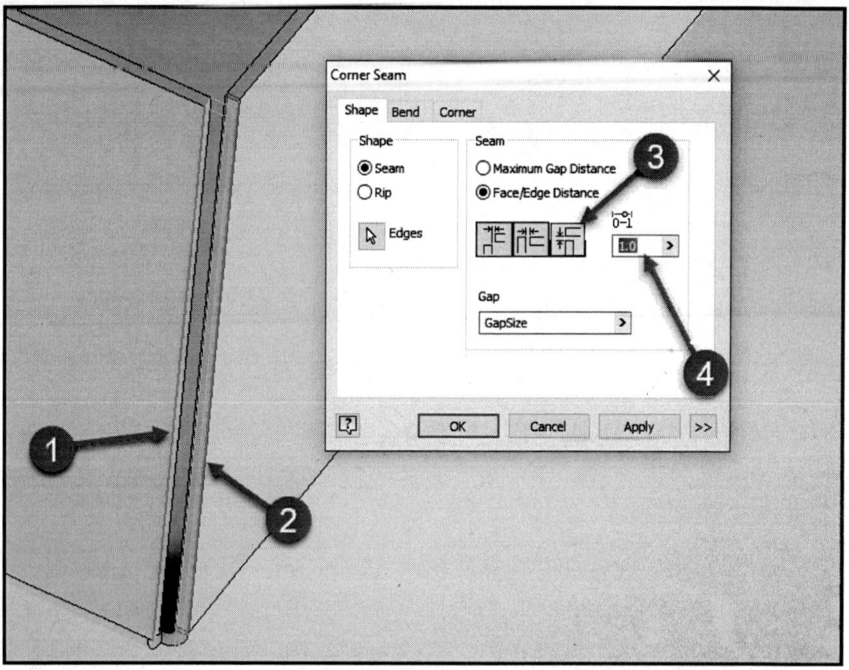

Step 5: Click "apply" and "ok" button.

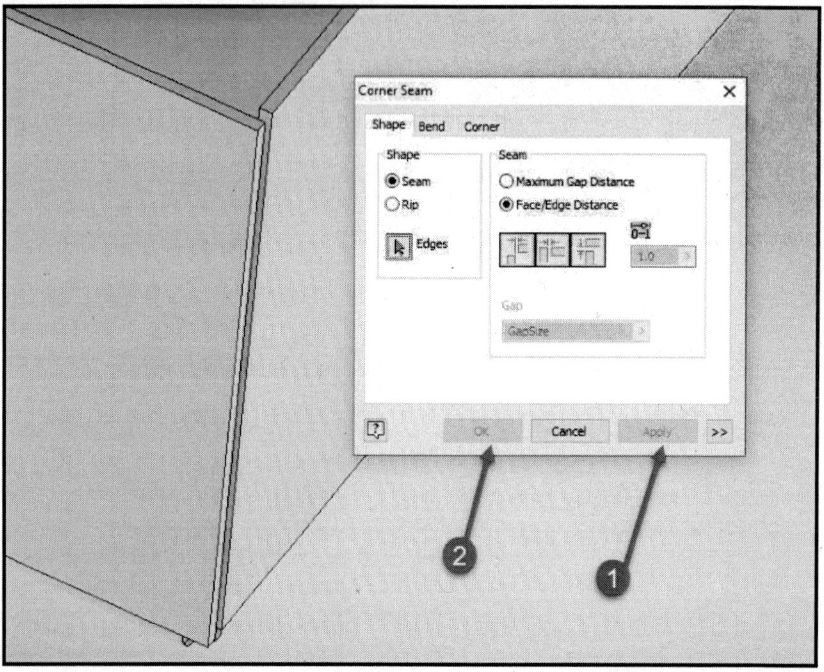

Punch tool

It is used to make a punch in sheet metal.

Step 1: If you already created a sheet. So, select a face on the sheet and make a point.

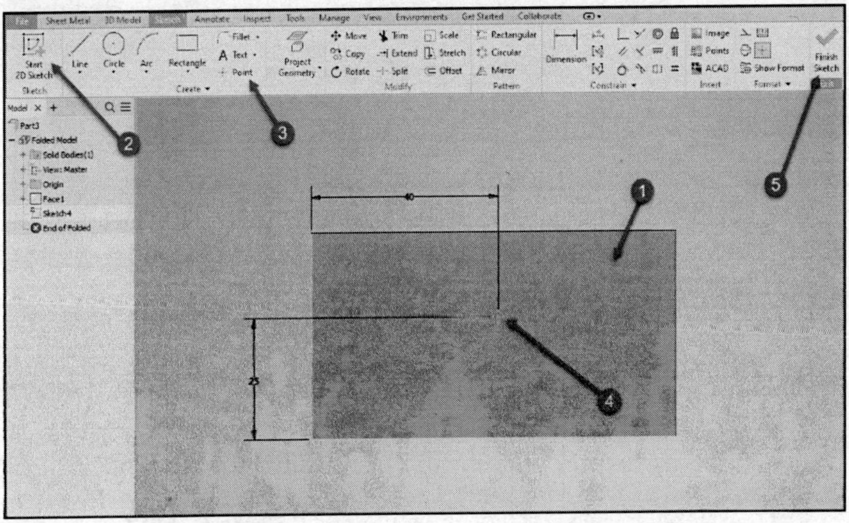

Step 2: Click the "Punch tool". and select punch type to the punch tool directory.

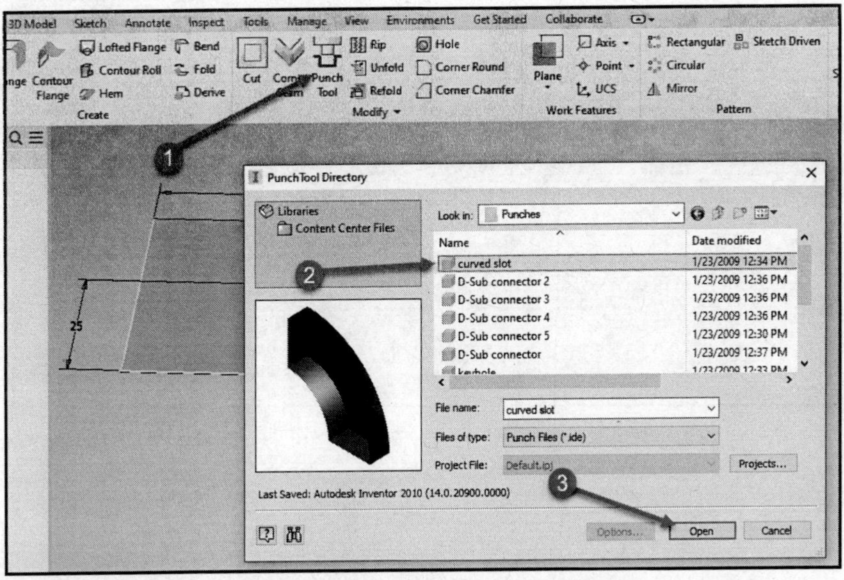

Step 3: Specify the size of the punch. And click "finish" button.

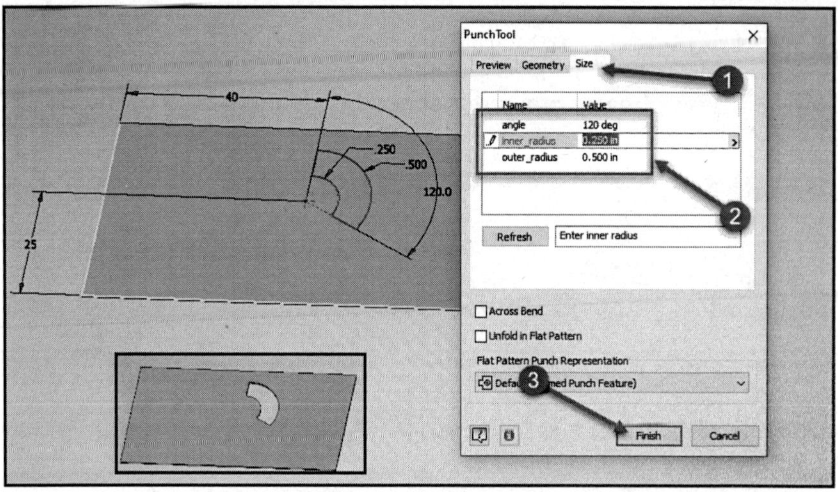

Rip

It is used for linear cut in the sheet. This is called the rip tool.

Step 1: First, Select side face of the sheet. And make a point.

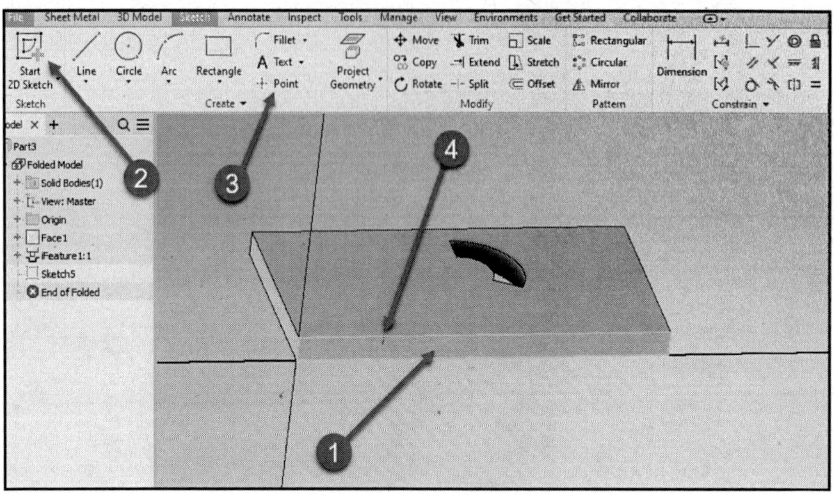

Step 2: Click the "Rip" tool. Then select Rip face and Rip point.

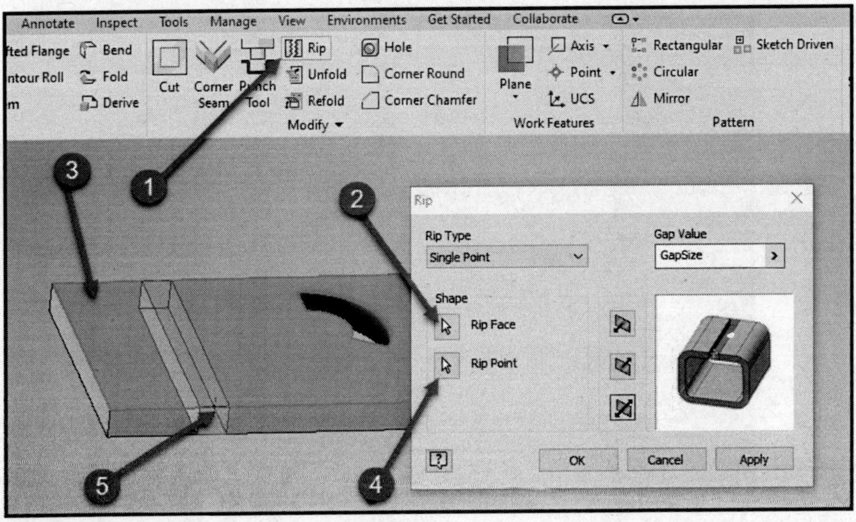

Step 3: Specify the Gap value. Then click "apply" and "ok" button.

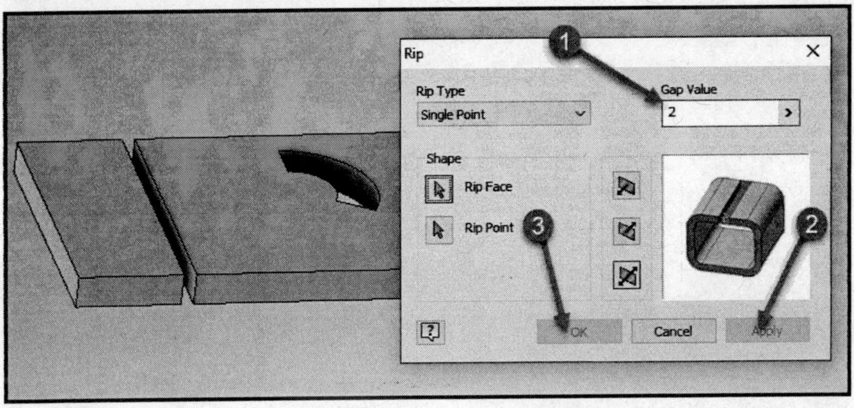

Unfold

It is used to Remove the bend. With this tool, we can flatten the sheet by choosing the bend according to us.

Step 1: First, make a sheet metal with some bend, as shown below.

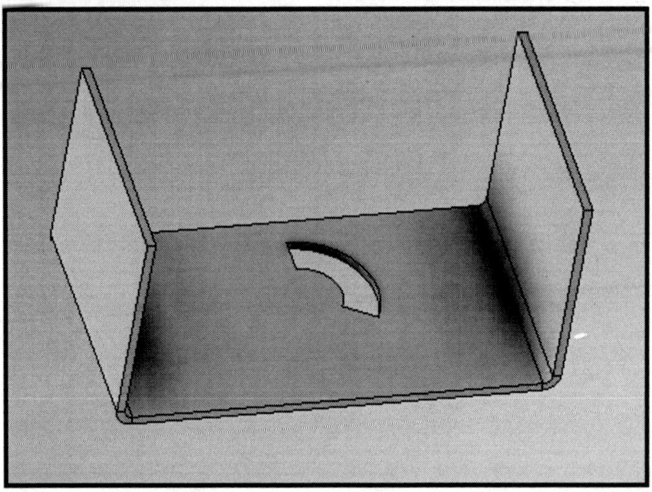

Step 2: Click the "unfold" tool, click the "stationary reference (A)" option, and select the sheet's face.

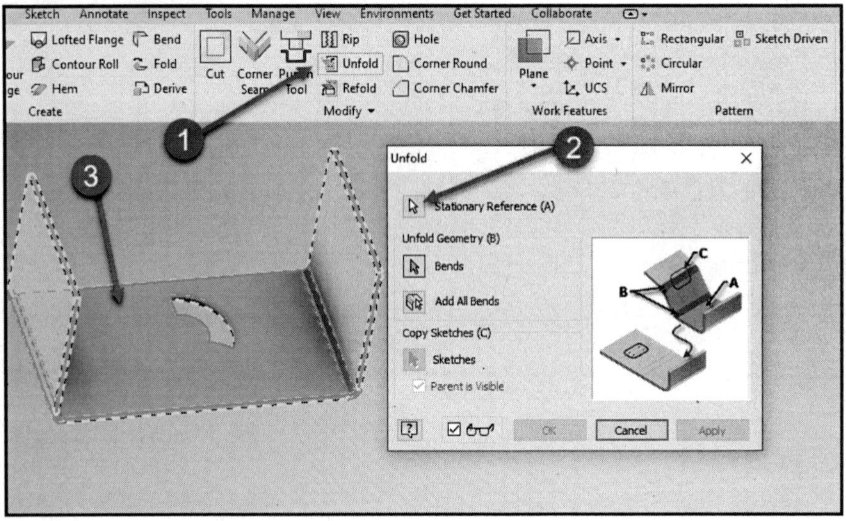

Step 3: Click the "bend" option. Then select the sheet's bend.

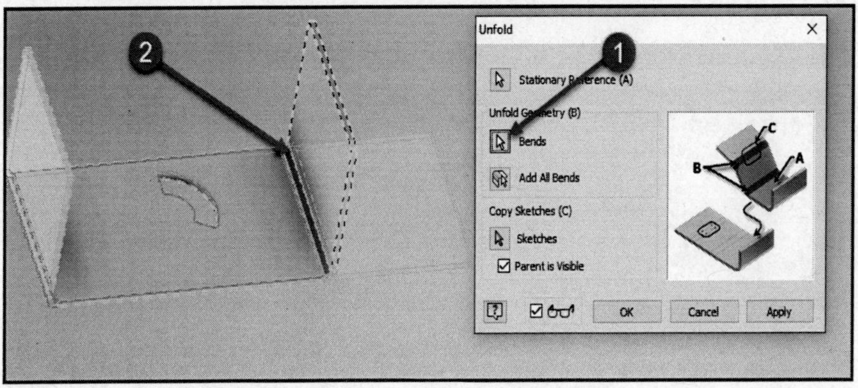

Step 4: After that, click "apply" and "ok" button.

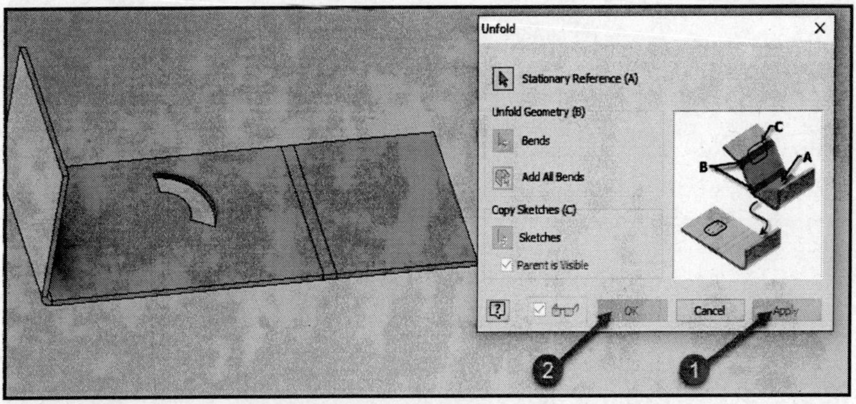

Step 5: After, you see a bend and flat sheet.

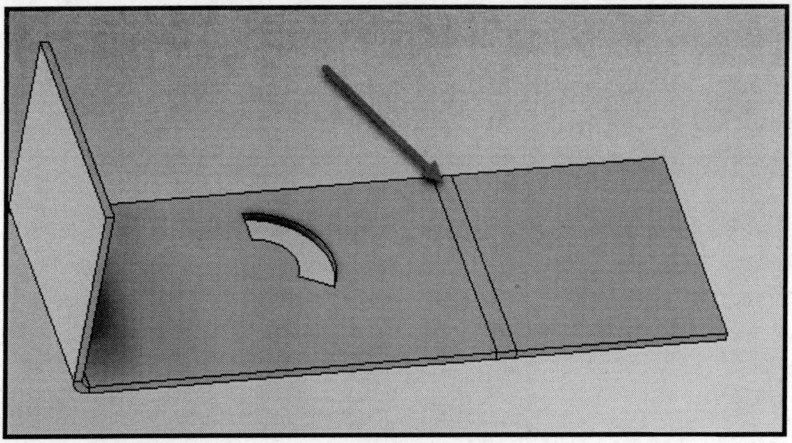

Refold

The "Unfold" tool is the opposite of the "Refold" tool.

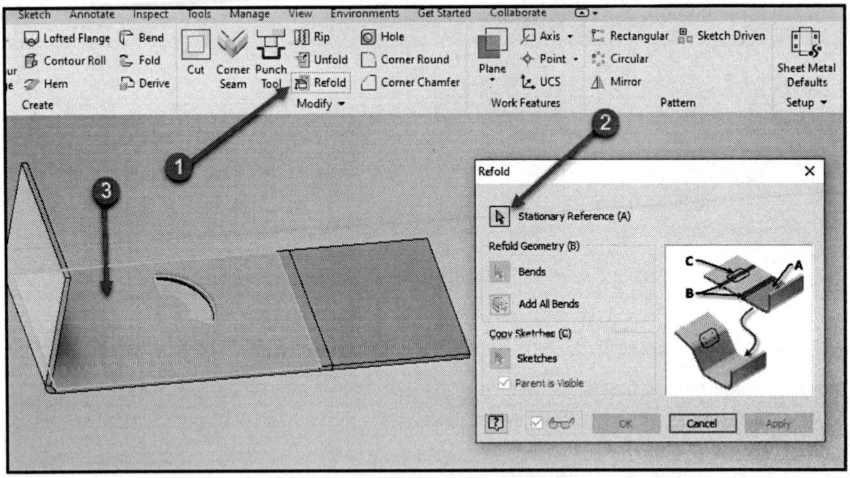

Step 2: Click the "bends" option. Select bending line. Then click "apply" and "ok" button.

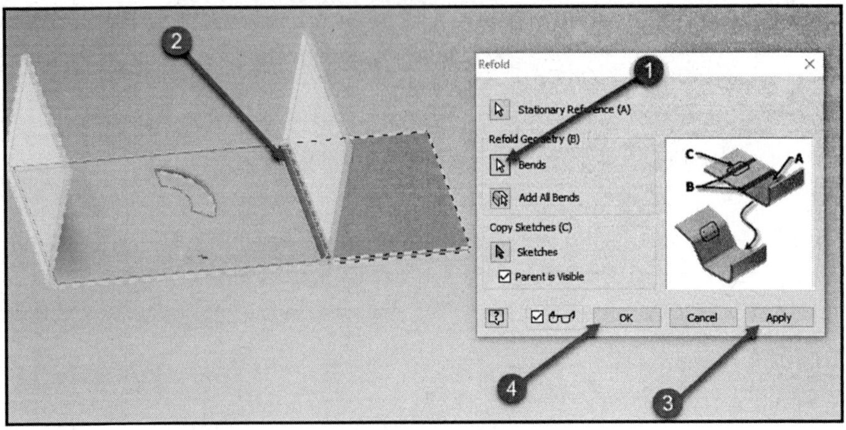

CHAPTER 9
Assembly

How to start ASSEMBLY?

Before starting the assembly, keep all the parts in a folder, then start from a new page.

Step 1: First of all, Click the "New" icon. In create new file tab, select "metric" and "assembly standard(mm)" option. Then click the "create" button.

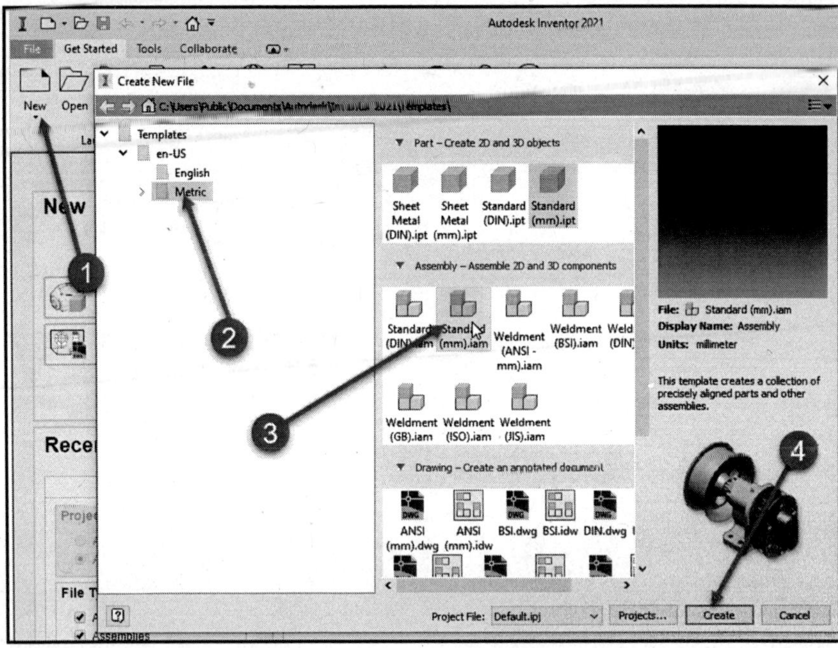

Step 2: After that, Click the "place" tool. And browse to the file you want to use as a part. Then click the "open" button.

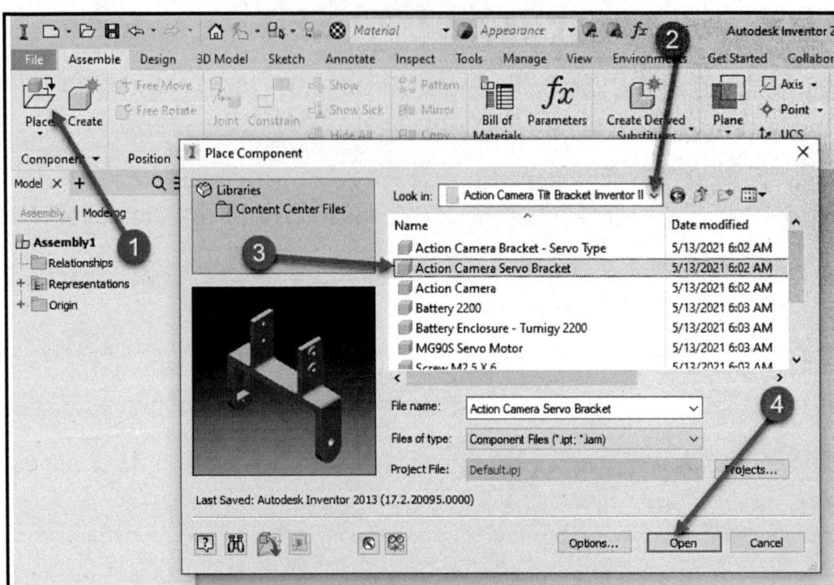

Step 3: Click on the screen to place the part.

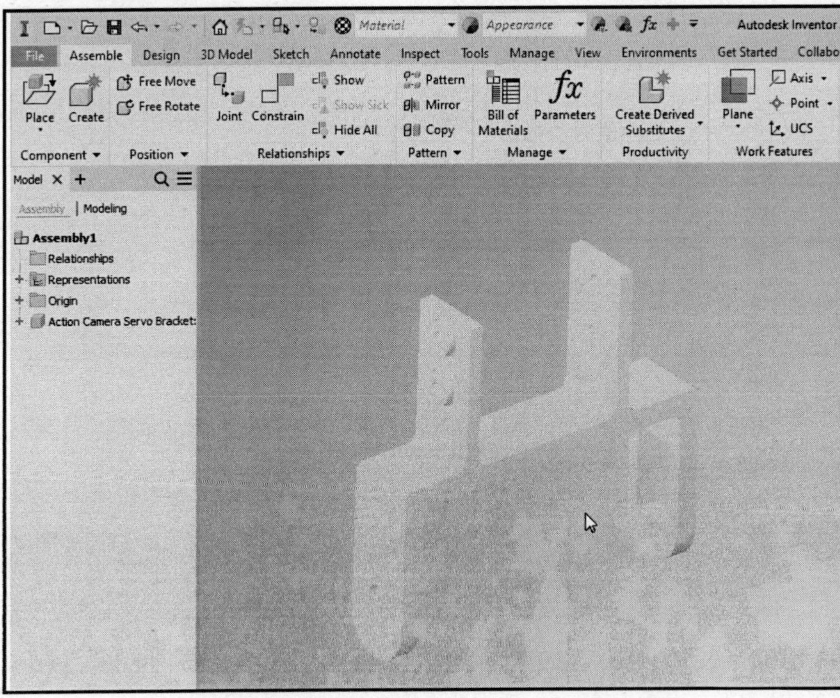

Step 4: Again, Click the "place" tool. And browse to the file you want to use as a part. Then click the "open" button.

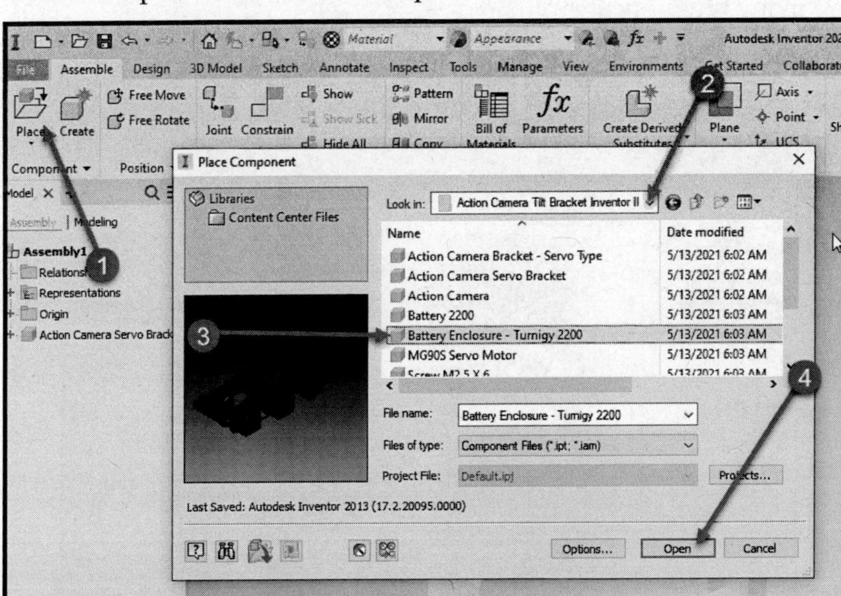

Step 5: Right-Click on the screen to Rotate the part.

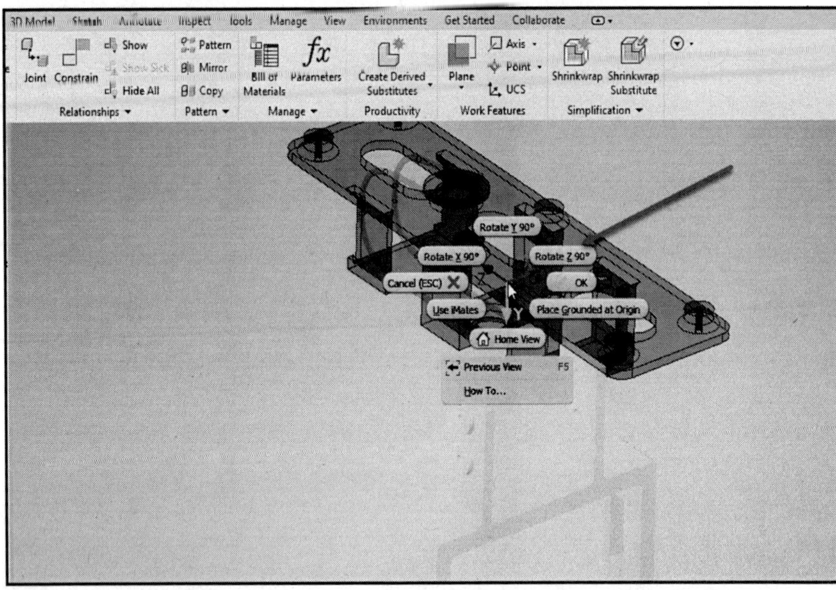

How to use constrain?

This tool is used to apply to constrain between the parts in the assembly. You can fix the part with the help of Constrain Tool. There are many types of constrain.

Step 1: First, Click the "place" tool. Then browse all file.

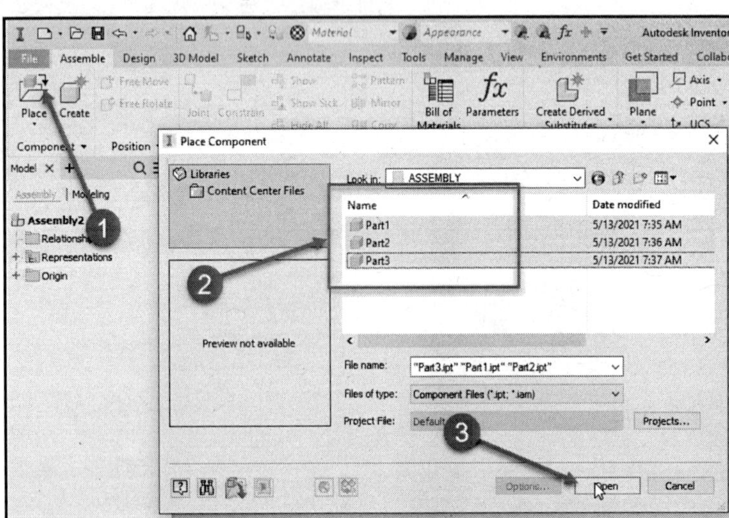

Step 2: Click on the screen to place the part.

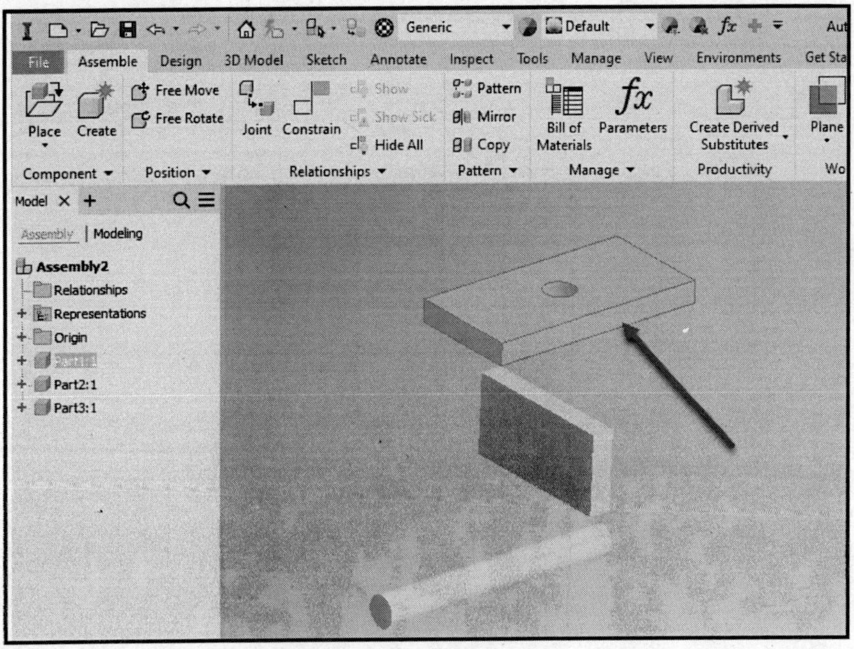

Step 3: Select one part. Then Right-click on the screen. And click the "grounded" option.

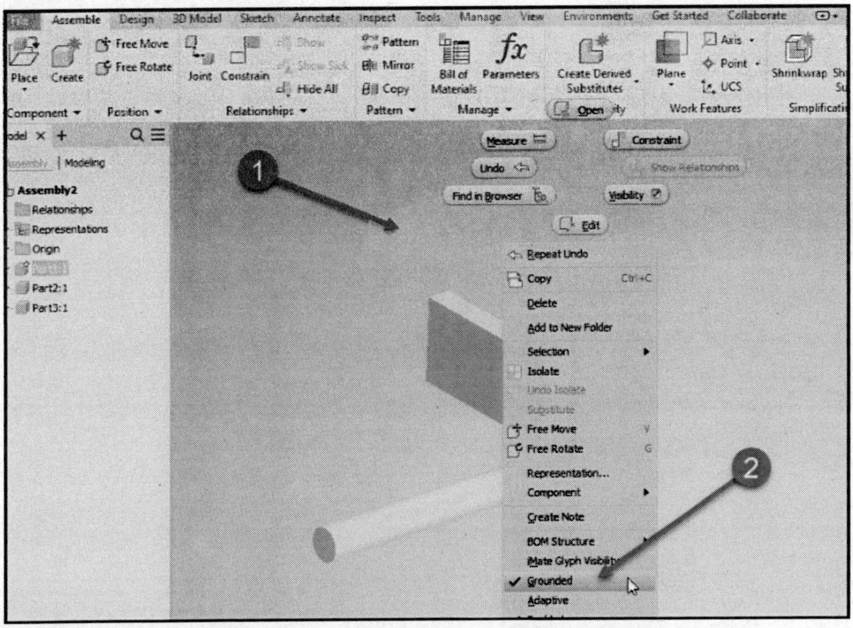

Step 4: Click the "constrain" tool icon, select "constraint" type on the place constraint. Then, Select two faces of different parts.

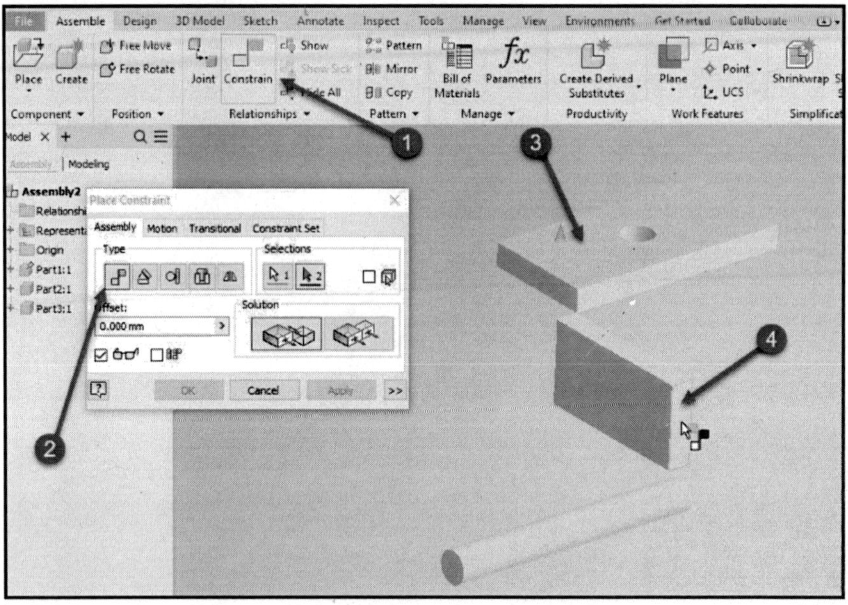

Step 5: Click "apply" and "ok".

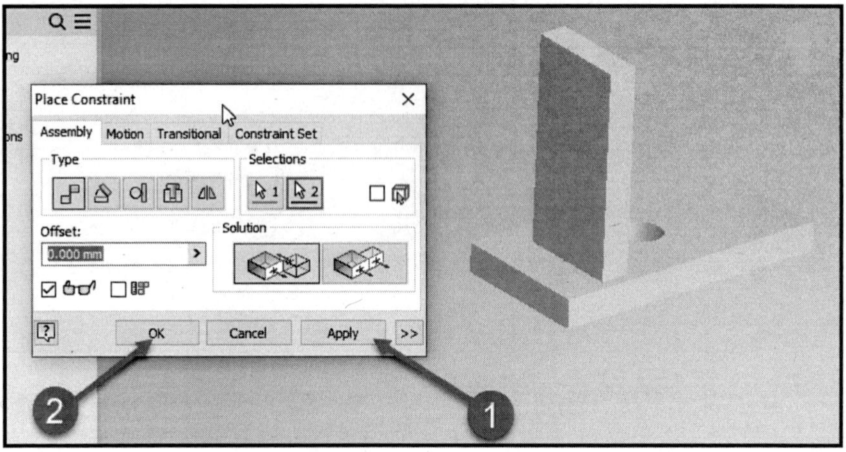

Step 6: Again, Use same step4.

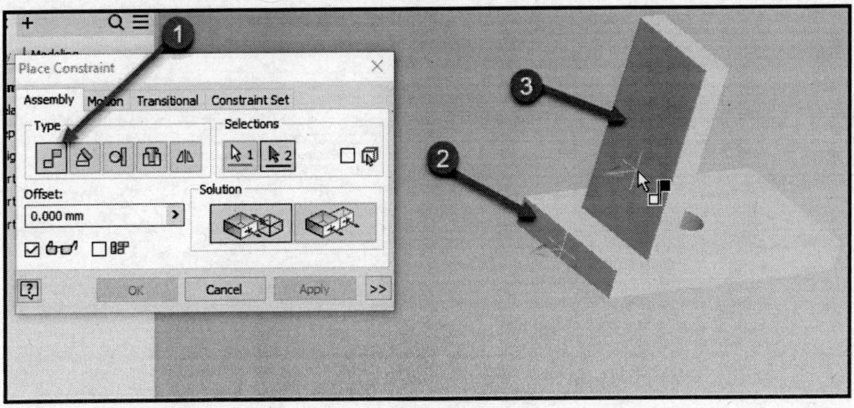

Step 7: Click the "flush" option on the "place constraint".

Step 8: Click "apply" and "ok".

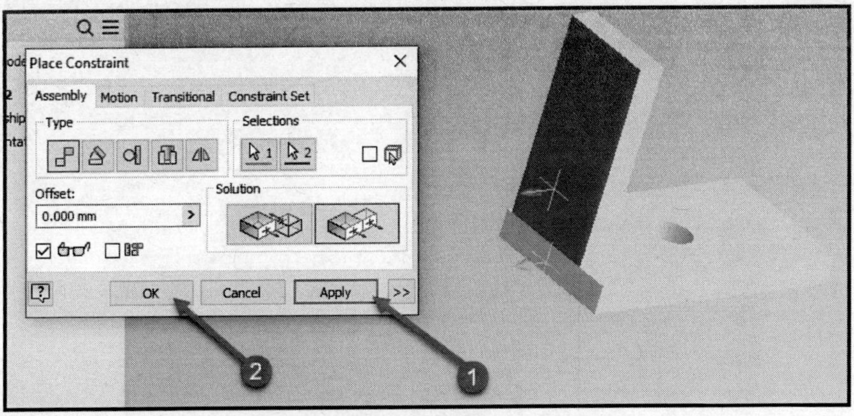

Step 9: Click the "Constrain" tool, select the "constraint" type on the "place constraint" tab, click the "flush" option. Then specify offset distance.

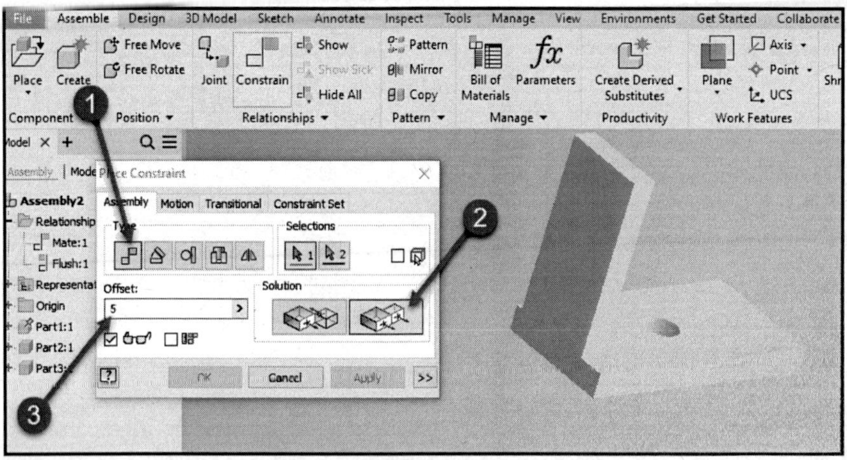

Step 10: Select two faces of different parts. Then click "apply" and "ok".

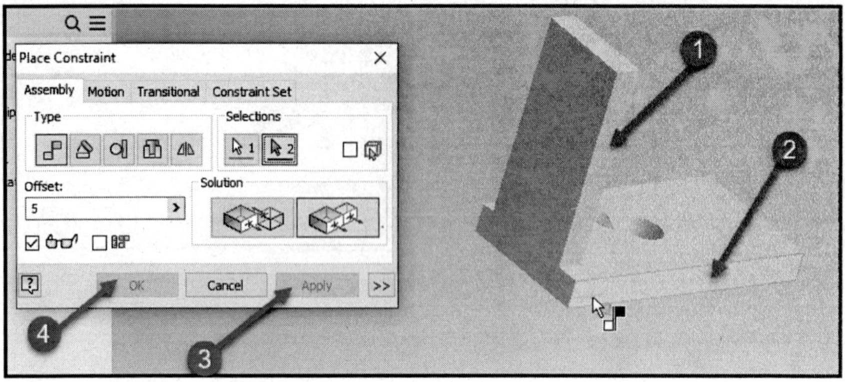

Copy

It is used to copy the part in the assembly.

Step 1: Click the "copy" tool. And select both objects. Then Click "next".

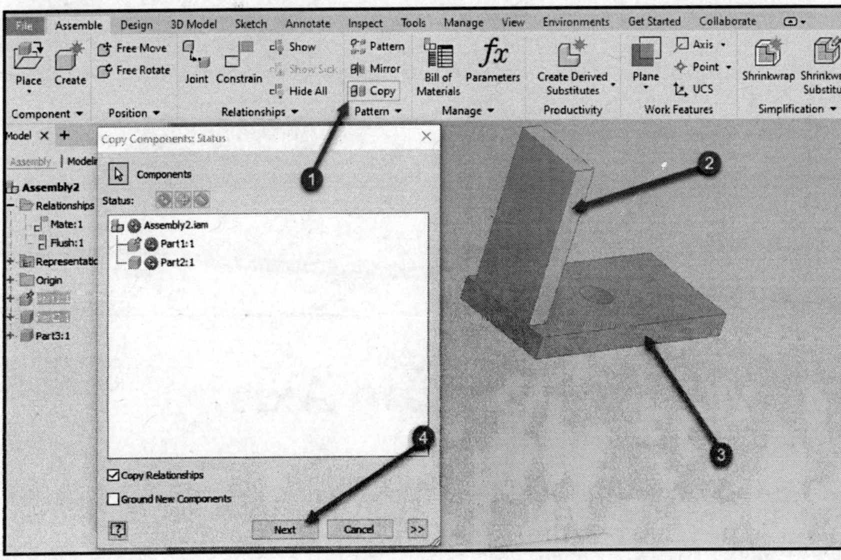

Step 2: Click the "ok" button.

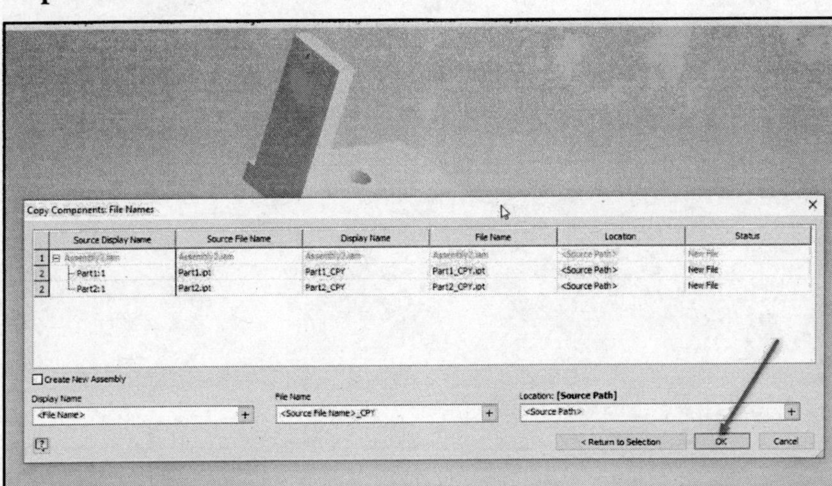

Step 3: Click on the screen to place the part.

How to use constrain Axis?

It is used to axis constrain. This is a type of constrain.

Step 1: Click the "constrain" tool. and select the "constraint" type. Then Select the box's hole axis and cylinder's axis.

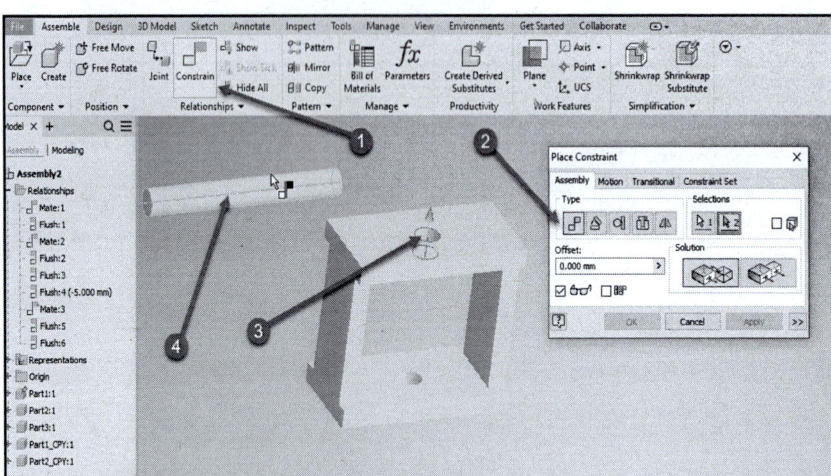

Step 2: Click "apply" and "ok".

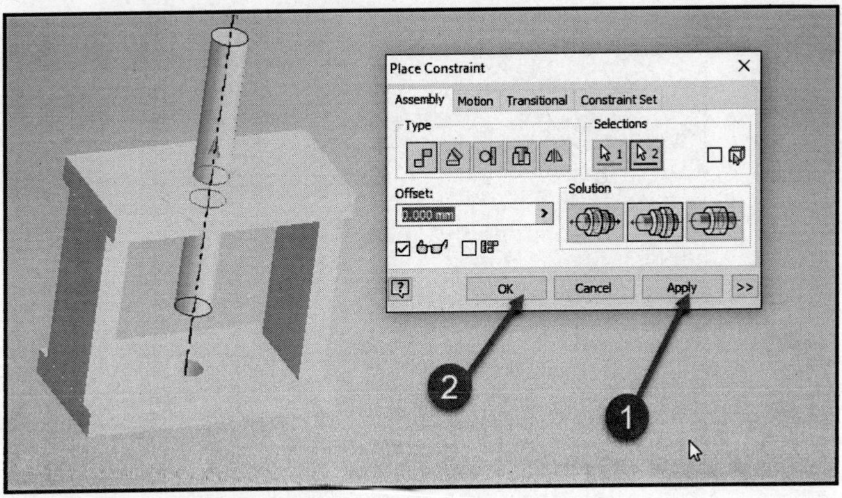

Move

It is used to move of part in assembly.

Step 1: First, Click the "Move" tool. And select the part.

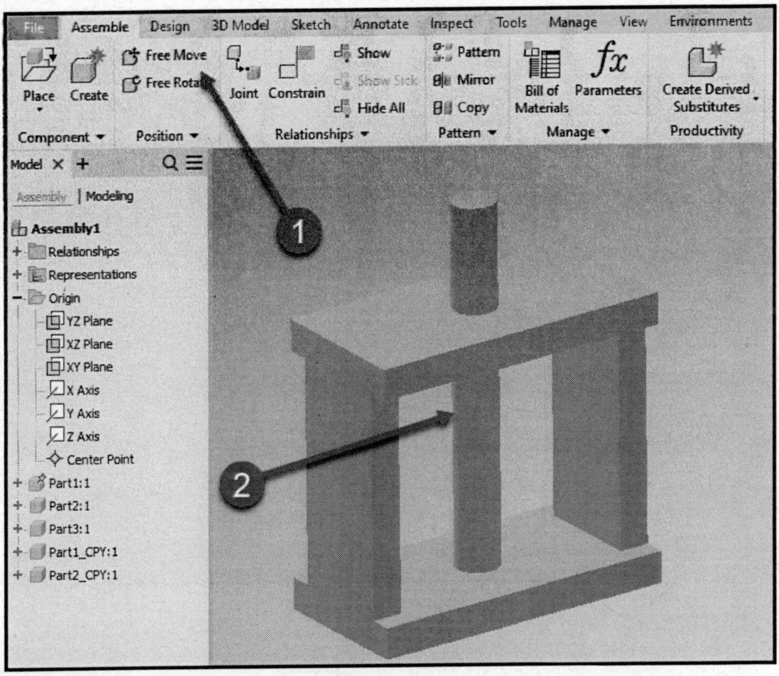

Step 2: After that, drag the part.

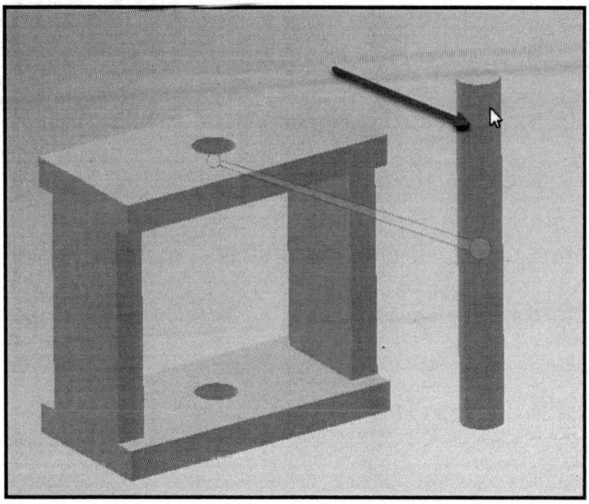

Rotate

It is used to rotate of part in assembly.

Step 1: First, Click the "Rotate" tool. then select the part and rotate.

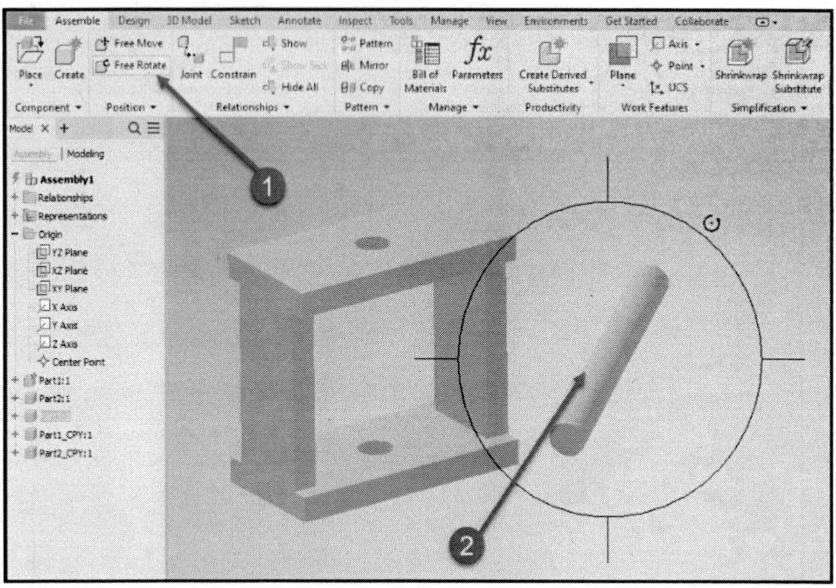

Grip Snap

Step 1: First, click the "grip snap" tool.

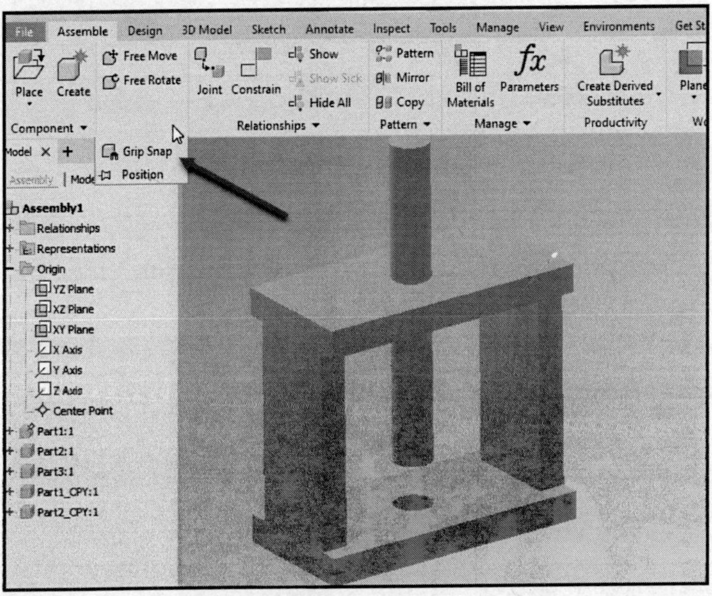

Step 2: Click on the corner of the part.

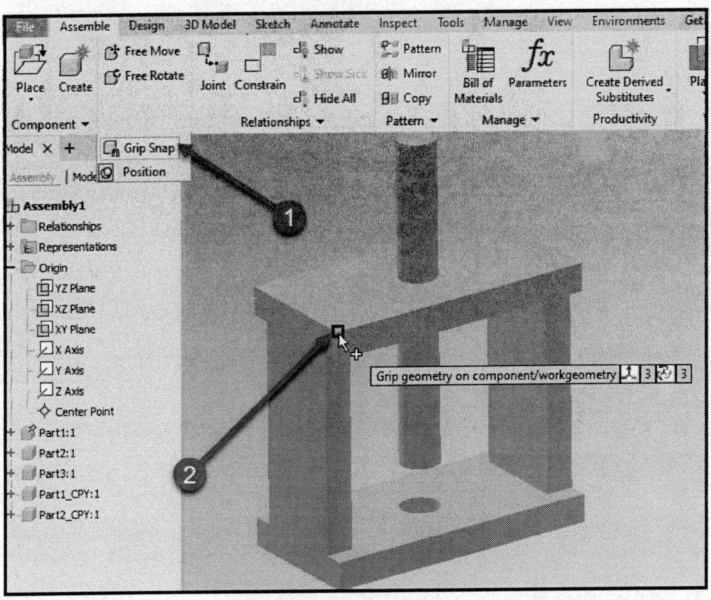

Step 3: Click the move option.

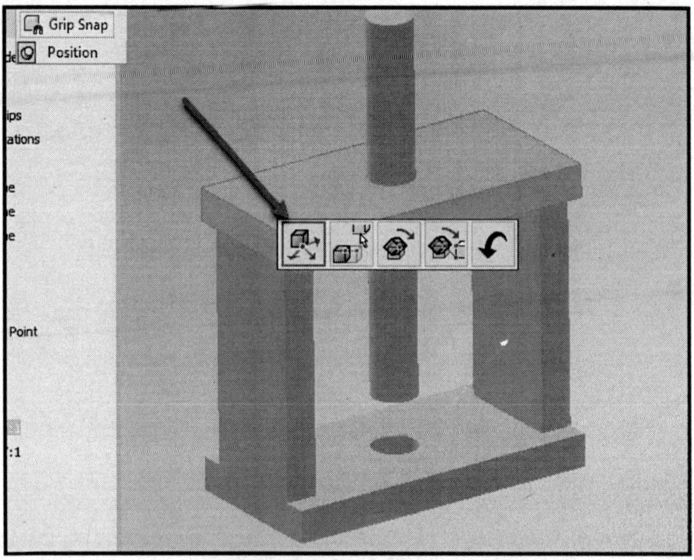

Step 4: Click on the corner of the other part.

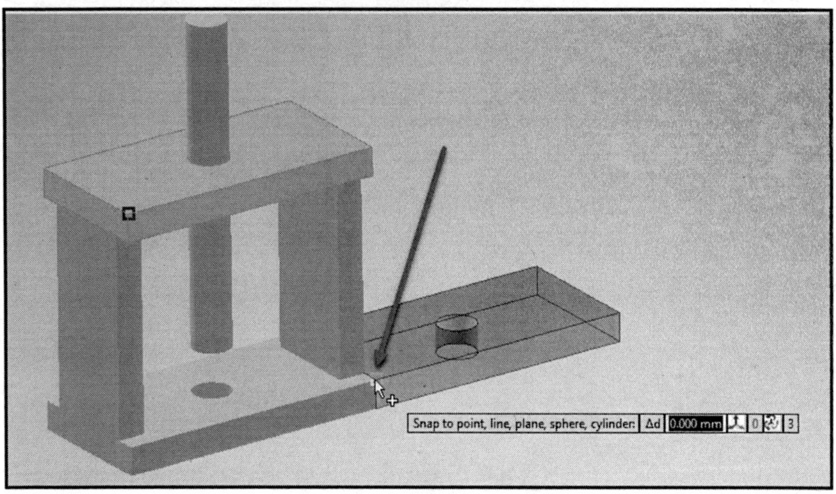

How to create new part in assembly?

Step 1: First, click the "create" tool. Then specify the name of the new part and specify the file location.

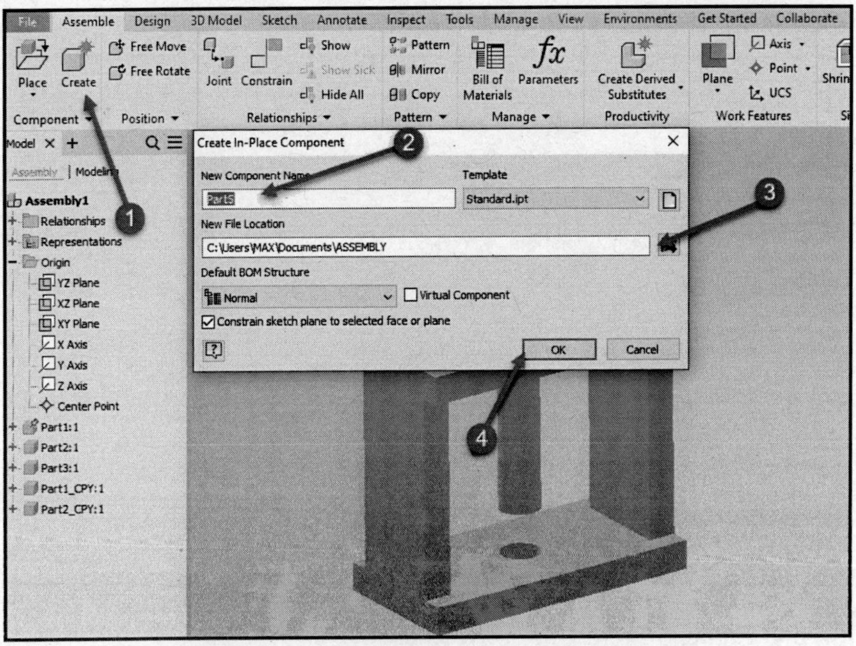

Step 2: Click on face of the part, As shown below.

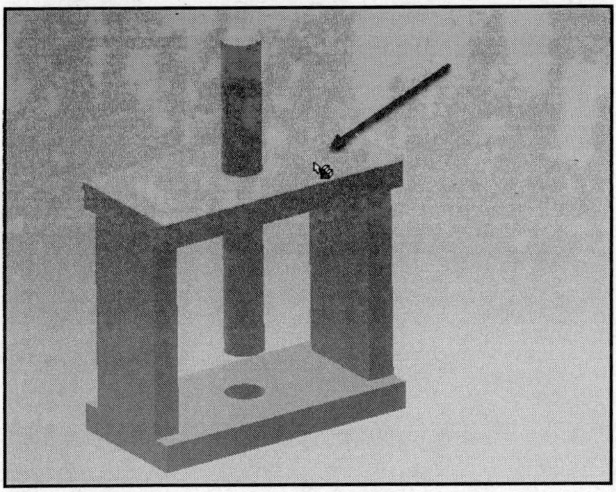

Step 3: Select a plane and click the sketch tool.

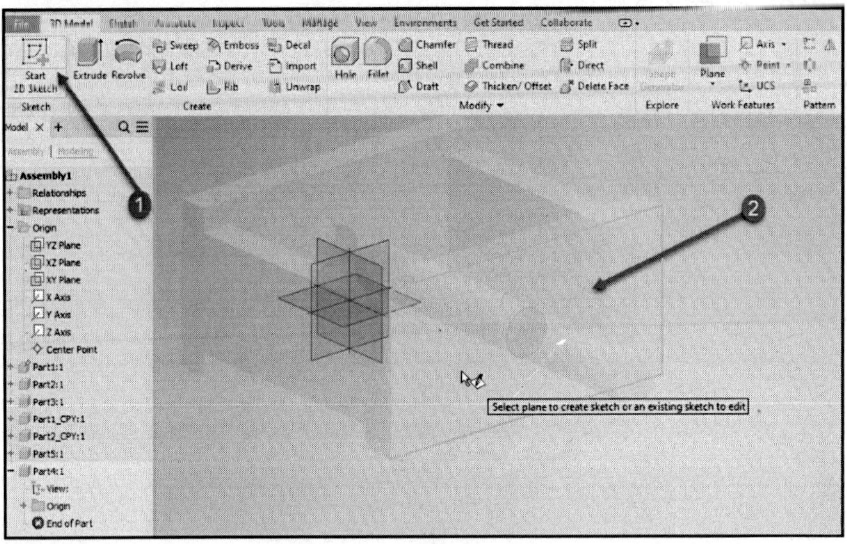

Step 4: Create a sketch, as shown below.

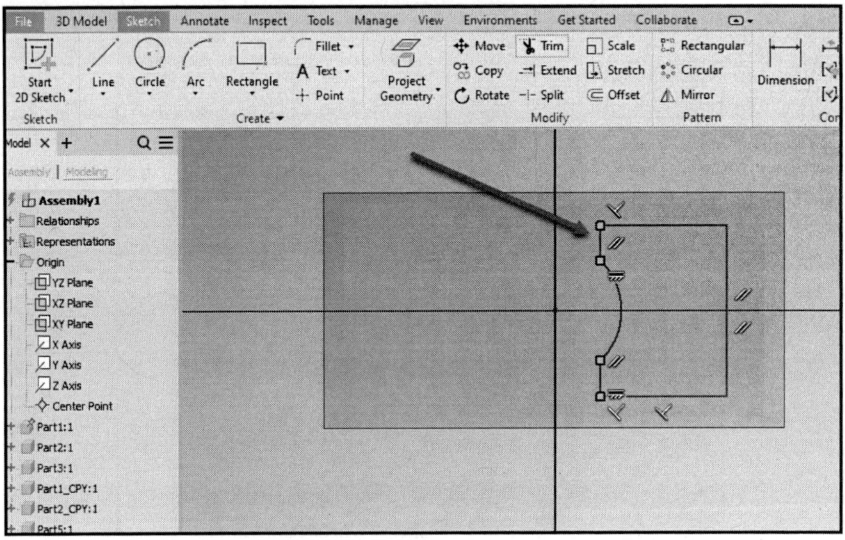

Step 5: Select the sketch. And click the "extrude" tool. then specify extrude height.

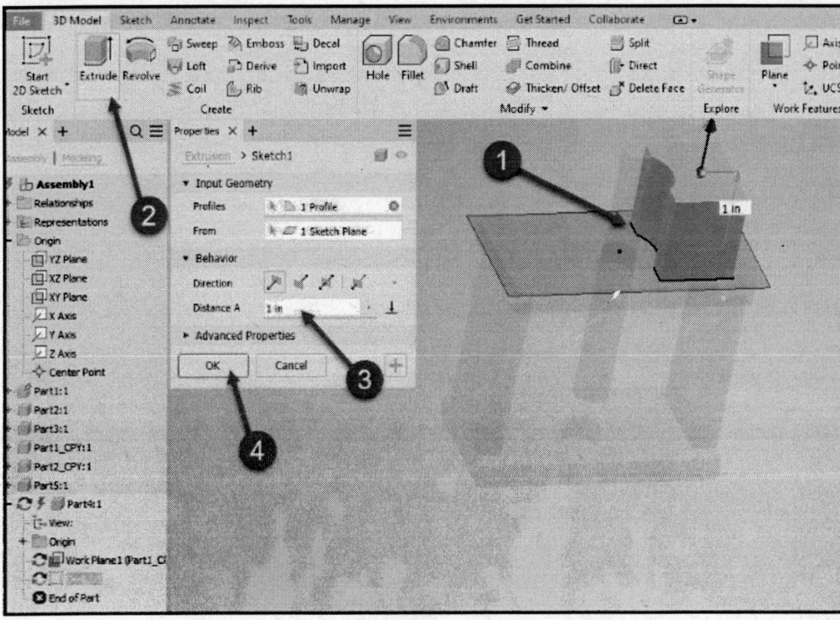